WINDOWS INTO OLD TESTAMENT HISTORY

WINDOWS INTO OLD TESTAMENT HISTORY

*Evidence, Argument, and
the Crisis of "Biblical Israel"*

Edited by

V. Philips Long,
David W. Baker,
and
Gordon J. Wenham

WILLIAM B. EERDMANS PUBLISHING COMPANY
GRAND RAPIDS, MICHIGAN / CAMBRIDGE, U.K.

Wm. B. Eerdmans Publishing Co.
255 Jefferson Ave. S.E., Grand Rapids, Michigan 49503 /
P.O. Box 163, Cambridge CB3 9PU U.K.

Printed in the United States of America

06 05 04 03 02   7 6 5 4 3 2 1

Library of Congress Cataloging-in-Publication Data

Windows into Old Testament history : evidence, argument,
and the crisis of "biblical Israel" / edited by
V. Philips Long, David W. Baker, and Gordon J. Wenham
p.   cm.
Includes bibliographical references.
ISBN 0-8028-3962-2 (pbk. : alk. paper)
1. Bible. O.T. — Historiography.   I. Long, V. Philips.
II. Baker, David W. (David Weston), 1950–   III. Wenham, Gordon J.

BS1180.W56 2002
221.9′5 — dc21
2002023821

www.eerdmans.com

Contents

CONTENTS

Abbreviations

AB	Anchor Bible
ABD	*Anchor Bible Dictionary*
AJA	*American Journal of Archaeology*
ANET	*Ancient Near Eastern Texts*
AOAT	Alter Orient und Altes Testament
BA	*Biblical Archaeology*
BARev	*Biblical Archaeology Review*
BASOR	*Bulletin of the American Schools of Oriental Research*
Bib	*Biblica*
BN	*Biblische Notizen*
BSac	*Bibliotheca Sacra*
BZAW	Beihefte zur *Zeitschrift für die alttestamentliche Wissenschaft*
CAH	*Cambridge Ancient History*
CBQ	*Catholic Biblical Quarterly*
CR:BS	*Currents in Research: Biblical Studies*
EA	El Amarna
ExpTim	*Expository Times*
HAT	Handbuch zum Alten Testament
HSM	Harvard Semitic Monographs
ICC	International Critical Commentary
IEJ	*Israel Exploration Journal*
JAOS	*Journal of the American Oriental Society*
JBL	*Journal of Biblical Literature*
JCS	*Journal of Cuneiform Studies*
JSOT	*Journal for the Study of the Old Testament*

JSOTS	*Journal for the Study of the Old Testament:* Supplement Series
JSS	*Journal of Semitic Studies*
JTS	*Journal of Theological Studies*
OBO	Orbis biblicus et orientalis
OBT	Overtures to Biblical Theology
OTG	Old Testament Guides
RB	*Revue biblique*
SBLMS	Society of Biblical Literature Monograph Series
SJOT	*Scandinavian Journal of the Old Testament*
TynBul	*Tyndale Bulletin*
VT	*Vetus Testamentum*
VTS	*Vetus Testamentum* Supplements
ZA	*Zeitschrift für Assyriologie*
ZAW	*Zeitschrift für die alttestamentliche Wissenschaft*
ZDPV	*Zeitschrift des deutschen Palästina-Vereins*

Introduction

V. PHILIPS LONG

Minimalism, Maximalism, and the Crisis in Old Testament Studies

It is not uncommon nowadays to hear that biblical studies in general, and OT studies in particular, are in a state of crisis. Old consensus positions have been abandoned, and questions formerly thought to be answered are again open for debate. In NT studies, the radical claims of the Jesus Seminar relating to the authenticity and historicity of the sayings of Jesus have gained a hearing even among the popular press (which gravitates naturally to the sensational). No less radical are the claims of some OT scholars regarding the historicity, or, more accurately, the nonhistoricity, of much of what the OT has to say about ancient Israel. Indeed, skepticism toward the historical value of the OT is very fashionable in some scholarly circles today. In the universities of Copenhagen and Sheffield, two of the most highly regarded centers of biblical studies in Europe, it is argued not only that the premonarchical traditions from Abraham to the judges are essentially fictional but also that the accounts of monarchical times are likewise inventions of Persian- and Hellenistic-period novelists.[1]

---

1. A steady stream of publications flows from Sheffield and Copenhagen, including scores of essays and numerous book-length treatments. The following recent titles offer a sampling of the latter: P. R. Davies, *In Search of 'Ancient Israel'*, JSOTS 148 (Sheffield: Sheffield Academic Press, 1992); N. P. Lemche, *Prelude to Israel's Past: Background and Beginnings of Israelite History and Identity*, trans. E. F. Maniscalco (Peabody, Mass.: Hendrickson, 1998); idem, *The Israelites in History and Tradition*, Library of Ancient Israel (Louisville: Westminster John Knox, 1998); T. L. Thompson, *Early History of the Israelite People: From the Written and Archaeological Sources*, Studies in the History of the Ancient Near East 4 (Leiden: Brill, 1992).

Most OT scholars stop well short of such extremes.[2] But scholars who hold a higher view of the historical worth of the biblical narratives, sometimes referred to as "maximalists," are occasionally accused by their "minimalist" counterparts of simply not knowing the facts, or of refusing to face them. In one of his more recent publications, N. P. Lemche of Copenhagen writes: "In the eyes of many 'scholars' of the past who have never looked out the window to perceive the world outside it, this biblical Israel was believed to have existed once."[3] In other words, those who believe that "biblical Israel" once existed simply have not bothered to look out the window to see the reality of the ancient Near Eastern world in which biblical Israel is supposed to have existed. Lemche's own "look out the window" discovers "a situation where Israel is not Israel, Jerusalem not Jerusalem, and David not David. No matter how we twist the factual remains from ancient Palestine, we cannot have a biblical Israel that is at the same time the Israel of the Iron Age."[4]

Lemche's insinuation that those who do not share his skepticism are either ignorant or obscurantist is astonishing, especially when one considers that skepticism regarding the historicity of biblical Israel is generally greatest among biblical scholars *without* specialized training in the languages and literatures of the ancient Near East. As J. K. Hoffmeier has recently observed:

> One reason for the disparity between historical maximalists and minimalists is that the former tend to be trained in Near Eastern languages, history, and archaeology with the Hebrew Bible as a cognate discipline, whereas the latter are largely trained in Old Testament studies in the nineteenth-century European mold and treat cognate languages and sources as ancillary rather than central to their discipline.[5]

---

2. For criticisms of "minimalism" implicit in the general Sheffield/Copenhagen approach, see, e.g., W. G. Dever, *What Did the Biblical Writers Know and When Did They Know It?: What Archaeology Can Tell Us about the Reality of Ancient Israel* (Grand Rapids: Eerdmans, 2001); W. W. Hallo, "Biblical History in Its Near Eastern Setting: The Contextual Approach," in C. D. Evans, W. W. Hallo, and J. B. White, eds., *Scripture in Context: Essays on the Comparative Method* (Pittsburgh: Pickwick, 1980), 1-26; idem, "The Limits of Skepticism," *JAOS* 110 (1990): 187-99; B. Halpern, "Erasing History: The Minimalist Assault on Ancient Israel," *Bible Review* 11, no. 6 (1995): 26-35, 47; J. K. Hoffmeier, "Of Minimalists and Maximalists," *BARev* 21, no. 2 (1995): 20, 22; J. K. Hoffmeier, *Israel in Egypt: The Evidence for the Authenticity of the Exodus Tradition* (New York and Oxford: Oxford University Press, 1997); I. W. Provan, "Ideologies, Literary and Critical: Reflections on Recent Writing on the History of Israel," *JBL* 114, no. 4 (1995): 585-606.

3. *The Israelites in History and Tradition*, 21.

4. Ibid., 166.

5. *Israel in Egypt*, 15.

In other words, maximalists tend to be found among those who have spent more, not less, time looking out the window onto the world of the ancient Near East. Lemche's remark also neglects the fact that what one sees when one looks out the window is in some measure a function of the eyes through which one looks. An absolutely "objective" look out the window is unachievable so long as a human subject is doing the looking. The best we can hope for is to become aware, ourselves, and to make others aware of our own subjectivity — particularly as this relates to our core convictions and background beliefs — and then, having acknowledged our subjectivity, to try to be honest with the evidence, even when it appears to go against what we would like to see. As Johan Degenaar succinctly remarks, "Theoretical self-reflection raises historiography to a higher level, for the historian can now take into account his (hidden) assumptions."[6]

Lemche does not offer an explicit statement of his core convictions and background beliefs, but his agenda is not difficult to discover. While noting that some scholars look to external evidence in the hope of supporting the notion that "a certain event narrated by the Old Testament really happened and that the narrative is for that reason a valuable [historical] source," Lemche, for his part, insists that "it is at least as respectable . . . to try to show that the text does not carry any information about the period worth speaking about."[7] Having set himself the task of demonstrating the historical worthlessness of the OT, Lemche pursues his aim unflinchingly, even when faced with such daunting counterevidence as the recently discovered Tel Dan inscription with its mention of the "house of David."[8] Lemche's approach to this piece of evidence — understandably embarrassing to minimalist scholars — appears to assume that it can be nullified simply by raising questions or presenting speculative scenarios of how the evidence, the realia, *might* be taken in some way other than at face value.[9] Whether the evidence in fact *should* be taken in one of the alternative ways is often not argued. To raise a question seems to suffice. It is left to individual scholars to decide which ex-

---

6. "Historical Discourse as Fact-Bound Fiction," in M. C. Doeser and J. N. Kraay, eds., *Facts and Values* (Dordrecht/Boston: Martinus Nijhoff, 1986), 76.

7. *The Israelites in History and Tradition,* 29.

8. For primary publication of the initial find and of the subsequently found broken fragment, see A. Biran and J. Naveh, "An Aramaic Stela Fragment from Tel Dan," *IEJ* 43 (1993): 81-98; idem, "The Tel Dan Inscription: A New Fragment," *IEJ* 45 (1995): 1-18. For a recent discussion and a listing of the burgeoning literature spawned by the discovery, see K. A. Kitchen, "A Possible Mention of David in the Late Tenth Century BCE, and Deity *Dod as Dead as the Dodo?" *JSOT* 76 (1997): 29-44.

9. For Lemche's discussion, see *The Israelites in History and Tradition,* 38-43.

planation of the inscription seems more probable. But, of course, what will seem probable to one scholar may seem improbable to another. For at a very deep level, what is deemed *probable* will be limited by what is believed *possible*. To those already convinced that there can be no *historical* counterpart to *biblical* David, any explanation — for example, the inscription is a fake, the reference is to a town or a temple — will seem more probable than that we have a ninth-century extrabiblical mention of the David of the OT, who *ex hypothesi* never existed. To those not already convinced, the *prima facie* reading will seem the more probable.

As hinted earlier, it is unlikely that the minimalist approach will find a wide following among today's scholars — least of all among those who have spent much time "looking out the window" onto the world of the ancient Near East, or, to reverse the image, among those whose acquaintance with the literatures of the ancient Near East provides a "window into the Old Testament." Nevertheless, the regularity with which a vocal minority declares the historical worthlessness of the OT has introduced a sense of uneasiness even among those accustomed to regarding the Old Testament differently, an uneasiness perhaps most pronounced among those less directly involved in the debate.

A Field-Encompassing Field

In this climate of uncertainty about the OT and history, the present volume offers solid encouragement. Comprising a collection of essays most of which were originally delivered and discussed by an international gathering of scholars at Tyndale House, Cambridge, in the summer of 1998, the volume seeks to open "windows" onto the ancient Near Eastern world of the biblical period and in so doing also to open windows into OT history. The essays cover a wide range of topics, and this is not surprising, as it is often said that the field of history — and this would include the historical study of the OT and of ancient Israel — is a "field-encompassing field." This means that historians, in seeking to reconstruct the past, must consider many kinds of evidence: textual and artifactual, literary and material, sociological and ecological. They must consider many kinds of influences on historical process: the general, *nomothetic* (law-giving) influences of climate, population growth, geography, and the like, the specific, *idiographic* (individualizing) influences of personal decisions and particular events, and the *institutional* and *societal* influences that fall somewhere in between. Given the multifaceted character of history as a "field-encompassing field," scholars interested in "ancient

Israel" can begin their investigations in any number of different areas. Important in the end is that all available evidence be considered.

For those whose interest in "ancient Israel" arises from a primary interest in the OT (i.e., for many believing Jews and Christians), a logical place to begin is with the OT texts themselves. For others, whose initial interest is not in the OT but in the history of Israel per se, the OT texts still constitute important evidence and must be considered at some point in the investigation (whether the OT should be regarded as "secondary evidence" depends on what exactly the designation means).[10] In any case, the importance of rightly discerning the texts' *truth claims* (historical or otherwise) cannot be overstated. This applies as much to extrabiblical textual evidence as to the biblical texts.

If we may adduce the oft-cited analogy between history and jurisprudence, the task of rightly understanding textual truth claims is like the task of understanding a witness on the stand — with the added difficulty that direct questions cannot be posed to the former as they can to the latter. Both historians and jurists seek to establish, on the basis of a fair assessment of all available evidence, the most likely scenario regarding the specific question(s) they are asking about the past. In the interrogation of witnesses, listening must precede judging. Irrespective of whether the text/witness is ultimately to be believed, the initial task is to listen carefully and fairly in order to understand as accurately as possible what the text/witness is *saying.* The importance of grasping the truth claims of text/witness should not be underestimated, and neither should the *difficulty,* especially when dealing with occasional documents in foreign languages from foreign cultures of long ago.

Once the testimony of all pertinent texts/witnesses has been heard and rightly understood, the historian/jurist is ready to begin to assess the *truth value* of the claims that have been made. A *necessary* condition of the truth value of testimony is that it be self-consistent and coherent. Testimony that contradicts itself discredits itself. But internal consistency alone is not *sufficient* to prove the veracity of the testimony. (Clever liars can keep their stories straight, as indeed can competent novelists.) The testimony of the individual text/witness must be compared with the testimony of all other credible texts/witnesses. If there is compatibility (we should not expect identity) among the witnesses, a case begins to build that the testimony is true, that its truth claims have truth value. In history, as in law, there is yet another category of evidence to be considered: the

---

10. If it simply means that the OT texts are not directly tied to the events they record in the same way that a victory stela or artifactual remains might be, then the designation seems unobjectionable. If the term is taken to mean that the OT texts are of secondary importance, then this needs to be argued, not merely asserted.

material evidence. The objects, architecture, and various other physical evidences brought to light by archaeological or legal investigation all must be considered before a reasoned judgment about what happened in the past can be reached. Sometimes material evidence is plentiful, sometimes there is none, but where it exists it requires *interpretation* no less than does the verbal evidence. Verbal testimony can provide guidance in the proper interpretation of the material evidence, and the material evidence, rightly understood, can provide a check on the veracity of the verbal testimony.

In considering both verbal and material evidence, the historian/jurist seeks to arrive at a sensible and defensible explanation of what happened in the past. It is seldom if ever possible to *prove* a particular reconstruction of events, but the goal is to arrive at the most probable reconstruction. But here a third factor (touched upon earlier) enters in, namely, the historian's/jurist's personal beliefs about what kinds of things *can* happen, what kinds of events are possible. Even a significant body of evidence and argument will have difficulty convincing one of an event's *probability*, if one believes such an event to be an *impossibility*. Because scholars embrace sometimes fundamentally different worldviews, a given scenario (whether offered by a text or the result of scholarly reconstruction) may strike one scholar as quite possible (and perhaps even probable) and another as utterly impossible.

In sum, the task of the historian, like that of the jurist, is threefold: first, to amass all pertinent verbal testimony and to come to a fair and accurate understanding of its truth claims; secondly, to test the truth value of these claims by applying internal checks (is the testimony self-consistent and coherent?) and external checks (how does the testimony square with whatever material evidence is available — which itself must be assessed, or interpreted?); and thirdly, to bring all the evidence (verbal and material) together into a reasoned account of what most probably happened with respect to a particular question about the past. At each stage, and particularly the third, the core convictions and commitments of the investigator inevitably, even if unconsciously, come into play. V. A. Harvey puts it plainly: "all our judgments and inferences [including historical ones] take place . . . against a background of beliefs. We bring to our perceptions and interpretations a world of existing knowledge, categories, and judgements. Our inferences are but the visible part of an iceberg lying deep below the surface."[11]

The essays collected in the present volume are arranged in a roughly logi-

---

11. V. A. Harvey, *The Historian and the Believer: The Morality of Historical Knowledge and Christian Belief* (New York: Macmillan, 1966; reprinted 1996), 115. I have argued elsewhere that scholarly understanding, if not agreement, will be greatly furthered as we pay

cal order. Given the importance of the "iceberg issue," we begin with a consideration of "models and methods." In the first essay, Danish scholar Jens Bruun Kofoed explores the philosophical and epistemological underpinnings of the so-called Copenhagen School (as exemplified particularly in the works of T. L. Thompson). Kofoed's study alerts readers to the link between general philosophical concerns and the specific judgments that scholars reach. Following Kofoed's investigation of the link between scholarly models and methods, we move to the question of how best to "hear" the verbal testimony. The second essay, also by a Danish scholar, Nicolai Winther-Nielsen, turns to matters linguistic and literary and seeks to show how "pragmatics" (i.e., the study of language use in real-life contexts) can help interpreters detect textual truth claims. He is particularly concerned with how we can judge the antiquarian intentions of ancient texts. Winther-Nielsen maintains that the pragmatics approach offers a more reasonable alternative to the absolute "verification principle" promoted, for instance, by the Copenhagen school. Once truth claims are discerned, their truth value can be tested. The next three essays relate in one way or other to the issue of testing truth value against the ancient Near Eastern context. Three authors, Richard S. Hess, Alan R. Millard, and Kenneth A. Kitchen, focus each in his own way on archaeological and comparative literary studies and illustrate how extrabiblical evidence can often clarify debated issues and elucidate questions raised by the biblical texts themselves. There then follow two sample studies, by Brian E. Kelly and Peter Williams. Each is a synthetic exegetical essay that deals with an aspect of the book of Chronicles and illustrates how biblical and extrabiblical evidence can be brought together to shed light on some of the vexed issues relating to Israel's history. The volume's final essay, by Iain Provan,[12] provides a fitting conclusion to the collection, bringing the reader full circle to a further, broader consideration of the kinds of fundamental epistemological and philosophical issues introduced in Kofoed's essay. We shall have more to say on each of the essays or essayists mentioned above as our discussion of the "crisis of history" currently animating biblical studies continues.

---

more attention to the subsurface portion of the iceberg; see V. P. Long, "Historiography of the Old Testament," in D. W. Baker and B. T. Arnold, eds., *The Face of Old Testament Studies: A Survey of Contemporary Approaches* (Grand Rapids: Baker, 1999), 145-75; more briefly, idem, "The Future of Israel's Past: Personal Reflections," in V. Philips Long, ed., *Israel's Past in Present Research: Essays on Ancient Israelite Historiography*, Sources for Biblical and Theological Study 7 (Winona Lake, Ind.: Eisenbrauns, 1999), 580-92, esp. 586-87.

12. Provan's essay (the only reprint in this volume) previously appeared as "In the Stable with the Dwarves: Testimony, Interpretation, Faith and the History of Israel," in A. Lemaire and M. Sæbo, eds., *Congress Volume, Oslo* (Leiden: Brill, 2000), 281-319.

Of Models and Methods

As noted above, it is now commonplace to hear that OT study is in crisis. Many former consensus positions have been abandoned. Everything seems up for grabs, and firm ground is a precious commodity. In such a climate, it is not surprising that calls for methodological discussion are frequent.[13] And discussion of methods is certainly to be welcomed. But as we have already noted, methodological discussion alone is only half the story. If there is to be true understanding among scholars, then not just methods but also models must be open for discussion. We shall never fully understand one another — why we agree and disagree — until we are willing to take our discussions to the deeper level of reality models, worldviews, philosophical presuppositions, and control beliefs (or whatever term we choose to describe who we are and what we believe at the core of our being).[14] The thought of such discussions is naturally threatening, but the fact is that every scholar comes to the table not just as a scholar but as a human being. Postmodernism, for all its excesses and misguided notions,[15] has at least driven home the point that scholarship involves a subjective element (a point, by the way, that seems to have eluded some, but certainly not all, scholars of past generations). No longer can appeal simply be made to "scholarly standards of historical research to which all legitimate scholars agree." From many directions we are reminded that who we are as whole persons affects how we approach and assess evidence.

Unless we live a bifurcated existence in which our beliefs about the fundamental realities of life are excluded from our scholarly practice, then our views about big issues, our philosophical or metaphysical commitments, inevitably affect our judgments on the smaller issues.[16] Absolute objectivity is

13. For example, P. R. Davies insists that "More discussion about historical method and less about the historicity of individual persons and events is badly needed" ("Whose History? Whose Israel? Whose Bible? Biblical Histories, Ancient and Modern," in Lester L. Grabbe, ed., Can a 'History of Israel' Be Written? JSOTS 245 [Sheffield: Sheffield Academic Press, 1997], 104-22; quotation from 110).

14. W. G. Dever, e.g., is to be commended for including in the Foreword to his recent book, What Did The Biblical Writers Know and When Did They Know It?, a sketch of his personal journey from a fundamentalist Christian upbringing to his conversion to secular (nontheistic) Judaism (ix-x).

15. For a recent critical appraisal of postmodernism and historical study, see P. Zagorin, "History, the Referent, and Narrative: Reflections on Postmodernism Now," History and Theory 38, no. 1 (1999): 1-24.

16. For a striking example of this fundamental point, see P. R. Davies' remarkably candid discussion and dismissal of the idea of "objective" history. Davies concludes: "When I claim, then, that there is no 'objective' history I am implying a world-view incompatible

an illusion. Those who lay claim to it, even as an aspiration, are simply over-looking (or obscuring) the fact that *scholarly methods themselves arise upon philosophical foundations.* The philosophical assumptions undergirding the methods we use may not always be as obvious as in D. F. Strauss's bold asser-tion that "all just philosophical conceptions and all credible experience" teach us that "the absolute cause never disturbs the chain of secondary causes . . ."[17] — but they are always there.

Recognizing that absolute objectivity is impossible does not mean that we should give up any notion of objectivity whatsoever. Just because *absolute* objectivity is a chimera does not mean that we must resign ourselves to *abso-lute* subjectivity, as some strains of postmodernist relativism would maintain. It means, rather, that when making historical judgments, we must remind ourselves that whether a particular reconstruction seems plausible, or proba-ble, *to us* is a function not just of the evidence before us but of the larger model of reality that we each embrace. Let us imagine, for instance, that someone claims to have had a religious conversion experience. Historians who are theists may be open to the possibility that God has done a work in the life of the claimant. Notice that I say "may be open to the possibility"; fur-ther questions may need to be asked and further observations gathered before anything approaching reasonable assurance that God has indeed been at work can be achieved. Historians who are not theists, if they are consistent, will discount the possibility that *God* (who does not exist) has actually been at work. Instead, they will appeal to psychological or emotional explanations. In both instances, historians draw conclusions in keeping with their larger views of reality. And while only one of the two opposing views on ultimate re-ality can be correct — either God exists or not —, there is nothing *logically* objectionable in historians maintaining a consistency between their general beliefs and their specific judgments. Less acceptable is the not uncommon phenomenon of even theistic historians employing historical methods with an in-built a-theistic premise (cf. the Straussian quotation above) and so rul-ing the God-at-work explanation out of court on methodological grounds,

---

with that of the biblical writings . . . for whom history was defined by divine deeds. . . . So a certain kind of religious belief *might* well dictate a certain definition of 'history' " ("Whose History? Whose Israel? Whose Bible?" 116-17). In a footnote Davies faults W. G. Dever and B. Halpern (both agnostics or atheists by Davies' account, based on personal communica-tions) for nevertheless espousing a "view of history that is theistic" (ibid., 117 n.19).

17. From Strauss's influential *The Life of Jesus Critically Examined,* trans. G. Eliot; ed. P. C. Hodgson (Philadelphia: Fortress; London: SCM, 1972), 88; for discussion see V. P. Long, *The Art of Biblical History,* Foundations of Contemporary Interpretation 5 (Grand Rapids: Zondervan, 1994), 108-16.

even though their metaphysical commitments make room for God and they may in fact believe that he has been at work! Despite their actual metaphysical convictions, they simply cannot allow God a place in *historical* explanation. In the name of rationality and methodological consistency, God-talk is systematically eliminated. No further questions need be asked; no further observations made. Whatever the *historical* explanation of the claimant's experience may be, it cannot involve God in action.

The point in all this is not that we must cease doing history until all can agree on a given model of reality and then conform our methods to it. There is nothing to suggest that this will ever be the case, as long as the world shall last. The point, rather, is that we shall make little progress in understanding one another and in intelligently debating our competing historical judgments until we are willing more openly to explore how our judgments are fundamentally affected by our core convictions.

The first essay in this volume, Jens Bruun Kofoed's "Epistemology, Historiographical Method, and the 'Copenhagen School,'" tackles the fundamental issues head-on. While my own comments at the beginning of this introduction focused on one leading light among the "Copenhageners," Niels Peter Lemche, Kofoed focuses on the other, Thomas L. Thompson. Welcoming the fact that the Copenhagen controversy has alerted many to the need for explicit discussion of philosophical and epistemological issues, Kofoed seeks to uncover the theoretical basis of the approach of Thompson and, by implication, of others like him. Kofoed contends that Thompson's approach rests on two foundations: (1) his historiographical method (specifically his view of the relationship between texts and artifacts); and (2) his text theory (specifically his theory of the composition and contribution of textual traditions). Thompson claims to attend equally to archaeology, ancient Near Eastern written sources, and the biblical material. In practice, however, Thompson regards the biblical texts as reflecting only the time and circumstances of their *composition* and thus as unlikely to yield useful information about the earlier periods they purport to describe. Further, even the ancient Near Eastern textual remains themselves, by Thompson's reckoning, are to be trusted only insofar as they can be verified by archaeological realia. Thus, in practice, Thompson's focus (at least in terms of Israel's early history) falls on non-written, material evidence.

Recognizing that Thompson's approach has been influenced by the thinking of Fernand Braudel and the Annales School, with its threefold emphasis on "structures" (i.e., "la longue durée" affected by large-scale elements such as geography and climate), "conjunctures" (i.e., economic and social trends), and "events" (i.e., specific, individual happenings), Kofoed argues in essence that Thompson's method is a truncated application of the

Annales approach, unnecessarily downplaying the significance of specific, individual events (idiographic factors) as causal elements in historical process and relying too exclusively on larger-scale, nomothetic factors. While the empirical, quantifying approach proved fruitful in Braudel's study of medieval history, it becomes much more problematical when applied to the sparser data of the ancient world. Moreover, Thompson's undervaluing of idiographic forces (and of texts, such as the OT, that describe them) derives not so much from Braudel as from Thompson's own materialistic and positivistic philosophy. In the end, Thompson's suspicion of textual evidence frees him to try to tell the whole story from nomothetic evidence alone. But such evidence, as Kofoed points out, is but a small piece of the overall jigsaw puzzle of Early Iron Age society.

In the light of Kofoed's appraisal of Thompson's historical method, it is worth noting in passing that many secular historians have long since significantly modified their understanding of the three tiers of the Annales approach. The original concept was that "structures," "conjunctures," and "events" existed in a kind of "standard hierarchical arrangement," described by Princeton University professor Lawrence Stone as follows:

> [F]irst, both in place and in order of importance, came the economic and demographic facts; then the social structure; and lastly, intellectual, religious, cultural and political developments. These three tiers were thought of like the storeys of a house; each rests on the foundation of the one below, but those above can have little or no reciprocal effect on those underneath.[18]

Already in 1979 when Stone's essay appeared, many secular historians were abandoning the above schema. Stone writes:

> Many historians now believe that the culture of the group, and even the will of the individual, are potentially at least as important causal agents of change as the impersonal forces of material output and demographic growth. There is no theoretical reason why the latter should always dictate the former, rather than vice versa, and indeed evidence is piling up of examples to the contrary.[19]

In short,

> The historical record has now obliged many of us to admit that there is an extraordinarily complex two-way flow of interactions between facts of popu-

18. L. Stone, "The Revival of Narrative: Reflections on a New Old History," *Past and Present* 85 (1979): 3-24; quotation from 7.

19. Ibid., 9.

lation, food supply, climate, bullion supply, prices, on the one hand, and values, ideas and customs on the other.[20]

Biblical scholarship is frequently criticized for lagging behind the secular fields from which it sometimes draws inspiration. Some excuse can perhaps be made, inasmuch as a "field-encompassing field" should hardly be expected to provide the cutting edge in each field with which it deals. Nevertheless, in the case of biblical scholars prone to dismiss Braudel's third tier in favor of the second and particularly the first, some catching up may be in order.

Returning to Kofoed's analysis of the fundamentals of Thompson's epistemology and historiographical method, we discover *inter alia* that "meaning" is not an attribute of "things as they are" but is created and attributed to them by the human mind, that "tradition" is able only "to evoke truth, not to recount it," that "true reality" is unknowable, and that texts can preserve little historical information about any period other the time of their composition. In Kofoed's estimation, these working principles arise in Thompson's work more by way of assertion than by virtue of compelling argument.

In sum, Kofoed's analysis of some of the philosophical and epistemological underpinnings of Thompson's work demonstrates the importance and impact of such matters on all attempts at historical reconstruction. And so Kofoed aptly concludes his essay with an appeal to those who produce the "multiplicity of histories" that have been predicted for the future not to fail to offer some explicit indication of their own philosophical and epistemological assumptions.

Detecting Truth Claims

Once we are clear on the fact that *who* we are and *what* we believe about big issues affects our judgments on particular cases, we are prepared to undertake the task of trying to understand the evidence. We can now proceed more objectively because we are more aware of our own subjectivity and thus less inclined to mistake emotional attachment for evidence or argument.

Chief among the verbal evidence that we must seek to understand are the texts of the OT. In approaching these texts, we must not underestimate the difficulty of rightly construing the texts' truth claims, as I have already remarked. It is not uncommon for scholars of various theological orientations,

20. Ibid., 8.

whether theists or nontheists, to misconstrue what the texts actually claim. For instance, a misreading of the book of Joshua has in the past led "conservative" as well as "liberal" scholars to assume that the book describes a rapid blitzkrieg involving extensive property destruction in many of the cities of Canaan. It is then assumed that the property destruction should have left an indelible mark in the archaeological record. A more careful reading of the Joshua texts, however, discovers much destruction of populations but only limited destruction of property.[21] The common misreading has led some scholars to misconstrue the archaeological evidence and others to dismiss the biblical evidence. In a nutshell, poor *literary* understanding of the Joshua texts allows the emergence of a "straw man" that liberals find easy to destroy and conservatives find difficult to defend. Recent advances in linguistics and literary studies are facilitating clearer perceptions of what the texts actually claim and, along with heightened awareness that archaeological remains are themselves also subject to interpretation, are beginning to suggest ways in which the former tensions might be relieved. The newer linguistics and literary studies come in a variety of forms and are not without their own hidden dangers.[22] Nevertheless, as the better conceived of the newer approaches come into their own, the future is likely to see many revisions and reversals of earlier conclusions drawn without benefit of the "literary competence" that the newer approaches afford. One potentially fruitful text-linguistic approach is what Nicolai Winther-Nielsen calls "pragmatics."

In the second essay below, Winther-Nielsen takes as his starting point Baruch Halpern's recent contention that the writers of the bulk of narratives found in the Hebrew Bible had genuine antiquarian intentions — that they were, in fact, the "first historians."[23] Concerned, however, that Halpern's case was partially based on historical-critical conclusions that are now discredited, Winther-Nielsen proposes that a better case can be made by bringing to bear the insights of modern "pragmatics," namely, the study of how language functions in actual, real-life contexts. He commends earlier studies that have stressed the fact that biblical narratives comprise a complex interweaving of

21. For discussion, see Long, *Art of Biblical History*, 160-67, and the literature cited there. Most recently and most fully, see E. H. Merrill, "The Late Bronze/Early Iron Age Transition and the Emergence of Israel," *BSac* 152 (1995): 145-62.

22. See A. C. Thiselton's evaluation of "problematic and productive aspects of the literary approach" in his *New Horizons in Hermeneutics: The Theory and Practice of Transforming Biblical Reading* (Grand Rapids: Zondervan; London: Marshall Pickering, 1992), 471-79.

23. B. Halpern, *The First Historians: The Hebrew Bible and History* (San Francisco: Harper & Row, 1988).

historical, literary, and ideological (theological) threads, but he fears that these approaches have sometimes left unresolved the question of how these three interact in practice. He contends that the emphasis of pragmatics, or discourse analysis, on beginning with the literary text and exploring it in the light of the insights of speech-act theory, for example, before then moving to a consideration of more specifically historical and theological questions, holds promise of enabling firmer conclusions regarding a text's actual intentionality and import. Using selected conversations from the book of Judges, Winther-Nielsen concludes that when subjected to scrutiny in terms of the two basic principles of modern pragmatics — namely, the "communicative principle" (focus on intentionality) and the "coherence principle" (focus on contextual constraints) — such conversations give the impression of reporting real-world events, albeit selected for their ideological value. He recognizes that it is not possible to *prove* that these chapters, with their obvious artistic design and rhetoric, represent essentially historical reportage. But, of course, absolute proof of historicity is seldom if ever achievable. What is required, rather, is evidence that will tip the balance in terms of the texts' apparent intentionality, followed by some judgment as to whether the textual testimony is to be trusted once its apparent intentions have (with the help of pragmatics) been determined. In a time when some scholars writing on the history of "ancient Israel" are insisting that texts (especially the biblical texts) cannot be trusted unless they can be *verified* by external, contemporary evidence, Winther-Nielsen's call to take seriously the literary task of rightly reading texts on their own terms and then deciding whether to believe them or not is most welcome. Were the "verification principle" to prevail, most knowledge of the past (at least the ancient past), dependent as it is on trustworthy testimony, would cease.

Testing Truth Value

Once interpreters have arrived at a reasonable understanding of the truth claims made by their written sources, it is time to decide what level of truth value should be ascribed to the claims. I have mentioned above some of the tests that can be applied in coming to a judgment, namely, internal consistency, external consistency, and (meta)physical possibility. Here it is worth noting some of the reasons why biblical texts are often regarded as lacking (historical) truth value. Occasionally they are dismissed simply because they are narrative in form and ideological in character. But as M. Z. Brettler has noted, "[O]utside of biblical studies, the ideological nature of much of history is recognized, and the narrative dimension of almost all history writing is acknowledged."[24] Another reason why the historical veracity of OT accounts is doubted is that the accounts are assumed to be very late in origin, and thus far removed from the events they ostensibly report. Apart from the illogic of assuming that late accounts cannot be true accounts (an assumption particularly odd among modern historians who, even farther removed from the events they purport to describe, nevertheless aspire to write accurate histories), it must also be noted that the late datings of many biblical texts are anything but assured. In an earlier time, it seemed sufficient simply to cite the late arrival of literacy on the scene as ample evidence that *texts* by definition are late and so are not to be trusted when they report *early* events, unless they are verified by external evidence contemporary with the events. While archaeological discovery has largely overturned such views, verificationist thinking still persists in some circles,[25] and the issue of literacy in ancient Israel remains a matter of debate.

In our third essay, Richard S. Hess explores the question of the nature and extent of literacy in Iron Age Israel. He takes as his starting point two recent articles by Ian Young in which the latter argues (1) that mass literacy could *not* have been a feature of Iron Age Israel and (2) that reading and writing must have been limited to scribes, priests, and administrators. Hess notes also the role of Jamieson-Drake's 1991 monograph in reawakening interest in the general issue of literacy in ancient Israel. In the face of Jamieson-Drake's contention that writing was largely absent in Iron Age Israel until after the eighth century BC, Hess offers a thorough survey of extrabiblical evidence for literacy first in "pre-Israelite Canaan" and then in Iron Age Israel, which he discusses in six divisions: twelfth-eleventh century, tenth century, ninth, eighth, seventh, and sixth.

For the pre-Israelite period, Hess presents evidence and argument for literacy on a wide scale "even in relatively small and isolated towns," thus undermining arguments against literacy based on low population. Indeed, "all

---

24. M. Z. Brettler, *The Creation of History in Ancient Israel* (London and New York: Routledge, 1995), 18.

25. Lemche, e.g., while allowing that "historical information may be present in a late text irrespective of how strongly edited this text may have been," nevertheless insists that, "in general, it will be necessary to provide contemporary evidence to say that a later source is delivering anything in the way of historical information." In other words, "the biblical text cannot in advance be accepted as a historical source or documentation; it has in every single case to prove its status as a historical source" (*The Israelites in History and Tradition*, 25-26, 29 respectively).

assumptions about illiteracy throughout Palestine for the thirteenth century as well as the early Iron Age (1200-1000 B.C.) must be questioned and re-examined." The extant extrabiblical materials suggest that writing was wide-spread from north to south in Canaan and that, furthermore, there was a shift following the Amarna period from Akkadian as the *lingua franca* to "the local scripts and languages of Palestine."

Turning to Iron Age Israel, Hess surveys the evidence for literacy in each of the six time periods mentioned above. With all their variations in detail, each of the periods from 1200 to 586 BC gives evidence of writing as a perva-sive phenomenon in ancient Israel, and not just in the larger population cen-ters. Nor does the evidence justify attempts to limit literacy to specific classes of people (e.g., priests, scribes, or administrators); rather, it appears that "many individuals . . . could write the simpler alphabetic script and . . . did so for a variety of reasons and purposes."

So, then, to draw some threads together: If a late text can offer accu-rate reportage, if late datings for many biblical texts are more often as-sumed than assured anyway, and if literacy rates in ancient Israel are unproblematic, then what further grounds are there for discounting the historical import of biblical texts? Sometimes cited is the belief that didac-tic intent and historical import stand in a kind of inverse relationship, and also the belief that in the absence of ancient Near Eastern analogues, it is inconceivable that the biblical texts could comprise true historiography. Both of these issues are addressed in our fourth essay, Alan Millard's "His-tory and Legend in Early Babylonia."

Recognizing that we have precious little Hebrew textual evidence outside the OT for reconstructing the history of ancient Israel, Millard sets out to as-say inscriptional and epic materials that might help decide how the biblical texts themselves should be viewed with regard to their historical import. In an earlier essay Millard considered the bearing of Aramaic materials relating to the (period of) the monarchy in Israel.[26] In the present essay he looks to the much earlier Babylonian inscriptional and epic materials relating to Sargon, the first "Semitic" emperor, and his grandson Naram-Sin. Epics known only from second-millennium copies mention a campaign to the far northwest into west-central Anatolia for both Sargon and Naram-Sin. Of these, only one epic poem survives (in a fourteenth-century-BC copy) to de-scribe Sargon's campaign, while Naram-Sin is better supplied with documen-tation. A question this raises is whether Sargon's Anatolian adventure actually

---

26. A. R. Millard, "Israelite and Aramean History in the Light of Inscriptions," *TynBul* 41, no. 2 (1990): 261-75.

took place or whether, as Mario Liverani has argued, it was forged to create a model to be emulated. Liverani's argument rests on three observations: (1) Naram-Sin claims to have been the first to "destroy" the sites in question; (2) no monumental inscription attributing such a campaign to Sargon has survived in copies or otherwise; and (3) there is no archaeological mark of a Sargonic conquest. Responding to each in detail, Millard argues (1) that we must distinguish between "conquering" (claimed for Sargon) and "destroying" (claimed for Naram-Sin); (2) that our lack of a monument recounting Sargon's campaign does not prove that one never existed, perhaps at the "new city at Akkad" that Sargon built but which has not yet been located; and (3) a conquest that did not include large-scale property destruction would not likely leave any archaeological mark. Thus, the arguments against the *possibility* of Sargon's northwest Anatolian campaign are not compelling. Moreover, since Naram-Sin's campaign in the same direction is supported not only by epic materials but also by original monuments, its essential historicity seems confirmed. If it appears, then, that Naram-Sin's campaign was not simply a scribal invention, then might this not also be the case for Sargon's campaign? An affirmative answer to this question would not deny, of course, that the epic materials also served didactic purposes. Comparative study such as Millard presents indicates the wrongheadedness of assuming, as biblical scholars sometimes do, that didactic purposes and historicity stand in an inverse relationship.

Another reason sometimes given for dismissing the biblical depictions of Israel's past is that they do not seem to fit what we know of the ancient Near Eastern world in the period in question. For instance, it is sometimes asserted that the biblical picture of David's and especially Solomon's Israelite empire is anachronistic, an imaginative retrojection of scribes familiar with the Persian Empire. Our fifth essay, Kenneth Kitchen's "The Controlling Role of External Evidence in Assessing the Historical Status of the Israelite United Monarchy," offers an alternative viewpoint.

Though not in so many words, Kitchen, like Lemche, also challenges biblical scholars to "look out the window" onto the world of the ancient Near East, especially in the period from the twelfth to the tenth centuries, to see what effect a broader view of the "facts" might have on one's assessment of the historicity of the biblical picture of the kingdom/empire of David and Solomon. Interestingly, although not surprisingly, Kitchen comes to conclusions radically opposed to the general direction of Lemche and others like him who find the biblical picture implausible and incredible. Drawing on both the biblical and the extrabiblical data, Kitchen builds a strong case for the view that the period in question, while it was a time of "Great Power–

eclipse" (i.e., some recession in the case of Egypt and Assyria and collapse in the case of Hatti), was *not* a "'dark age' throughout the ancient world," as claimed, for instance, by J. M. Miller.[27] It was, rather, a period that saw the temporary flourishing of "mini-empires" comprising "heartland" along with conquered territories and "subject-allies." Drawing on whatever biblical and extrabiblical evidence is extant, Kitchen argues for the existence of three such "mini-empires" in the Levant in the Late Bronze Age — namely, Tabal in southeast Anatolia, Carchemish on both sides of the west bend of the Euphrates in north Syria, and subsequently Aram-Zobah, beginning in its homeland in the Beqaʿ valley and extending by conquests northeastward toward the Euphrates and southward toward Maacah and Geshur and including subject allies in Aram-Damascus to the east and Hamath to the north (maps are included with Kitchen's essay). Given the presence of these three mini-empires in the period in question, could there not have been a fourth — that is, the relatively short-lived but territorially extensive mini-empire of the Israelite United Monarchy under David and Solomon? Combining forceful argumentation with characteristically forceful rhetoric, Kitchen answers with a resounding Yes! Kitchen is particularly vexed by those in the ranks of biblical scholars who

> fail to weigh the *nature* of evidence, and not merely its quantity. They continually set up "straw men" — erroneous ideas of what *they* think the biblical writers say (or should say . . .), which they then knock down, and (hey presto!) the Bible is wrong — but alas, it is their *misrepresentation* that is proven wrong, and not necessarily the biblical text, into which the misinterpretation in question has been read.

Thus, Kitchen ups the ante, challenging biblical scholars not only to "look out the window" onto the broader world of the ancient Near East but also to look more carefully, competently, and objectively at the biblical texts themselves. Few scholars come close to having spent as much time exploring the ancient Near Eastern world of the Bible as Kitchen, and it is instructive to note, as already mentioned, that his conclusion regarding the historical plausibility of the biblical picture of the United Monarchy is diametrically opposed to that of Lemche.

---

27. J. M. Miller, "Separating the Solomon of History from the Solomon of Legend," in L. K. Handy, ed., *The Age of Solomon: Scholarship at the Turn of the Millennium*, Studies in the History and Culture of the Ancient Near East 11 (Leiden: Brill, 1997), 13-14.

Sample Studies

The next two essays in the volume provide examples of synthetic approaches that seek to draw on a variety of evidence, biblical and extrabiblical, to build a case. In his consideration of "Manasseh in the Books of Kings and Chronicles," Brian Kelly shows how attending to both the extrabiblical context and the specific purposes and literary methods of a biblical writer can yield surprising results. Beginning with the recognition that biblical historiography (as indeed all historiography) is selective and interpretative, Kelly takes up the Chronicler's account of Manasseh as a test case of the historical reliability of Chronicles. He notes that although the scholarly appraisal of the historical value of Chronicles has been rather negative since de Wette and Wellhausen, recent decades have seen some reversal of this view. Turning specifically to questions of Manasseh's defeat by Assyria and deportation to Babylon, his repentance and return to Jerusalem, and his building activities and cult reforms — all mentioned in 2 Chron 33:11-17 but not mentioned in Kings —, Kelly canvasses five commonly cited grounds for dismissing the Chronicler's depiction: it is theologically motivated; Kings is silent; Assyrian records make no mention; imprisonment in Babylon seems curious since Nineveh was the imperial capital; the theology, style, language, and subject matter (building works and cult reform) are all suggestive of Chronistic invention as opposed to reliance on sources. Kelly then responds to each in turn, drawing on a wide range of (biblical and extrabiblical) textual evidence and on available archaeological evidence. He argues that neither singly nor in combination are the grounds for discounting the historicity of the Chronicler's account of Manasseh compelling.

The historicity of the book of Chronicles is also at issue in Pete Williams's essay, "Israel outside the Land: The Transjordanian Tribes in 1 Chronicles 5." Selecting 1 Chronicles 5 almost at random, with the sole criterion being that it is "generally without direct parallel within the OT," Williams begins by exploring the unity of the passage. He finds that both spelling and phraseological characteristics suggest that the chapter is a unified and integral part of the Chronicler's work. Williams then traces the historical development implied when the Chronicles passage is compared with other biblical materials (Numbers 32; Joshua 13; Isa 15:16; Jeremiah 48) and the Mesha Stela. When arranged in *prima facie* chronological order, the biblical texts indicate a shift from Israelite to Moabite possession of many Transjordanian sites — a shift verified by the Mesha Stela. Finally, Williams examines the names used in 1 Chronicles 5 and discovers that they well suit "the date, geography, and tribes to which they are assigned." While admitting that the argument is largely circumstantial and that it is possible to imagine alternative explanations of some of the data, Williams contends that an economic and justifiable approach to the various indicators is to assume that the Chronicler had access to independent, reliable information from the preexilic period.

Clarifying the Fundamental Issues

The final essay of the volume is Iain Provan's "In the Stable with the Dwarves: Testimony, Interpretation, Faith, and the History of Israel." In many respects, this essay would have served well to lead off the present volume and would have nicely complemented Kofoed's exploration of the working assumptions of T. L. Thompson and the Copenhagen School. It is included last, however, to provide a kind of final clarification of fundamental issues and to offer a philosophical and methodological footing upon which historical study of ancient Israel might fruitfully proceed. Provan boldly challenges the "rules of the game" by which so much historical study since the Enlightenment has been pursued and asks to what degree, if at all, they are capable of doing justice to reality. In particular, he queries whether "principled skepticism" can be logically and epistemologically defended, especially when it is applied with greater rigor in respect to the biblical testimony than to other ancient Near Eastern texts. It is, after all, largely through testimony that we know most of what we believe to be true about the past. Insistence on a hard "verification principle" as a prerequisite for accepting testimony would leave historians in the dark about most everything. Provan prefers instead to apply a falsification principle, whereby testimony from the past is given the benefit of the doubt, unless and until grounds for suspecting it are discovered. Ultimately, there is no substitute for careful, thoughtful judgment of each case on its own merits. Epistemological openness, not naive credulity or undue skepticism, is the order of the day.

Conclusion

The variety and magnitude of current disagreements about how to assess OT history and how to reconstruct the history of ancient Israel are sufficient to justify the notion that these areas of study are in crisis. As I argue elsewhere,[28] however, it is not necessarily a bad thing for a discipline to be in crisis, or, less dramatically, in a state of flux, especially when the discipline has followed

28. For example, "Historiography of the Old Testament," passim.

some wrong leads and developed some bad habits. A time of reflection, reappraisal, and renewal may well set the discipline on a firmer footing, or at least alert those willing to inspect the foundation of where cracks and design flaws may exist.

The essays in the present volume support this line of thinking in various ways. Kofoed stresses the importance of taking a direct look at the epistemological and methodological underpinnings of historical reconstructions currently being advanced. Winther-Nielsen reminds us of the challenge of listening well and of rightly interpreting ancient documents, and he presents "pragmatics" as a potentially fruitful approach. Hess adduces a considerable body of evidence to counter the notion that literacy was severely limited in ancient Israel. Millard shows how careful analysis of ancient Near Eastern texts can teach us to assess biblical texts more accurately on their own terms. Kitchen combines biblical and extrabiblical evidence to demonstrate that, far from being an anachronistic and fantastical retrojection, the Bible's description of the "empire" of David and Solomon accords nicely with evidence of other Near Eastern "mini-empires" during the same period. Kelly advances arguments that engender confidence in the historicity of even one of the more disputed episodes in the book of Chronicles — Manasseh's repentance. Williams explores a more or less randomly chosen passage from the material unique to Chronicles and discovers many indications that the Chronicler had access to reliable traditions from the period of the United Monarchy. And finally, Provan reminds us one last time of the fundamental issues that guide and divide biblical scholars.

From many different angles, these essays stimulate a more positive attitude toward the historical import of the biblical texts than is often displayed in current writing on the subject. They explore philosophical and hermeneutical issues, they advance improved literary approaches to texts, they open windows onto the ancient Near Eastern world of the biblical period, and they demonstrate synthetic approaches that combine textual and material evidences in arriving at well founded reconstructions. In all these ways they open windows into OT history.

Some readers of this volume may be more attracted to the generalizing discussions of the big issues. Others may find the presentations of hard data and specific evidence more exciting. But the best approach will recognize the importance of both the general and the specific. Theorizing without sufficient grasp of the data will devolve into mere fantasy. The accumulation of data without adequate understanding of the theoretical issues involved in reconstructing history will lead to mere confusion. If I may wrench out of context a line from Qoheleth: "It is good to grasp the one and not let go of the other" (Eccl 7:18). If in some small way the present volume challenges readers to take OT history more seriously and helps them to set out in fruitful directions, it will have accomplished its purpose.

Epistemology, Historiographical Method, and the "Copenhagen School"

JENS BRUUN KOFOED

Introduction

If one were to point out one characteristic of reviews on the historiography of Israel's history in recent years, it could very well be the addition to the scholarly vocabulary of words like "the Copenhagen School," "the Copenhageners," or "the Copenhagen Twins." And though the scholars in question have not invented, let alone advocated, these designations themselves, no scholar dealing with the history of Israel can now be ignorant that they refer to Niels Peter Lemche, Thomas L. Thompson, and to a lesser degree Fred Cryer — in the Department of Old Testament at the University of Copenhagen.

When Thomas L. Thompson and Niels Peter Lemche joined forces at the University of Copenhagen, they had already for a long time presented to the scholarly community a view on Israel's history that was highly critical of the traditional view of the established historical schools of Alt and Albright. It was therefore natural to use their new partnership at Copenhagen to make a bridgehead for their shared innovative approach to Israel's history. And though both Lemche and Thompson have opposed the above-mentioned designations,[1]

---

1. For the reason that they tend to underestimate the differences in methods used and views held by supposed adherents of the Copenhagen School. See, e.g., Thomas L. Thompson's response to Iain Provan, 1995a, 683-705, and — if able to read Danish — Niels Peter Lemche's reply to a Danish colleague on the same subject, 1996a, 6-8.

I am much indebted to my fellow lecturer, Henrik Bartholdy, for improving my English.

they have nevertheless, through their engagement in the scholarly debate, shown that designations like "The Copenhagen School" and "the Copenhageners" are in no way misnomers.

Their engagement in the *bytdwd* discussion,[2] to mention only one example, gave the academic community a brilliant opportunity to experience "The Copenhagen School" in action, so to speak. Characterizing the approach of the resident Copenhageners to the history of Israel as school-like and labeling their partnership "the Copenhagen School" does not mean that the same nomenclature automatically is applicable to other scholars however much they share the views put forward by the "resident" Copenhageners. But though Thompson, in his reply to Iain Provan, has made great efforts in accentuating more the differences than the similarities between the "Joycean Catholic Irish-American emigrée, a Welsh atheist, a happy Protestant Dane, and a rather disrespectfully Protestant Swede,"[3] referring to himself, Philip R. Davies, Niels Peter Lemche, and the late Gösta Ahlströhm respectively, there can be no doubt that it is both appropriate and necessary to talk about an international group of scholars who have taken a new Copenhagen School–like approach to historical studies relating to the Bible. Thompson is of course right that certain — and indeed important — differences exist between the above-mentioned scholars, but the debate on the Tel Dan stela — not to mention the strong representation of the Copenhagen School–like approach in the recently established European Seminar on Historical Methodology — is both a visible and legible witness that such a group exists.[4] So, even though it could also be justified to associate other scholars — nonresident "Copenhageners," if you like — with the "Copenhagen School" or even — as a matter of convenience — label them together with the "real" Copenhageners as the "Copenhagen School,"[5] the term will be used in

---

2. For example, the joint article by Lemche and Thompson, 1994, 3-22, and, in a broader perspective, also the launch in 1997 of the Copenhagen International Seminar series published by Sheffield Academic Press.

3. Thompson 1995a, 696.

4. Papers read at the inaugural meeting of the 1996 SBL International Meeting in Dublin have been published by Lester L. Grabbe 1997. Though the contributors are allowing the biblical records to carry different weight as historical witness and thus do bear witness to the differences mentioned by Thompson, there can be no doubt that the more skeptical Copenhagen-like approach to the biblical texts is dominant. A list of members (membership is by invitation) can be found in Lester Grabbe's introduction on p. 12.

5. One argument would be that though others have put forward similar views, thus making their own contribution to the forming of a new international direction in the study of Israel's history, the "Copenhageners" have played so prominent a part that this "direction" ought to be named after them. Another argument would be that several schol-

what follows in the more narrow sense, referring exclusively to Lemche and Thompson.

The views put forward by Lemche and Thompson have from the beginning been controversial,[6] and the present article adds to the list of critical articles assessing the approach of the Copenhagen School,[7] the present writer having at least two obvious reasons to deal with the Copenhagen School. First, theological students at the University of Copenhagen are now being taught almost exclusively that biblical Israel was never more than a literary construct of the biblical writers.[8] *In Search of Ancient Israel* by Philip R. Davies is, just to mention one example, now being used as one of the basic textbooks in OT introductory courses. So if theological students in Copenhagen, being forced by the Danish educational system to graduate from the state faculty, are ever to be aware of other approaches than Lemche and Thompson's, someone in the Danish scholarly community must challenge, assess, and dispute their views and try to put forward an alternative. That is clearly one of our obligations at the Copenhagen Lutheran School of Theology.

Second, the "Copenhagen School" has, in its very thorough rebuttal of the assumptions underlying classical form-criticism and tradition-history,[9] allowed some fundamental questions concerning historiographical method to surface in the scholarly debate. And no one should regret either that we again are allowed to discuss the epistemological aspects of the biblical texts or that archaeology and the so-called social sciences have established themselves as independent disciplines over against the literary criticism of biblical studies. For these reasons I find it not only interesting and challenging on a personal level but also necessary on a scholarly level to discuss the views of the "Copenhagen School." Even if their conclusions indeed may be disputed, they have raised a number of important questions with which a historian of Israel has to deal.

In unearthing the methodological assumptions underlying the approach of the Copenhagen School, I will deal primarily with the literary production

---

ars have given extensive support to the views put forward by Lemche and Thompson in the scholarly debate, thereby associating themselves with the "Copenhagen School."

6. That the controversy is still alive and kicking can easily be observed in the most recent scholarly debate. So, e.g., in the recent critique by W. G. Dever, 1998, 39-52.

7. A nonexhaustive list would include I. W. Provan 1995, 585-606; Provan 1998; A. R. Millard 1995, 209-17; H. H. Klement 1997/98, 7-41 (esp. 10-15); K. A. Kitchen 1999.

8. To such a degree that colleagues with different approaches have begun to react. Cf. Jesper Høgenhaven 1996, 156-69, and Niels Peter Lemche's reply, 1996c, 6-8.

9. Cf. Thomas L. Thompson 1998.

of Thompson and refer to Lemche's writings only sporadically or when they differ from those of Thompson.

The "Thompson Tel"

Digging through the literary Thompson Tel, one will sooner or later strike the methodological bedrock of his historiography. And let it be my opening thesis that the methodological Hinnom and Kidron valleys embracing his historiographical Ophel are his historiographical method and text theory. That is: his assumptions regarding the nature of and relationship between artifactual and textual remains on the one side and his understanding of how ancient texts were composed on the other.

The most conspicuous of Thompson's historiographical works[10] is no doubt his 1992 attempt to write an independent history of Iron Age Palestine[11] depending on the so-called primary sources, which are claimed to be "a) archaeological excavations and their analysis, the classification and interpretation of archaeologically derived realia and archaeological surveys and the settlement patterns of ancient Palestine understood regionally and geographically; b) the wealth of ancient written remains directly and indirectly related to ancient Palestine: the people, its neighbours, its economy, religious and political structures, modes of life and known events; and c) the biblical traditions that reflect explicitly and implicitly the world in which they are formed and which portray that understanding of Israel whose origin we are seeking."[12]

Though a first reading of this paragraph could lead one to believe that the biblical records are included in what Thompson calls "primary evidence," a reading of the book as a whole makes it clear that an apparent corollary in his heuristics to the stress that he lays on structures and developments over longer periods as decisive for history, as opposed to events, is that non-written, artifactual remains are preferred to written sources. The archaeological remains are realia, while the biblical records are traditions that portray only an understanding, not the origin, of the Israel "whose origin we are seeking." And, moreover, events described in the "wealth of ancient written re-

10. Thomas L. Thompson 1992.
11. This is his most extensive treatment, but see also Thompson 1999. In the 1992 volume he states in his concluding chapter (405) that "What we need to overcome this crisis in the historiography of early 'Israel' is a structurally dependable, correctable and expandable history, which, independent of biblical historiography, might render the context of the tradition's formation and the background of its referents. . . ."
12. Thompson 1992, 127.

mains" are reliable only when they are "known events," that is, known from the archaeologically derived realia. A close reading of this paragraph as well as of the book as a whole reveals, then, that in reality it is the archaeologically derived realia that are used as the basis and point of departure for his Iron Age Palestine history. They form the interpretative context for his considerations on the kingdoms of Israel and Judah.[13] The question still not answered, however, is on what basis Thompson writes off the biblical "traditions" in favor of the archaeological realia. In order to answer the question we will now turn to a closer look at the way he seeks to integrate the biblical and extrabiblical data into a reconstruction of Israel's history (historiographical method) and his understanding of how and for what purpose the biblical texts were composed (text theory).

The French Connection

In the above-mentioned reply to Iain Provan, Thompson gives his approval of the historical orientation of the so-called Annales School. In doing so he points not only to the "essentials" of his own historiographical method and historical understanding but also to one of the main reasons for the more general reorientation of historical method in relation to biblical studies that has been going on since at least the beginning of the 1970s.

When in 1929 Lucien Febvre and Marc Bloch started publishing the *Annales* magazine, history had become a social science with open borders to geography, sociology, anthropology, and archaeology. This multidisciplinary "new history" was a reaction against the idiographical focus on the extraordinary history of kings, states, and nations of historicism and romanticism. It is this reaction that penetrated the study of Israel's history when, in the course of the early 1970s, more and more scholars recognized the independence of archaeology and the so-called behavioral sciences from the literary criticism of biblical studies. The fact that classical literary criticism at the same time was deadlocked, and that the views of the well-established historical schools in the field since the beginning of the '60s had been heavily attacked, only accelerated the development. Hitherto archaeology and the behavioral sciences had been used — more or less — as subdisciplines to biblical studies, answering the questions raised by literary criticism. Now they were recognized as disciplines in their own right. The starting point of the historiographer was no longer a primary and textual pool of evidence brought forth by biblical literary criti-

13. To this see also Thomas L. Thompson 1991, 65-92.

cism but several pools of evidence, the results of literary criticism being considered "evidence" on equal terms with reports from archaeological excavations and results from sociology, anthropology, and the like. History had become "multidisciplinary," and the task of the historian was now to integrate the results from these different disciplines in a comprehensive synopsis of Israel's history, a so-called "total history."

It is this historical reorientation that Thompson acknowledges,[14] just as in his re-presentation of Iron Age Palestine he takes as a starting point the three-tier model for historical explanation developed by one of the representatives of the Annales School, Fernand Braudel. Braudel, in Hans Barstad's words, "apparently has become the hero of quite a few biblical historians during recent years."[15] In his model, Braudel distinguishes between levels of historical analysis that work with different sets of data, use different research strategies, and arise, to a certain extent, from different theoretical perceptions of history.[16] These levels of historical analysis correspond with three levels of historical development, designated "structures," "conjunctures," and "events," using Braudel's terminology.[17] At the most basic level are the "structures" or "la longue durée," the long-term level, that is, those phenomena that lasted for generations if not for centuries — for example, climatic or geographic conditions that determined the patterns of people's lives over extended periods of time. At the second level one finds the "conjuncture," that is, the economic and social trends that may rise and fall in importance and popularity over the course of a generation. On the third level is the "event," those historical phenomena that are most familiar to us but that are of the shortest and most insignificant duration, a day, a week, or at most a few years.[18]

In a most illuminating article, Ernst Axel Knauf has described Braudel's model and its possible implications for the reconstruction of Israel's history.[19] About the first two levels of Braudel's model he states that " 'Structures' and 'conjunctures' describe a state of the world beyond the individual's reach, changing in terms that far surpass one human's lifetime and experience. But accumulated actions of individual persons can create 'structures' in the course

14. Thompson 1995a, 687, 692.

15. Hans Barstad 1997, 49.

16. Lemche, Thompson, Ahlström, Davies, and Knauf all refer to Braudel's historical levels, which are developed and applied in Braudel 1972. For a shorter presentation of his theory see Braudel 1980.

17. F. Braudel 1980, 25-54.

18. Braudel 1980, esp. 27-34, 74-76.

19. Ernst Axel Knauf (now Axel Knauf-Belleri), "From History to Interpretation," in Edelman 1991, 26-64.

of the millennia. History as a process describes our common fate beyond the influence of conscious decision-making."[20] Then he goes on to make two very important points that, as we shall see shortly, very well describe how Thompson is applying the model when he deals with the artifactual and textual evidence in his historiographies. First, it is on the level of this processual history that "we may expect answers to the questions of Israel's origin, the origin of its religion, and the emergence, rise and fall of Israelite states. Whatever the achievements of some individuals in these processes were, . . . there are structural reasons for their success or the reception of their ideas."[21] Second, "as the construction of any chain of events is based on a collective or individual decision about what is meaningful and relevant, the eventual level of history is textual by nature. Meaning is not an attribute of 'things as they are'; meaning is attributed to certain things by the human mind that perceives meaning by creating it."[22] Knauf adds in a footnote: "Ancient Near Eastern historiography (including biblical and early Islamic historiography) is not concerned with what actually had happened. Rather, it is interested in stating what should have happened in order to construct a 'correct' world."[23]

Now, it is not difficult to see how Thompson is putting the reorientation of the Annales School in general, and Braudel's model of historical explanation in particular, into practice. In the concluding chapter of his 1992 volume, "The Independent History of Israel," he deals explicitly with the influence of the more general reorientation of historical studies on biblical studies. Here he refers to his own (and Lemche's) historiographical method as a "spectrum studies approach," describing it as a method

> based on efforts to interrelate a wide variety of taxonomies or spectra which organise ancient data that are potentially related to our historical questions and hence to our reconstructive interpretations. The integration of our analysis of multiple, overlapping spectra brings into our historical purview hundreds of data-sensitive variables relating to such important historical factors as economics, politics, social organisation, linguistics, religion, ethnicity, art and material culture. When these spectra can be isolated in discrete chronological units, our analysis becomes open to the intrinsically historical issues of stability, development and change.[24]

20. Knauf in Edelman 1991, 43.
21. Knauf in Edelman 1991, 44.
22. Knauf in Edelman 1991, 45.
23. Knauf in Edelman 1991, 46 n. 1.
24. Thompson 1992, 405.

A reading of his 1992 volume as a whole makes it obvious how he also uses Braudel's three-tier model. He moves from the basic "structure" level through the "conjuncture" level in order to create a more or less normative and fixed context for the understanding of the "eventual" level. This level is by nature textual and accessible to us only through a number of subjective, selective, and, according to Thompson, variant historiographical traditions: Genesis-Kings and Chronicles-Ezra in their Masorete, Qumran, and Septuagint variants, the book of Maccabees, the book of *Jubilees,* and so on.[25] The emphasis in Thompson's description of historical development in Iron Age Palestine is clearly on the so-called structures (especially climatic changes) and conjunctures (changes in political, socioeconomical conditions) with a corresponding emphasis on sources considered relevant to such changes and conditions, namely, the non-written, artifactual remains. According to Thompson, then, the most basic explanation of the demographic movements in the early history of Palestine is not a change in economic conjunctures and commercial relations, but climatic changes, or, to be more explicit, the great Mycenean drought from 1250 to 1050 BC. It is this drought that, according to Thompson, is decisive for changes in both the economic conjunctures and the demographic movements in the period discussed.

How are we, then, to judge Braudel's model of historical explanation and, not least, Thompson's application of it in his historiography? Is it the "French connection" that governs his use, or rather nonuse, of texts? There can be no doubt that a multidisciplinary "new history" or "total history" approach in some form must now be deemed necessary in historical studies and that Thompson's application of it in his "spectrum studies approach" is one of the best examples hitherto of how it can be applied to the history of Israel. The history of Israel is not an exception alongside histories of other nations or ethnic groups. Its history may very well be exceptional, but a description of its "exceptionality" must be based on the same historical inquiries as are used to write histories of other nations and ethnic groups. Furthermore, a broader perspective focusing on the geographical, anthropological, and societal structures of ancient Syro-Palestine as the inseparable and indispensable context of the more regional histories is a plain necessity if we want to elucidate "the conditions and limitations, the possibilities and impossibilities under and among which the people of the past had to live and had to make their decisions."[26]

Thompson's 1992 volume is at least to be commended for making this

25. On "variant traditions" see Thompson 1992, 383-99; cf. Thompson 1987, 41-59; Thompson 1991, 65-92.

26. Knauf in Edelman 1991, 44.

point. The different climatic, socioeconomic, and political factors are consequently seen over against the regional heterogeneity of Palestine. Severe drought had, of course, other consequences in the Judean hills than was the case in the Southern Negev region. Thompson consequently avoids applying the same yardstick to all geographical regions in heterogeneous Palestine, as has often been done in archaeological surveys. The point, however, is whether texts are relevant and consequently should be taken into consideration when such a processual or structural history is being written, or whether a processual history written exclusively on the basis of artifactual evidence should be seen as the normative context for the interpretation of the textual evidence, not least the biblical texts.

It is important to notice that Braudel's model does not in itself demand that all answers to the questions of Israel's origin must be found in the so-called "structures" and "conjunctures," nor that there can be no possible epistemological coherence between the historical events and the textual re-presentation of them in much later texts.[27] Though the model admittedly does emphasize the importance of structural and conjunctural history, the structures or conjunctures are not necessarily to be understood as the absolute determinatives of human behavior, since the model (at least in principle) leaves room for interaction between the structural, conjunctural, and eventual (human) actors of the different historical levels.[28] However, if determinism, materialism, and sheer positivism are to be avoided in the application of the model on ancient history, two important caveats must be kept in mind. First, though Braudel's stress on the need to use empirical, quantifiable data in order to describe the structures and conjunctures underlying *l'historie eventiellement* has proved very helpful in his own studies of medieval history, it is highly problematic in the study of the ancient world, since the sources of, for example, Israel's history are scattered, sparse, and, not least, event-oriented. And, as Barstad and others have shown, we do not have enough evidence from the Early Iron Age to do for example, statistics in the same way as is possible in the medieval period. Applying Braudel's model too rashly to the textual evidence from Iron Age Palestine could therefore easily result in an unnecessary and methodologically highly problematic dismissal of, for example, the biblical historiography.[29]

27. Contra what Knauf seems to imply in his explanation of the model in Knauf in Edelman 1991, 43-44.

28. Though being praised for his distinction between historical times in his description of the Mediterranean world, he has also been criticized for not being willing (or able) to bridge the gap between *la longue durée* and *l'histoire eventiellement*. Cf. G. G. Iggers 1984, 56-79, esp. 59.

29. Cf. Iggers 1984, 65ff.; Barstad 1997, 49-50; R. S. Bagnall 1995, 112-17.

Second, if historiographers using Braudel's model discard the human factor as decisive for historical development, or deny textual evidence any possibility of adding much to an overall understanding of the historical development of Iron Age Palestine, it is not so much because of the model itself as it is because of the historiographers' own philosophical presuppositions. And any historiographer using Braudel must therefore be aware of how his own philosophical presuppositions influence his understanding of the causal and epistemological relationships between the above-mentioned levels. We have to realize that we are entering nothing less than the well-known discussion between empirical and nomothetical-oriented positivism on the one hand, and idealistic and idiographical historicism on the other. For even if Braudel's three-tier model seems very useful or even indispensable, "we need," as J. Maxwell Miller once put it, "to be reminded that methodologies are ways of examining evidence and never should be mistaken for evidence itself."[30] Methodologies are governed by philosophies, in Thompson's case by the view that structures and conjunctures are basic to the understanding of the Iron Age history of Palestine, that the event-oriented textual evidence is to be considered "secondary" or "intellectual" history, and that an analysis and interpretation of the artifactual data therefore must serve as the interpretative context for the textual data, not least the "biblical traditions."

Such a weighing and use of artifactual and textual evidence is, as we have seen, not necessary from Braudel's model, but is a materialistic or positivistic use of the model.[31] I see no problem in analyzing the evidence from a nomothetical perspective, or, for that matter, in using Ernst Troeltsch's principles of causality, analogy, and immanence in order to describe what, on the basis of well-known sociological patterns and the natural laws, can be said about the conditions, possibilities, and impossibilities under which the people of the past had to live and had to make their decisions. There can be no doubt that artifactual remains are crucial to such studies. A problem does arise, however, when such nomothetically oriented methods (not least those of Troeltsch) are used to answer questions they are incapable of answering, namely, what people choose and why they sometimes choose the unexpected and, according to the nomothetical thinking scholar, the impossible. People sometimes make unexpected choices, as we know from experience (after all, football wouldn't be worth watching if they didn't!). Artifactual remains are certainly capable of describing the possibilities and impossibilities under

---

30. "Is It Possible to Write a History of Israel?" in Edelman 1991, 100.

31. Here Provan is obviously right. Cf. Provan 1995, 585-606. A fact that has also been admitted by Hans Barstad; cf. Barstad 1997, 49-50.

which the people of the past had to live and make their decisions, but they cannot and do not tell what choices people actually made and they certainly do not explain why they made them.

When Thompson states that "the biblical concept of a *benei Israel* . . . is a reflection of no socio-political entity of the historical state of Israel of the Assyrian period, nor is it an entirely realistic reflection of the post-state Persian period in which the biblical tradition took its shape as a cohering self-understanding of Palestine's population,"[32] it is an assertion highly dependent on his view on artifactual evidence as the interpretative context for textual evidence. A few quotations will illustrate this. In his discussion of Albrecht Alt's "God of the Fathers" and of a God giving laws by command, he states that "if we do not have corroborative evidence from the real world that such deities and laws existed . . . then we can hardly have any form-critical or literary and interpretative ground for using such materials for historical reconstruction."[33] And, later in the same volume, criticizing Mendenhall and Gottwald: "their focus on anthropology, sociology and economics, however, is of immense importance, since most atextual approaches to historical change and development must proceed á la longue durée; i.e., more in terms of societal and structural changes than in terms of events and personages." Why? Because, "What we need . . . is a structurally dependable, correctable and expandable history, which, independent of biblical historiography, might render the context of the tradition's formation and the background of its referents. . . ." And from another contribution: "If we are ever to achieve our exegetical goal of allowing the biblical narrative to be heard and understood within the modern context of our discipline, the first and primary need is to establish, in all the fullness and detail possible, an independent history of early Palestine and Israel that might serve as the historical context from which these narratives speak. Without such an interpretative matrix, we continue to read the biblical tradition in faith — as through a glass darkly."[34]

So even though Thompson does distinguish between primary and secondary texts and between different genres of texts (historiography, origin traditions, inscriptions, etc.), it is nevertheless the atextual approaches to historical change and development that are given precedence over against the results from any form-critical and literary-textual approach. Even if the oldest known biblical manuscripts were not so far removed in time from the events they purport to describe, there would still, according to Thompson, be

---

32. For example, Thompson 1992, 422.
33. Thompson 1992, 29.
34. Thompson 1991, 92.

no form-critical, literary, or interpretative grounds for using such materials for historical reconstruction, if "we do not have corroborative evidence from the real world," that is, the artifactual remains.[35] Analysis and interpretation of the material remains function as the interpretative context and background of the textual remains. In other words, artifacts are always the interpretative context, while texts are the interpreted context.

Herein lies the first decisive methodological problem in Thompson's historiography. As mentioned above, the material remains have no doubt enabled us to paint a better picture of the so-called "structures." There can be no doubt, either, that these "structures," that is, climatic and ecological disturbances, had great impact on the "conjunctures"; an impact observable not least in the settlement patterns. Though Thompson's efforts to describe these demographic movements and changes in settlement patterns with regard to the regional differences in Palestine must be praised, they are but a little piece of the Early Iron Age jigsaw puzzle, and we are lacking more pieces than we have. Kenneth Kitchen's well-known dictum, that "absence of evidence is not evidence of absence," of course applies here.[36]

We have to be content with what we can say and leave the rest open. Take the well-known Iron Age settlements in the Judean hill country. Drought may very well have caused radical changes in settlement patterns all over Palestine, and the so-called Israelite Iron Age settlements could very well be the result of drought causing overpopulation in other regions of Palestine. But other factors, which we do not and cannot know from material remains, may have been operating as well. This makes it impossible from the artifactual remains alone to identify with certainty who those settlers were and precisely why they chose to settle as they did. My point here is not to argue that these settlers were Israelites or non-Israelites, but that it is not obvious that the biblical text should be excluded as a witness to identify who they might have been and why they chose to settle there. Whether the texts should be included in or excluded from the pool of primary evidence is not a given, but is to be considered on the basis of one's understanding of the epistemological capability and literary form of the texts. So, when Thompson excludes the biblical sources from the primary pool of evidence, we must correspondingly seek the arguments for doing so in either his epistemic standing or his literary criticism. Since we shall deal more thoroughly with his understanding of the texts in the next section, suffice it to say that if he fails to argue that the biblical texts necessarily must be seen as "traditions" that have their origin and find their

35. Cf. N. P. Lemche 1996b, 26-27.
36. For example, Kitchen 1995, 50.

meaning "within the development of the tradition and within the utopian religious perceptions that the tradition created, rather than within the real world of the past that the tradition restructured in terms of a coherent ethnicity and religion,"[37] then he is using the kind of circular argumentation for which he so often criticizes others. He is using his own reading of the biblical texts to ascertain that his interpretation of the scattered and fragmentary artifactual evidence is correct, namely, that biblical Israel did not originate or ever exist in Early Iron Age Palestine. We can find exactly the same circular argumentation in Lemche. In *Die Vorgeschichte Israels* he states that "historisch betrachtet, vermögen die alttestamentlichen Erzählungen nur wenig oder gar nichts zur Geschichte der Bronzezeit vor der Entstehung Israels beizutragen."[38] Why? Because there is no extrabiblical evidence of a literary class that, in Lemche's opinion, was capable of writing such sophisticated literature as the biblical narratives. Again, the absence of evidence becomes the interpretative context, a "norma normans," for what is reliable or not in the biblical narratives.

The Creation of Meaning

In order to answer the question why Thompson does not put faith in the biblical narratives as reliable sources for ascertaining conditions and events in Early Iron Age Palestine, we need to uncover the philosophical and epistemological assumptions underlying his above-mentioned description of the biblical texts as "traditions." It seems to be in full accord with Knauf's explanation of how the textual nature of Braudel's eventual level can be applied to biblical studies when Thompson states that "in history, meaning is created, arbitrary and additional,"[39] or when he writes that

> the traditions are not so much a direct reflection of or reference to either periods of origin and composition as they are an explanation that gives meaning to them. That is, the ideological and theological Tendenz of the received or extant traditions, to the degree that they are oriented to the world of the final stages of the tradition's formation, may well preclude their use for any historical reconstruction based on assumed events from a greater past. For such past worlds refracted from the redactions are constructs of a world contemporary to the redaction. Indeed, they stand outside of any historical field

37. Thompson 1992, 422.
38. Niels Peter Lemche 1996d, 208.
39. Thompson 1992, 405.

of reference other than intellectual history. The historical significance of the received tradition, holistically perceived, lies primarily in its dual functions as meaningful literature and as library in post-compositional times. . . . One must indeed incline towards the Persian period for the historical context in which our narratives have their significance as a tradition of Israel. . . .[40]

"Unlike events of history," which can only be affirmed by the artifactual evidence, "events of tradition," that is, according to Thompson, events that are not confirmed by the artifactual evidence

do not share in reality through their own individuality or significance. Rather, the referent of the Bible lies quite far from both this world and its events. 'History', the past of human affairs, is, for the ancient traditionist, illusory — like the whole of this material, accidental and refracted world. Events in time are but a distorting glass through which we can but see partially. True reality is unknowable, transcendent of experience. Tradition is important in order to bring understanding: to evoke truth, not to recount it. Reality is not part of this traditional world of human creation. Not even the tradition's gods are truly real in themselves, but are only manifestations of God. Yahweh is god for Israel.[41]

The crucial question is, of course, whether Thompson is evoking the biblical text's own voice or reading it with "postmodern glasses." Though Thompson — not surprisingly — claims the former, he nowhere gives us compelling arguments. In excluding the biblical texts from contributing to the understanding of the historical context of the texts, Thompson uses a highly problematic circular argumentation, where the political, intellectual, social, or religious *Sitz im Leben* of the text is determined by comparing the texts with a reconstruction of Palestine's history without allowing the texts to play any role in this interpretative reconstruction. And, just to mention one example, because we have found no reference to, say, King Solomon in the sparse and scattered extrabiblical sources, he is interpreted by this very absence of evidence to be pure invention, a literary construct of a much later period, thus preventing the biblical record from being the hitherto only source that mentions his name. So, even though it must be taken into serious consideration that the oldest manuscripts are very late indeed compared to the persons and events they purport to describe, it cannot be taken as a given, as Thompson seems to do, that late biblical texts cannot at one and the same

40. Thompson 1991, 85.
41. Thompson 1996b, 247.

time be addressing contemporary issues by using traditions or historical accounts and render reliable accounts of a distant past. This is a *non sequitur.* He, and anyone else dealing with the question of historical consciousness in the biblical texts, must at least as a starting point be open to the possibility that the biblical texts both are capable of and conscious about rendering the past in a reliable and, to the modern historiographer, useful way.[42] That is clearly not what Thompson is doing in his *a priori* exclusion of the texts as contributors to a reconstruction of, for example, Israel's history.

If, however, the biblical texts were allowed the possibility of contributing to the reconstruction of Palestine's history, a very different understanding of Israel's history would have been achieved, an understanding that would not allow Thompson to discard the biblical accounts as unreliable, fictive, inventions. His reading must therefore at the outset be considered questionable and suspect. Rather than evoking the text's own voice, Thompson is doing the same thing that he claims the biblical authors did, namely, reading their accounts through the lens of a much later period and using them for his own purpose without being concerned with their original historical context. Or, to use more philosophically loaded language: he is taking Immanuel Kant's transcendental philosophy to its logical conclusion and applying it to the OT texts. "True reality," Thompson's equivalent of Kant's *Ding an Sich*, "is unknowable, transcendent of experience."[43] Because of this transcendence, *truth,* in Thompson's opinion, can only be created (or categorized — to use another of Kant's key terms) by the ancient biblical writers. Such a Kantian understanding of humanity's epistemological capacity has only natural bearings on the understanding of the biblical texts and on the relationship between the biblical texts and other ancient texts — in other words, on the concept of "canon."

1. The biblical texts are the perceived history, or, to use Kant's terminology, the categorized reality of its last known author(s) or redactor(s), namely, in the Hellenistic period.[44]

2. As a collection of texts they are, for the same reason, nothing but an expression of how available fragments of the past (oral or written) were used — regardless of their origin and primary context — to express what was considered meaningful and important by a particular author or group of authors. In

42. The question of an open epistemology is a very important and noteworthy argument of Provan, who most kindly provided me with a draft version of his 1998 IOSOT paper (see below, 161-96).

43. Thompson 1996b, 247.

44. Used as an important argument against form-criticism and tradition-history in Thompson 1987, 62. Cf. Thompson 1992, 353-66.

a recent article so far published only in Danish, Thompson compares these fragments with the well-known Danish lego blocks and describes the compositional techniques of the ancient authors as if they were using these fragments as lego blocks in order to "bring understanding, to evoke truth, not to recount it."[45] "For," to recall Thompson's words cited above, "such past worlds refracted from the redactions are constructs of a world contemporary to the redaction. Indeed, they stand outside of any historical field of reference other than intellectual history."[46]

3. Such a collection of texts must be considered not prior or normative but parallel to other contemporary collections: Qumran, Samaritan, Maccabean, and the like. They are to be considered variant traditions, different but parallel expressions of fragments considered useful to express the perception of reality of a given author, group, or society.[47]

4. The primary goal of exegesis is, therefore, on the basis of what we "know" about the "structures" and "conjunctures" in Hellenistic period Palestine, to identify the motives and ideas that have governed the compositions of the biblical authors.

Thompson's understanding of the epistemological capacity of humans and the compositional techniques of the biblical writers has wide implications not only for historical studies and biblical exegesis but also for biblical theology — implications that Thompson is well aware of himself. Discussing the goal "so dear to the reformers," Thompson has the following to say about the possibility "that Yahweh — or indeed Jesus — could somehow be translated and become our god, without substantial loss or distortion": "This fundamental assumption (and, I would say, arrogance) of biblical theology had at its core a belief in the inadequacy of the worldview of the ancients, but at the same time it maintained a blind faith that this same primitive world's religious perception could be a saving perception for our world."[48] If the presupposition is right, namely, that the religious perception of a given biblical

45. Thomas L. Thompson 1996c, 233-41.

46. Thompson 1996b, 247

47. In their overall historiographical method Lemche and Thompson share — as we have noticed — the "new history" or "total history" approach of the Annales School, and though they also have quite similar views on the late compositional date and the nonhistorical character of the biblical narratives, they argue for them in quite different ways. Though Lemche argues more on the basis of comparative historiography and conventional literary criticism, he nevertheless shares the view that the biblical narratives are almost exclusively invented stories composed for contemporary or future political, intellectual, or religious purposes.

48. Thomas L. Thompson 1996b, 246.

writer is founded on evoked truth and grounded in a created reality, it can be maintained — as Thompson does — that (a) it did not matter for the ancient writer and does not matter for us whether any correspondence or coherence can be created between created reality in the texts and true reality outside the texts, and (b) the religious perception of the text must be regarded as authoritative, that is, "canon," only for a very limited group of people in Palestine during the Hellenistic period. What is at stake, then, is not just an outdated picture of Israel's past and ancient composition techniques, but nothing less than the authority and status as "canon" of Scripture for ancient as well as modern man.

In a word of assessment, however, it has to be held that Thompson's presupposition is neither necessary nor likely. It is true, of course, that "events in time" — as they are experienced by human beings — are "a glass through which we can see but partially," but in no way does it follow that this glass is a "distorting" one and that the ancient writer was indifferent to whether his perception of reality was distorted or not. Reading the biblical texts, one almost intuitively gets the impression that it did matter, that it did make a difference for the biblical writer (and his audience/readers) whether his characters and accounts were factual or fictitious. And — in addition — one might very well ask how Thompson himself would respond if his own historiography were measured by the same skeptical epistemological yardstick? Does it make a difference for Thompson whether the Albrecht Alt referred to in his writings is a factual or fictitious character? For his readers? I think so. It would have been very compromising for Thompson's historiography if he had referred to fictitious scholars as a part of his argument. His scholarly integrity would no doubt have been questioned, and his historiography would most probably have been rejected as an interesting but nonetheless unreliable contribution to the study of Israel's history. Or, in Steven Shapin's words, "A person who would not take information on the same bases as others would not know what others knew, and, accordingly, would not be accounted a competent and reasonable member of society."[49] Is it likely, then, that a reference to past events and characters as employed in the biblical texts could have achieved such an authoritative status as they did if they were indifferent to whether their perception of reality was distorted or not? That is only one of many questions one could — and should — ask in an assessment of the presupposition underlying Thompson's text-theory.

49. Steven Shapin 1994, 204.

Concluding Remarks

It has been the aim of the present essay to uncover and assess the methodological bedrock of Thompson's historiographical works. Thompson and the school he represents have offered us no new and compelling evidence for their thesis that the biblical concept of Israel is the construct of a second-century-B.C. Jewish-Hellenistic writer or group of writers and that they for the same reason are to be excluded from the pool of primary witnesses to the history of an Early Iron Age Israel. What is new — or at least different from the old, well-known schools — is Thompson's epistemic stand in preferring artifactual evidence to textual, and his assumptions regarding the compositional techniques of the biblical authors — assumptions that, we have seen, are highly questionable, resulting in circular argumentation. In this enterprise, Thompson represents a peculiar combination of Braudel's model of historical explanation in a positivistic outlook and a postmodern, Kantian approach to the understanding of texts. Since the materialistic and positivistic use of Braudel's model functions as Thompson's overall historiographical method, Barstad is quite right when he says that Thompson and Lemche represent "the first of the last modernists" and are "still profoundly marked by the nineteenth-century absolutist/historicist/positivist understanding of what it is to be scientific." Their contributions to biblical historiography cannot be characterized as a "paradigm shift" since they still, "in Kuhnian terminology, qualify as 'normal historians.'"[50]

Barstad is no doubt right when he predicts that the future of biblical historiography will be "a history characterised by a multiplicity of methods."[51] And Davies' plea that what we need are "multiple histories" so that we "may learn in how many different ways 'history' may be represented"[52] may be a good one. We do need a multiplicity of new histories with different perspectives on, for example, Israel's history. They are only to be welcomed. What we do not need, however, are histories that do not present a full discussion of the philosophical and epistemological assumptions that have determined their choice of methods and assertions.[53] Though neither Thompson's nor Lemche's contributions

50. Barstad 1997, 50-51.// 51. Barstad 1997, 51-52.

52. Philip R. Davies, "Whose History? Whose Bible? Biblical Histories, Ancient and Modern," in Grabbe 1997, 104-22.

53. It is thus not sufficient when Davies quotes Diana Edelman in a praising note (Davies in Grabbe 1997, 120 n. 21) for having stated that "There can never be a definitive reconstruction of the past; there can only be a range of creative associations by individuals who have been influenced by their own life experiences as well as by the data they believe

meet this standard,[54] they must, after all, be considered most welcome because they have opened up a discussion of historiographical method — and, not least, of the deficiencies of any method not epistemologically open to the possibility that the biblical texts will and can contribute to a modern reconstruction of Israel's history.

Bibliography

Bagnall, R. S.
1995   *Reading Papyri, Writing Ancient History.* London and New York: Routledge.

Barstad, H.
1997   "History and the Hebrew Bible." L. L. Grabbe, ed., *Can a 'History of Israel' Be Written?* JSOTS 245. Sheffield: Sheffield Academic Press, 37-64.

Braudel, F.
1972   *The Mediterranean and the Mediterranean World in the Age of Philip II.* 2 vols. London: Collins; New York: Harper & Row.
1980   *On History.* Chicago: University of Chicago Press.

Dever, W. G.
1998   "Archaeology, Ideology and the Quest for an 'Ancient' or 'Biblical' Israel." *Near Eastern Archaeology* 61/1: 39-52.

Edelman, D. V., ed.
1991   *The Fabric of History.* JSOTS 127. Sheffield: Sheffield Academic Press.

Grabbe, L. L., ed.
1997   *Can a 'History of Israel' Be Written?* JSOTS 245. Sheffield: Sheffield Academic Press.

Høgenhaven, J.
1996   "Det gamle Testamente og teologien — efter 'Københavnerskolen.'" *Fønix* 3: 156-69.

Iggers, G. G.
1984   *New Directions in European Historiography.* Middletown, Conn.: Wesleyan University Press.

---

to be reliable and choose to link together in chains of meaning," since the phrase "life experience" is too loose and at least has to be qualified. Whenever we choose data "to be reliable," we do so on the basis of a certain epistemology, and any historiographer owes the readers a clarification of this basis.

54. On the contrary, Lemche and Thompson often present their views in an assertive way as if the discussion on the epistemological capabilities of the biblical texts ought to be a closed matter. Cf. Lemche 1996b, 27-28; 1996d, 208-24.

Kitchen, K. A.

1995   "The Patriarchal Age: Myth or History?" *BARev* 21/2 (March/April): 48-57, 88-95.

1999   "Egyptians and Hebrews, from Ra'amses to Jericho." In S. Ahituv and E. Orens, eds., *The Origin of Early Israel: Current Debate. Biblical, Historical, and Archaeological Perspectives.* Levi Sala Seminar. Beersheva: University of the Negev Press, 1998, 65-131.

Klement, H. H.

1997/98 "Gott und die Götter im Alten Testament." *Jahrbuch für evangelikale Theologie*, 7-41.

Lemche, N. P.

1984   "On the Problem of Studying Israelite History Apropos Abraham Malamat's View of Historical Research." *BN* 24: 94-124.

1985   *Early Israel: Anthropological and Historical Studies on Israelite Society before the Monarchy.* VTS 37. Leiden: Brill.

1988a   *Ancient Israel: A New History of Israelite Society.* Sheffield: Sheffield Academic Press.

1988b   *The Canaanites and Their Land.* Sheffield: Sheffield Academic Press.

1989   "On the Use of 'System Theory', 'Macro Theories' and Evolutionistic Thinking in Modern Old Testament Research and Biblical Archaeology." *SJOT* 4: 73-88.

1991   "The Development of the Israelite Religion in the Light of Recent Studies on the Early History of Israel." In J. A. Emerton, ed., *Congress Volume: Leuven.* VTS 43. Leiden: Brill, 97-115.

1993   "Kings and Clients: On Loyalty between the Ruler and the Ruled in Ancient 'Israel.'" *Semeia* 66: 119-32.

1996a   "Clio Is Also among the Muses! Keith W. Whitelam and the History of Palestine: A Review and a Commentary." *SJOT* 10/1: 88-114.

1996b   "Early Israel Revisited." *CR:BS* 4: 9-34.

1996c   "Københavnerskolen — og Jesper Høgenhaven." *Arken* 3: 6-8.

1996d   *Die Vorgeschichte Israel's: Von den Anfängen bis zum Ausgang des 13. Jahrhunderts v. Chr.* Biblische Enzyklopädie, Band 1. Stuttgart-Berlin-Köln: Verlag W. Kohlhammer.

1998   "The Origin of the Israelite State — A Copenhagen Perspective on the Emergence of Critical Historical Studies of Ancient Israel in Recent Times." *SJOT* 12/1: 44-63.

Lemche, N. P., and T. L. Thompson

1994   "Did Biran Kill David?" *JSOT* 64: 3-22.

Millard, A. R.

1995   "The Knowledge of Writing in Iron Age Palestine." *TynB* 46/2: 209-17.

Provan, I. W.

1995   "Ideologies, Literary and Critical: Reflections on Recent Writing on the History of Israel." *JBL* 114/4: 585-606.

2000   "In the Stable with the Dwarves: Testimony, Interpretation, Faith and The History of Israel." In *Congress Volume of the Sixteenth Congress of the International Organisation for the Study of the Old Testament Held in Oslo 1998.* VTS 80. Leiden: Brill, 281-319, reprinted here on 161-91.

Shapin, S.

1994   *A Social History of Truth.* Chicago and London: University of Chicago Press.

Thompson, T. L.

1974   *The Historicity of the Patriarchal Narratives: The Quest for the Historical Abraham.* BZAW 133. Berlin: Walter de Gruyter.

1978a   "The Background of the Patriarchs: A Reply to William Dever and Malcolm Clark." *JSOT* 9: 2-43.

1978b   "A New Attempt to Date the Patriarchal Narratives." *JAOS* 98: 76-84.

1979   "Conflict Themes in the Jacob Narratives." *Semeia* 15: 5-26.

1987   *The Origin Tradition of Ancient Israel.* JSOTS 55. Sheffield: JSOT Press.

1991   "Text, Context and Referent in Israelite Historiography." In D. V. Edelman, ed., *The Fabric of History.* JSOTS 127. Sheffield: Sheffield Academic Press, 65-92.

1992   *Early History of the Israelite People.* Leiden: Brill.

1994   "Some Exegetical and Theological Implications of Understanding Exodus as a Collected Tradition." In Niels Peter Lemche and Mogens Müller, eds., *Fra Dybet.* København: Museum Tusculanum, 233-42.

1995a   "Critical Notes: A Neo-Albrightean School in History and Biblical Scholarship?" *JBL* 114/4: 683-705.

1995b   "The Intellectual Matrix of Early Biblical Narrative: Inclusive Monotheism in Persian Period Palestine." In D. V. Edelman, ed., *The Triumph of Elohim.* Kampen: Kok Pharos, 107-24.

1995c   "How Yahweh Became God: Exodus 3 and 6 and the Heart of the Pentateuch." *JSOT* 68: 57-74.

1995d   " 'House of David': An Eponymic Referent to Yahweh as Godfather." *SJOT* 9: 59-74.

1996a   "W. G. Dever and the Not So New Biblical Archaeology." In V. Fritz and Philip R. Davies, eds., *The Origins of the Ancient Israelite States,* JSOTS 228. Sheffield: Sheffield Academic Press, 26-43.

1996b   "He Is Yahweh: He Does What Is Right in His Own Eyes: The Old Testament as a Theological Discipline, II." In L. Fatum and M. Müller, eds., *Tro og historie.* Copenhagen: Museum Tusculanum, 246-63.

1996c   "4Q Testimonia og Bibelens affattelse: En københavnsk legohypotese." In Niels Hyldahl and Thomas L. Thompson, eds., *Dødehavsteksterne og Bibelen.* Copenhagen: Museum Tusculanum, 233-41.

1999   *The Bible in History: How Writers Create a Past.* London: Jonathan Cape.

Fact, Fiction, and Language Use: Can Modern Pragmatics Improve on Halpern's Case for History in Judges?

NICOLAI WINTHER-NIELSEN

1. Introduction:
Fact or Fiction and the Game of Language

Fact or Fiction is the name of a popular game. Three people explain the same word in different ways. They all pretend to tell the truth and sound very convincing, yet only one of the three intends to tell the truth, while the other two intend to lie and persuade. Could this also be the name of the game of the Bible: everything was communicated with conviction, some of it to tell the facts, the rest to convince of its fiction?

In wide circles this used to be accepted as the model for the game: make your decision on true or false in the Bible as best you can, and then wait for the verdict of the academy or the church. An increasingly popular model is to decide in advance that the Bible is a literary fiction without a factual basis, as many literary critics and even a few historians claim. The opposite option is

This article has been fundamentally changed from the paper read before the Tyndale Fellowship OT group in July 1998. I wish to thank Cynthia Miller, Kenneth E. Bailey, Ben Carter, as well as Danish colleagues and students, especially Hans Jørgen Ladegaard, Jens Bruun Kofoed, and Hans Ole Bækgaard, for playing along with me on the present version, though none of them, of course, can be blamed for doing so. Ulrik Petersen checked my English.

to decide that everything in the Bible must be pure and simple empirical fact, as some fundamentalists might claim.

However, no matter how one plays the game of fact or fiction in the Bible, the problem is much too complex to be judged on presuppositions alone. We have to decide, yet it is very hard to make a choice between fact or fiction and to tell what would count as evidence in either direction. Some ten years ago Baruch Halpern's *The First Historians* (1988) opened a new round in this game by claiming that we do not even have to choose between fact and fiction, but rather that we are to play a game of fact or fable (1988: 8). We are to choose between fact and fancy, not between history and artistry (Long 1994: 65). During the course of his argument, Halpern then made the very interesting claim that many players in the game have a serious problem of communication. This is the language game that we are going to play in the following.

My intention in looking at the language game in narrative texts from the Hebrew Bible is not to fool anyone into believing that I hold the winning joker in the game of fact or fiction. I assume, however, that historical narrative in the Hebrew Bible is an intricately woven material or "texture" of historical, literary, and ideological threads. Because it narrates about persons and events in written language, it is also possible to go beyond a naive, positivist dichotomy of false or true and look at this fabric from the perspective of language use and thus explore the relation between fact and fiction in terms of communicative action. Even if this is only an offer to look at our narrative fabric from a particular perspective, I believe this project to be a natural, and indeed necessary, follow-up on the game opened by Halpern, but also an interesting new variant of the game, because our material is not usually inspected by scholars in relation to language use.

Stated differently, my objective is to take seriously the hint by Halpern that we are facing a problem of communication, and therefore need to scrutinize language use in the narrative of the Hebrew Bible in order to explain how it communicates intentions and refers to real contexts through actual language. I will present current theories on language use in pragmatics and then look at how principles of communication and coherence may have a bearing on the relationship between historical fact and literary fiction in the Hebrew Bible. My point is that modern pragmatics may help us to clarify how language is used by writers and readers and how language users refer to the world and other important contexts. I use Judges from the Hebrew Bible in my attempt to test Halpern's case for authorial intention and historical context, because Halpern opened the study with that case.

2. The Challenge by Halpern:
Fact, Fiction, and Communication

Halpern's provocative monograph was an important contribution in support of the essential historical truth of the historical books of the Hebrew Bible. From the book of Judges onward Halpern argued that we find much historically reliable information in Hebrew narrative because the narrators intended to take their task as historians seriously: "The ancient Israelite historians . . . had authentic antiquarian intentions. They meant to furnish fair and accurate representations of Israelite antiquity" (1988: 3).

Halpern formulated this defense of *an author-centered intentional approach* to historical narrative in a frontal attack on text-centered approaches. The historians of ancient Israel did not distort facts into imaginative fancy "presented in the garb of prose fiction" (1988: 5). Halpern of course agrees with reader-response critics like Gunn and Fewell (1993: 6) that Hebrew narrative is selective, dramatized, and ideological and only the story of some happening.[1] No historian can ever be comprehensively accurate, and every story-teller must employ fictional and imaginative techniques of presentation (Halpern 1988: 6-8). Yet these storytellers were honest men who wrote authoritatively on real events and met high standards of history writing in working with the evidence.[2]

Halpern is confident that the tools of historical criticism are appropriate for probing into the original legitimate meaning intended by the author, and vigorously rejects any method that in advance would "deny that readers can construe what the Israelite historian meant" (1988: 13). His entire project would fail if we were to assume "that texts are multivalent and their meanings radically contextual, inescapably bound up with their interpreters" (Gunn and Fewell 1993: 9). Yet this has been the dominant trend in historical studies for the last decade. In the *postmodern view of history* we are not dealing with

---

1. The reasoning of Gunn and Fewell is as follows: "All history writing involves defining and selecting 'events' and interpreting their relationships, which means constructing a plot and positing the motivation of the participating characters. All authors and editors serve ideological agendas, expressed or unexpressed, and shape their account accordingly. In practice, then, there must always be a distance between the narrative world and the world of 'what actually happened'. Indeed, . . . there are only stories (or histories) of what happened, always relative to the perspective of the story-teller (historian)" (1993: 6).

2. The Israelite historians' work can be tested in "its reconstructive logic, its relationship to the evidence of sources" (Halpern 1988: 13), and it will prove that historian(s) organized "available evidence (sources) into coherent narrative *about* events susceptible to reconstruction from the sources" (1988: 12). When they had no sources, they wrote what they had good reason to believe was true.

factual reference but with rhetorical representation (Berkhofer 1997: 60), and, like literary fiction, it depends on arrangement and argument (Berkhofer 1995: 76-105). Historical facts are reduced to constructions and interpretations of the past (1995: 53-58). Old Testament theology is also changing with the collapse of history under the weight of ahistorical fictional readings without any grounding in historical factuality (Perdue 1994: 7-11 and 231-38). All this is part of a major intellectual shift toward a subjective epistemology that is rapidly gaining momentum in biblical criticism.[3] Halpern's case for fact in fictional historical narrative is therefore as relevant today as it was more than ten years ago when he entered the game, and the main issue is whether his case could still be made today, given the tremendous shifts in perspectives on history, knowledge, and the world at present.

Halpern's response to the challenge from modern ahistorical subjectivism and reader-centric relativism is highly interesting. His first step is to analyze the gapping between the ancient historians and the modern readers as *a breakdown in communication*. Present controversies on historical method in the study of texts from ancient Israel are evidence of miscommunication because modern readers do not understand that the ancient authors intended to "communicate information about specific phenomena outside the text, in the text" (1988: xvii, cf. 3-5).[4] This crisis in communication can find a solution only if the modern reader tries to understand his ancient communication partner. He must understand how speaker, world, and hearer are involved in communication on history. An ancient historian must have serious and reliable intentions, "*mean* to be accurate in representing the past" (1988: 7), and, "conditioned by a culture, must persuade other historians, whom the culture conditions differently, that one construction is accurate" (1988: 13). He refers

---

3. Gunn and Fewell follow Stanley Fish and Richard Rorty and reject "self and society as objective realities in a world of ostensible, essential truths and values" and instead view modern man as fashioning "the world through language, manipulating reality rather than discovering it" (1993: 10). History is merely an "ideological and social construct, inevitably subjective" (1993: 11), and Hebrew narrative is told by literary narrators about literary characters, none of them real people (1993: 51, 53). Accordingly, the modern reader is left to his own psychologizing (1993: 47-50) and production of ideological meaning (1993: 191), helped along by a multi-vocal Bible that provides its own clues to its deconstruction (1993: 204-5).

4. In his delightful and vivid language Halpern nicknames the modern miscommunicators as "the confessionalists, negative fundamentalists, Pyrrhonists, and social scientists" (1988: 6). Confessionalists approach the Bible in an ahistorical search for present and eternal meaning, historical critics apply a principle of scientific scepticism denying historical value, and literary critics deny all possibility of acquiring significant and reliable knowledge of the past (1988: 3-5).

to the world insofar as "historians try to communicate information about phenomena extrinsic to the text" (1988: 11). Finally, the reader of his history is also involved in a communicative process by "determining what data its author meant the reader to extract" (1988: 11).

Halpern (1988: 10, 28) even takes a second important step forward by insisting on an "epistemologically based" view of *human knowledge of the past*, challenging positivist skeptics as well as postmodern reader-response critics. He rejects the value of both approaches for an inquiry into historical narrative because they both demand illusory and illogical absolute proof of veracity in history writing that no historian could ever meet. A historian can only have recourse to testimony of the past, be it his own or that of others (1988: 28). In court, it would mean the end of justice if witnesses and testimonial evidence were ruled out in advance as suspicious and unreliable and therefore inadmissible. Furthermore, most human beings get along happily in their daily lives — positivists, relativists, or neither — trusting and acting on the basis of less than absolutely verified data, and their access to personally experienced reality is an ideal model for their access to historical evidence.[5]

This is how far Halpern's communicative perspective on history writing goes. In essence the problem of fact and fiction is a matter of how ancient writers can communicate and how modern readers can communicate with them! In the following we intend to enter into this communicative process and bring a pragmatic perspective on communication to the forefront of the discussion in order to discuss the nature of authorial intentions and the contexts illustrating the world of Judges.

3. Communication in Narrative: The Three Dimensions and Language Use

If, as Halpern suggests, understanding historical narrative resembles the way human beings understand and communicate effectively about the past and present of their everyday lives, we will have to consider pragmatic aspects of the problem. Understanding history writing is then a matter of how people contextualize meaning through their linguistic interaction.

Halpern's case for historical communication will have to be restated in

5. Humans live "relying on subjective observations and culturally conditioned analyses . . . on the basis of a preponderance of evidence. Our understanding of human history resembles our knowledge of the contemporary world" (Halpern 1988: 28). The only consistent alternative would be to dismiss anything unproven and totally "reject the claims of normal certainty" (1988: 28).

terms of current developments in the understanding of language, especially because the case partially rested on older historical-critical views of religion and redaction that are increasingly discredited.[6] Yet, even if we reject two centuries of historical criticism that has "proved mainly inconclusive" (Gunn and Fewell 1993: 5), this does not necessarily license us to relativize all stable meaning along with current reader-response critics. There are at least three possible alternatives to deconstruction to consider if we do not want to get entirely trapped in modern ideology. We may work our way forward from history to literature (the historiographical approach), we may posit history and literature along with ideology as distinct and equally important dimensions (the three-dimensional approach), or we may work our way back from literature to history (the pragmatic approach).

The first solution is to *underpin the historiographical position with comparative evidence.* Briefly stated, a responsible use of comparative evidence can provide much useful supportive evidence from ancient Near Eastern sources, and archaeological excavations in general illustrate the material culture of ancient Israel very well. Yet this evidence is only interpretive evidence.[7] Because archaeological remains are totally mute and texts from other cultures speak another language, more texts or artifacts will not bring any help, if the problem is that we miscommunicate with ancient documents.[8] An increase in the number of texts or artifacts will not really bring any help, and perhaps even blur the picture, if the real problem is how to participate in a communication and benefit from it epistemologically. When Lemche argues that "extrabiblical sources do not often verify social and political relationships in the biblical narratives" (1998: 64), it is clear that sociolinguistics and intra-Israelite political developments are not taken into account and the ar-

---

6. Halpern (1988: 11) only reluctantly admits the ideological goals of the antiquarian historian and insists that political-historical themes are sure signs of historiographic intentionality (1988: 13), as if the religious or cultic topics of history were less intentionally antiquarian. He defends Noth's hypothetical first historian as the writer of an equally hypothetical deuteronomistic work (1988: 30-33).

7. The last word on this matter cannot be Halpern's summary rejection of Albright's approach as a "crypto-fundamentalist philological program heavily laced with archaeology" (1988: 25). Note especially the discussions of the evidence in the contributions in Millard (1994) as well as Bunimovitz (1995: 96), who is prepared to allow textual evidence as a significant and indispensable part of the evidence besides the archaeological data. Provan (1997: 47-52) warns against some of the theorizing necessarily involved.

8. Comparisons can be made only on the basis of what current translation theory has called a "dynamic functional equivalence." Cultural pragmatics has shown that it is not possible to equate superficially similar forms across cultures without taking the functions of communication into account (Blum-Kulka 1997: 54-57).

gument apparently rests on the curious notion that unless proved to be true by sources from the ancient Near East the data in the Hebrew Bible are false.[9]

A second solution is to *strike a balance between history, literature, and ideology.* Due to the obvious shortcomings of a one-sided use of an author-centered historical approach or a text-centered literary approach, some scholars combine the two and even add the message of the texts as a third and equally important dimension. These scholars work from Sternberg's (1985: 362) synthesis of a literary approach emphasizing that aesthetics, ideology, and history are the three prominent impulses in the Hebrew Bible.[10] The three-dimensional approach is well illustrated in a recent, readable introduction to Kings by Provan (1997). The book of Kings is read as *narrative* literature telling a story of persons and events in a chronological framework and linked thematically into a larger whole (1997: 27). It is also read as *historiographical* literature depicting real events in the history of Israel rather than in a fictive world devoid of historical reference (1997: 45-46). Finally, the book is read as *didactic* literature teaching about God and his deeds in the course of its story line (1997: 23-25).

A three-pronged literary, historical, and theological study of historical books from the Hebrew Bible forms a tool that can dig deep into a book as a story, a history, and an ideological piece of writing. Yet it is not clear how these three distinctive lines of inquiry interrelate (Sternberg 1985: 41), as in cases in which names or numbers could count both as factual information and as fictional patterning. Brettler (1995: 8-19) also approaches the Hebrew Bible as history, ideology, and literature, yet he does not view this as a guarantee of historical reliability (1995: 1-2). The dominance of reader-response criticism on the current scene also indicates that at least some literary approaches seriously undermine a historical approach.[11]

A third solution is to reverse the process and *work from the literary text into historical evidence.*[12] Sternberg's (1985) original synthesis of a literary

9. In the words of Coady, this kind of scholarship is "haunted by Cartesian or incorrigibilist standards of rationality and knowledge" (1992: 144).

10. Long (1994: 71) uses the historiographical, theological, and literary impulses in a discussion of constraints by subject matter, point of view, and aesthetic choices in relation to portraiture. The prongs are developed further by Provan (1995 and 1997: 20-25). Based on Ricoeur, Watson defends the study of theology in "a historiography enriched by fiction and not subverted by it" (1997: 57).

11. Burke O. Long (1991) is very critical of the "new" approaches of Alter and Sternberg because they leave out deconstruction and feminist and reader-response criticism. Both are repressive hermeneutics hiding old-fashioned positivistic and truth-intentional skeletons in their closet.

12. Cf. V. P Long (1994: 159-60): "Careful literary reacting is a prerequisite of responsi-

approach included the communicative situation, because Hebrew narrative discourse was viewed as a historical use of language by writers and readers in a specific time and space. When the modern reader decodes the historical author's intention and perceives the artistic patterns of meaning and effect in the text, he is aware that the author tries to persuade him of the truth of his religious and moral issues (1985: 13-14). Sternberg suggested that discourse analysis can both reconstruct the source as a linguistic system and explore its cultural setting, theology, dating, canonical setting, origin, and transmission.

This perspective guides Hardmeier's (1990) work on the communicative function and structure of Hebrew narrative texts from the perspective of the ethnography of communication (1990: 26, 33).[13] Hebrew narrative is viewed as written communication intended for a general audience and reflects condensed speech situations (1990: 24) as well as oral narration and its repertoire (1990: 25). Hardmeier's theory of text and communication is closely tied to the author's intentional communication in a specific historical context. Narrative texts are explored as integral wholes in a concrete communicative setting and prior to any attempts to reconstruct historical events and social circumstances behind the text (1990: 6, 11-12, 17). The time of text production becomes the central focus for any reconstruction of the author's perspective, his purpose, and the text's original situation (1990: 29).

Hardmeier's approach brings the narrative text back to the center of the stage in full force as communicative discourse, but it is at the cost of the facts of the past, which are only indirectly represented in the memory of the writer insofar as they are relevant for his contemporary concerns (1990: 27-28).[14] The flawed logic appears to be that the greater the distance from the past situation, the less factual the narrative is and the more prominent fiction is. Then it serves only to support the author's argumentation and instruction in his own historical

---

ble historical reconstruction. That is to say, a conscientious, fair-minded attempt to understand a biblical text on its own terms is logically prior to any historicizing about it. Therefore, the more skilled biblical interpreters become in reading texts *literally*, the more competent they will become in assessing them *historically.*" Cf. also Long's frequent stress on the necessity of developing, as far as possible, an "ancient literary competence" (1994: 33-34, 42-43, 56, 112, 149, 179).

13. For a presentation of the ethnography of communication, see conveniently Schiffrin (1994: 137-89). Hardmeier exploits German research on communication (J. S. Schmidt mainly) and on the pragmatics of narrative (especially the work of U. Quasthoff and W. Kallmeyer).

14. The Hebrew Bible contains only recorded historical narratives based on second-hand knowledge of events, not spontaneous stories in face-to-face conversations (Hardmeier 1990: 49), nor biographical and personally experienced narratives (1990: 51).

situation (1990: 54).[15] However, Coady (1992: 146-47) has argued convincingly that testimonial memory has its own epistemology and that in our daily communication we usually learn without having first to establish the truth of various propositions (1992: 142-43).[16] Hardmeier's approach may easily reduce the communicative situations of the past to oblivion, and it runs the risk of predetermining a late dating much as current minimalist approaches to the history of Israel do.[17] Finally, he seems to focus so sharply on the alleged author's mind that he can hardly escape the charge of committing the intentional fallacy.[18]

A communicative approach to Hebrew narrative will therefore prove useful only if it is not haunted by Cartesian ghosts so that the past is written off in advance and if the writer's intentions, context, and addressee-hypothesis are construed by taking all the narrative data into account. The main issue is whether it is possible to bridge the gap between the antiquarian authors' intentions and their past historical context and the modern reader, as envisioned by Halpern. Discourse analysis, the pragmatics of narrative, and other theories of communication and context should not have been left out in the new formulations of a three-pronged approach. If we dispense with Halpern's one-sided focus on antiquarian interests at the expense of literary features and ideological persuasion, it may be possible to propose a new understanding of sincere and accurate narrative communication inspired by current work on language and context within pragmatics.

15. Hardmeier nevertheless defends fiction in the sense of *Dichtung* as an indispensable part of the narrator's unique communicative contribution and as integral to his perspective on events, "untrennbar in- und miteinander verwoben," designed for purposive effect (1990: 50). He rejects "zweifelhaften, von außen an die Erzählinhalte herangetragene Tatsächlichkeitskriterien" (Hardmeier 1990: 51; cf. 30).

16. Indeed, "it would be irrational to the point of insanity to withold [*sic!*] assent pending investigation" (Coady 1992: 144). The epistemological flaws in the demand for absolute verification have been pointed out by Halpern (1988: 28; see above) and Provan (1995, 1997).

17. Note amazing statements like "the use of biblical historiographical narrative for critical reconstruction of periods that it describes (rather than periods in which it was written) is precarious and only possible where there is adequate independent data" (Davies 1997: 104-5) or, comparing the Pentateuch with film and novels, the claim that "(t)he past can only be summoned up to understand the present" (Lemche 1998: 65). When statements are made in such general terms, the most serious problem is that it is not acknowledged that they are equally relevant for minimalist beliefs, if writers can provide only understanding of the present or their own contemporary situation.

18. Note the most recent presentation and discussion by Vanhoozer (1998: 82-85 and 240-63), and especially the contrast between the communicative intent and the intentional fallacy (1998: 285). Not even Hirsch expressed intentions in terms of the author's consciousness (1998: 74-75).

4. Constraints on Language Use: The Basic Principles of Modern Pragmatics

If communication really is the missing link in a new case for historiographic intentionality in Hebrew narrative, we must now turn to pragmatics as defined below in order to broaden the perspectives inherent to earlier literary and narrative theories. It goes well beyond Halpern's somewhat unsophisticated idea that the modern reader should read Hebrew narrative as "history on the basis of its author's perceived intentions in writing, the author's claim that the account is accurate in its particulars, the author's sincerity" (1988: 8).

Pragmatics, literally meaning "the art of acting right," has become the technical term for the modern perspective on how the use of language is constrained by its actual use in specific contexts. Modern pragmatics has its roots in classical logic and rhetoric, but it currently covers a broad range of modern studies of language and communication. The study of linguistic pragmatics focuses on the role of beliefs, intentions, plans, and acts in human verbal interaction, and can be defined as "the successful interpretation by an addressee of a speaker's intent in performing a linguistic act" (Green 1996: 1). In a broader sense pragmatics may cover any aspect of goal-directed action performed in "the study of understanding intentional human action" (1996: 2), and not just the linguistic means of action and interaction. A pragmatic approach does not deal with sentences as linguistic units, but rather as utterances that are "inherently contextualized units of language use" (Schiffrin 1994: 39). Pragmatics is the science of language in relation to its users (Mey 1993: 1, 5) and the "study of linguistic communication in context" (Blum-Kulka 1997: 38).[19] Its goal is, in short, to study intentional and contextual language use.

The modern study of pragmatics grew out of *philosophical and sociological investigation* of intentions and social actions (Clark 1996: 56). Language philosophers, in an effort to explain the relation between linguistic signs and their interpreters, realized that language use influences meaning far beyond the form and contents of language studied in syntax and semantics.[20] The founding fathers of pragmatics developed theories of cooperation and speech acts, and later research has turned to politeness systems and interaction in conversation.

---

19. Note also *metapragmatics,* which studies our language about what happens in language (Mey 1993: 269) and about its principles and rules (1993: 272), and in this sense is "reflections on the language users' use" (1993: 181).

20. For an introduction to Peirce's theory of signs and a new application, see Clark (1996: 155-88). Charles Morris popularized pragmatics for language philosophy. On Austin, Searle, Morris, and Grice, see now conveniently Schiffrin (1994: 49-96, 190-231).

Following the later Wittgenstein's understanding of language as a form of life, or a game, Austin wanted to explain how words can effectively perform things in the world, or *How to Do Things with Words,* to quote the title of his famous work from 1962. The language philosopher H. P. Grice had since 1957 tried to explain how hearers work out the meaning of signs in contexts. Hearers are chiefly being guided by assuming that they interact with reliable conversation partners. They therefore figure out meaning on the basis of a so-called "cooperative principle" and rely on conversational implicatures.

The pragmatic views of Austin and Grice inspired Searle to propose his "speech act" theory as a systematic classification of the basic units of intentional communication. The theory explained how language could perform communicative acts and how such acts were encoded by linguistic means in context. It appears that people use utterances to get their partners in communication to believe what they assert, follow their advice, comply with their requests, and answer their questions. They also express their own feelings and name or judge persons or objects. An utterance is not just a saying with sense and reference in its predicating and referring expressions (technically the propositions as *locutionary acts*), but also a doing or acting by performing an intended function (the *illocutionary force;* e.g., in a certain context, a simple statement of fact functions as a *directive,* just as readily as an imperative would — "It's cold in here"). However, the force of a linguistic expression is in effect only with the right participants under the right circumstances, that is, if it meets the right contextual conditions (as specified in *felicity* or *appropriateness conditions*). The goal of language use (its *illocutionary point*) is to communicate a publicly intended effect by committing a speaker and getting a listener to do something (Clark 1996: 134-35).

After the early phase of pragmatic research into cooperative principles and speech acts pragmatics gradually turned its focus toward the functions of politeness strategies and conversation, but still largely in terms of grammaticalized aspects of language and context (Levinson 1983: 9). The basic assumption was always that language users can also access external and factual reality through language, even if they also may mean more and imply all sorts of different things.[21]

We may also explain pragmatic principles in an informal way by illustrating how pragmatics would bear on the first dialogue exchange occurring in Judges. Caleb has just given Othniel his daughter Achsah in marriage as a prize for the conquest of Kiriath-sepher (1:12-13). Achsah jumps off her donkey and thereby corners her father into asking her,[22] "What do you wish?" Interpreting

---

21. According to Levinson, users have the "ability to compute out of utterances in sequence the contextual assumptions they imply: the facts about the spatial, temporal and social relationships between participants, and their requisite beliefs and intentions in undertaking certain verbal exchanges" (1983: 49).

22. Usually translated "When she came to him, she urged him to ask her father for a field" (1:14 RSV), but it should be rendered ". . . she urged her father by asking for a field" (Winther-Nielsen 1995: 255 and n. 42).

her act as intentional in this specific context, her father's question is not just a request for information but an invitation for her to ask some favor. She is then free to state her request as another directive speech act: "Give me a present; since you have set me in the land of the Negeb, give me also springs of water" (1:15). Caleb's answer is not recorded, but his compliance is noted in the sequel.

Current versions of pragmatics include sociocultural issues and broaden the perspective to the understanding of human discourse and interaction in a very broad sense. Pragmatics as set out in Mey now moves away from the former focus on the *force* of speech acts residing in abstract contexts of isolated sentences and asks about *effects* of speech acts in surroundings (1993: 148). It is now realized that Grice's maxims of cooperation are subject to contextual and cultural variation (1993: 41) and that speech acts should be treated as pragmatic acts dependent on the context of interaction (1993: 257, 261). Furthermore, while former approaches tried to formulate rules and principles for cooperation or expressibility, Mey now emphasizes the central role of *pragmatic constraints.* The idea is that language use must be understood in terms of what users can and normally will do rather than as a rule-governed behavior (1993: 277-78). Constraints tell us how we in a given actual situation "can identify the possible ways to proceed towards the goals we want to obtain" (1993: 264). People don't do correctly performed, abstract speech acts; they do pragmatic acts to achieve their goals in the actual situation. The pragmatic constraints on language use have important implications:

> All pragmatic acts are heavily marked by their context: they are both context-derived and context-restrained. That means, they are determined by the broader social context in which they happen, and they realize their goals in the conditions placed upon human action by that context. (1993: 264)

Due to such contextual constraints on language Mey proposes *two new key principles* for pragmatics focusing on the effect and efficiency of language use.[23] The "all-important factor" in language activity is a *communicative principle,* "the intention to communicate something to somebody" (1993: 55), which is constrained, however, by the fact that people may mean more than they say or may be incapable of stating what they really mean. The second fundamental principle is that both conversation and discourse are governed by a *coherence principle* (1993: 237) that captures the fact that meaning is always specified in a textual or situational context. Conversational utterance pairs make sense once they are placed "in the proper context, either in physi-

23. Note also that Mey (1993: 276) exchanges Grice's cooperative principle for principles of efficiency and economy in language use.

cal reality or in the universe of discourse" (1993: 240-41).[24] Utterances mean what they end up meaning in a total context (1993: 251).

Along with these new principles of pragmatics there are three important trends within pragmatics and related areas of research. First, the emphasis is now on how meanings are communicated in relation to *social patterns, cultural beliefs, and extralinguistic knowledge* (Yule 1996: 4-5). Pragmatics draws on related fields working with language as a social and cultural phenomenon, and the influence of the ethnography of communication formulated by Hymes and others is particularly strong (Blum-Kulka 1997: 38-39).[25] In Mey's definition, pragmatics is the study of the conditions of human language as these are "determined by the contexts of society" (1993: 42). Society, with its economic, political, and cultural values, norms, and conditions, is integrated as a context for all human activity and visible in our use of language (1993: 186-87). People influence each other through a prefigured context molded by society and perform pragmatic acts in interpersonal involvement in contexts that both provide a repository of earlier experience and a toolbox for change in the future (1993: 263).[26]

Second, contemporary pragmatics broadens its research scope from isolated utterances to *analysis of discourse* as the "extended sequences of actual text and talk" (Blum-Kulka 1997: 38) and through cross-cultural pragmatics studies discourse and actual use across languages (1997: 55-56). Pragmatics is thus closely related to modern discourse studies, which also focus on the use of forms and functions in contexts. The study of discourse is not only a study of how syntax functions in sequential ordering of utterances but also of how semantics and pragmatics, as "the meaning and use of particular expressions and constructions within certain contexts, allow people to convey and interpret the communicative content of what is said" (Schiffrin 1994: 41).

---

24. Mey's focus on effective responses in dialogue reduces the value of speech act analysis as utterances in context: "which speech act one actually is looking at depends very much, if not exclusively, on that particular context" (1993: 250). Illocutionary force is also problematic because "what really counts is how a speech act functions" (1993: 251).

25. For the ethnography of communication, see also the remarks on Hardmeier above. Assigning context a central role in social interaction "does not rule out a discourse pragmatics approach to the study of the negotiation of meaning unfolding within the event. In fact future research in discourse pragmatics may be much enriched by incorporating ethnographic viewpoints and procedures in its study of social interaction" (Blum-Kulka 1997: 58).

26. Pragmatic acting "relies on the context of goals, not just the communicative ones, but in general, the goals of the interaction" (Mey 1993: 262). In this sense pragmatic acting is "contextualized adaptive behavior: adapting oneself to a context . . . adapting the context to oneself" (263). In this sense society speaks through convention, culture, social structure, and felicity conditions.

Third, pragmatics plays an important role in current work on *collabora-tion in interaction*. In a major new synthesis of language use, the psycho-linguist Clark (1996) defines language use as activities based on "the joint ac-tion that emerges when speakers and listeners — or writers and readers — perform their individual actions in coordination, as ensemble" (1996: 3). Clark insists that a complete picture of language use must include both the thoughts and the actions of individuals as they act in pairs. The social, interactional, and cognitive aspects of language use are captured in three cen-tral propositions (1996: 23):

1. Language fundamentally is used for social purposes: it is an instrument in social activities.
2. Language use is a species of joint action: it always has two agents (real or imaginary, or institutions viewed as individuals). Even writing to others over vast stretches of time and space requires coordination.
3. Language use always involves speaker's meaning and addressee's under-standing: both have certain intentions and use mechanisms to coordinate effectively. It is critical to language use to mean something for another who is in a position to understand.

To summarize, pragmatics defined in a broad sense according to current developments informed by studies of society, discourse, and interaction ex-plains how language use is constrained by the principles of communication and coherence. Pragmatics explores how the intentions of language users are tied to references to the world inside and outside of the discourse and its sur-rounding situations. Our survey of pragmatics has emphasized two new prin-ciples of pragmatics that may help us to structure the following discussion of constraints on communication and coherence in narrative. In this way we can reformulate Halpern's view of authorial communicative intention and refer-ential coherence in Hebrew narrative on the basis of current pragmatics.

The prospect of this sort of work is that pragmatics may help us to un-derstand the role of speakers and hearers and their interaction in oral and written contexts in the Hebrew Bible. One of the chief characteristics of this approach is that it focuses on human intentions and interaction in context in contrast to most current literary and semiotic models of language. It is not a reader-centered but an author- and context-centered approach. In several ways this proposal is similar to the recently published, exhaustive presenta-tion of a modern pragmatic hermeneutics by Vanhoozer (1998), which inde-pendently reaches the same conclusions on communicative action and authorial intention, though from the opposite direction, that is, on philosophical, literary, and theological grounds in contrast to the present proposal based on linguistic, textual, and cognitive studies.

5. The Communicative Principle: Intentions, Modes, and Writers and Readers

In the test of the pragmatic case for Halpern's view on communication in Hebrew narrative, we will first turn to the communicative principle in order to explain how and by whom meaning is established in written Hebrew narrative, and whether this has any significant bearing on our understanding of fact and fiction. The following will show that the pragmatic relation between the speaker and the hearer within the narrative in many ways resembles the relation between the writer and his first audience as well as between him and the modern reader.

Halpern proposes the following crucial test of historiographic intention: "Whether a text is a history, then, depends on what its author meant to do" (1988: 8). In contrast to Brettler's (1995: 12) contention, the problem is not that Halpern puts so strong an emphasis on intentionality but rather that his particular version of authorial intention falls short of a modern view of intentional communication. The interdependence of speakers and hearers is a central and indispensable focus in pragmatics.[27] Pragmatics does not focus on isolated speaker intention or abstract sentence meaning, but on speaker meaning in terms of what is said, meant, and interpreted in a given context.[28] A sensible modern pragmatics would hardly try to trace the intentions of an illusive author named "Noth's Dtr" (Halpern 1988: 30), but would rather leave this to theologians with a particular scientific inclination.[29]

---

27. Note that pragmatics is about "what the utterer believes about what the addressee believes, and about what effect the utterer intends the utterance to have" (Green 1996: 10).

28. Cf. Blum-Kulka: "Linguistic knowledge alone will provide *sentence meaning* (information . . .); considering the *circumstances* of the utterance . . . will help in deciphering the *speaker meaning* . . . whether the utterance was meant as an invitation, a request or something else. . . . Pragmatic theory is concerned with explaining how interlocutors bridge the gap between sentence meanings and speaker meanings" (1997: 39). "Pragmatics views understanding as an interactive, inferential process which necessarily involves a constant matching of what is said with what is meant" (1997: 58).

29. Note the rejection of the Romantic emphasis on an author's mind (Vanhoozer 1998: 74-76) and the problem with interpretative foundationalism or Cartesian biblical criticism: in postmodern terms it is simply an institutionalized reading in a particular reading community (1998: 286-87), but it is also a naive denunciation of the modern reader (1998: 162).

Initially we may illustrate how important it is to communicate intentions properly by retelling a joke told by Yule (1996: 36). A man and a woman with a dog sit down at a table in a restaurant. The man asks, "Does your dog bite?" and the woman says, "No." The man reaches down to pet the dog and is instantly bitten. Surprised, he cries out, "Ouch! Hey! You said your dog doesn't bite." The woman answers, "He doesn't. But that's not my dog." There is a serious problem in communication in that the man assumes more than is said while the woman communicates less information than expected. Otherwise the point of the joke would have been lost.

An example from Judges shows that miscommunication can be deadly serious. When the Israelite forces were rallied for a punitive expedition against the lawbreakers from Gibeah in Benjamin, they consulted Yahweh by lot at Bethel before the initial assault (20:18).

20:18a	The people of Israel:	"Which of us shall go up first to battle against the Benjaminites?"
18b	Yahweh:	"Judah shall go up first."

Yet, this smooth dialogue between Israel and the divine decider ends in total disaster the next morning when the soldiers from Gibeah kill 22,000 soldiers of Israel in their counterattack. Why?

In the communicative context this example illustrates how downright fatal it can be when mutual cooperation does not succeed. The Levite had been cross-examined on the events leading up to his concubine's murder in Gibeah, and the Israelites had reacted spontaneously to his partisan account of the incident. They seem to be in such a hurry to attack that they do not care to listen to Yahweh, in complete contrast to their obedient listening in a similar situation at the opening of the book (1:1-3). All Israel goes into battle, not the tribe of Judah first and alone as their representative. Yahweh immediately strikes back to stop them in their ill-founded euphoria. The next morning Israel is much more careful to listen when it asks for direction. Yahweh gives them his "Go ahead" (20:23), but does not communicate his full intention. The surprise is that he is dead-serious about his intent still to punish them for their disobedience, and 18,000 men are lost. Only on the third morning, when the seriousness of God has finally dawned on Israel, does Yahweh communicate in full and clear directives properly backed up by promises, "Go up; for tomorrow I will give them into your hand." He finally means what Israel understands him to communicate.

This is an example of how meaning evolves in oral interaction when we have access to an event only in the form of the pragmatics of a written communication. Yet there is no absolute and fixed border separating spoken and written text and talk. Discourse studies have worked intensively on the use of language in two different *modes* investigating the differences between face-to-face conversation and storytelling in conversations (Schiffrin 1994: 80-84, 87, 204), and how oral interaction relates to written communication (Renkema 1993: 86). Written discourse lacks contact with an audience, is planned over time, and has a complex hypotactic grammar with integration through subordinate clauses. Oral interaction, on the other hand, is still intentional but instantaneous, and it has a simple paratactic grammar with clause fragmentation. Frequently the involvement of the audience includes references to interlocutors and mutual comments on the topic of conversation. The shared situation of the interlocutors plays a prominent role and even allows for quick responses to nonverbal events through intonation, body language, posture, and gestures.

Many scholars treat the Hebrew Bible solely as written communication without paying attention to the interactional features in the narratives. However, there are many similarities between language use in spoken and written settings.[30] Formal genres of oral discourse are usually well prepared and not spontaneous at all, while written personal letters can be more open and oral than conversation (van Dijk 1997b: 4). Cognitive research confirms that oral and written texts can vary in the degree to which they rely on contextual information — oral speech may be relatively independent of context, while private letters may depend on shared contextual knowledge (Gibbs 1994: 72-73).[31] In addition, authors usually write for some audience and try to anticipate expected reactions from their readers in their writing (Renkema 1993: 87). An author never creates text for those who actually read it, but instead uses a strategy to imagine a reader (Coulthard 1994: 4). Written texts are often part of ongoing communicative interaction, representing strategic and stylized answers to questions posed by a specific situation (Ochs 1997: 188), and narrators usually blend the written and spoken modes (1997: 186).

Oral conversation and written communication are also subject to similar *pragmatic constraints* on language use. Mey explains that the writer and the reader can "participate" in a literary work only if they "accept a set of con-

30. Note especially the survey of oral and written arenas in Clark (1996: 4-7). Written communication demands the same coordination as oral interaction (Clark 1996: 90-91), and the cooperative principle, politeness, cohesion, coherence, and style variation are common to both (Renkema 1993: 86-87).

31. Readers "assume a great deal about what even anonymous authors know, and what these authors may assume about them as readers" (Gibbs 1994: 73). Such assumptions range from competence in language to specific details of conceptual knowledge necessary for inferencing.

straints governing the use of that world, . . . relating that universe to language" (1993: 280).[32] A writer manipulates a set of literary constraints that governs his literary world, and this constrained world in turn manipulates the reader, who is completely between the mighty paws of the author, even if he must still accept the world between those paws voluntarily.

One problem with Mey's pragmatic account of literary communication, however, is that he assumes that hearers and readers are free to construe any meaning they want from a conversation as well as from a literary work of art.[33] In Halpern's terms this would be miscommunication, and he would insist that the reader instead has to "accurately construe the author's intent" (1988: 9). In this respect Halpern is in good company with the pragmatics of Searle, which focuses on the speaker's intentions, but he is flatly rejected by the ethnography of speaking. Goodwin and Duranti (1992: 18) argue that intentions do not have a central role in all societies and that recipients define meaning collaboratively through interaction in order to achieve coordinated social action and establish mutually acceptable evidence and truth.[34] In their view, written discourse would also be conditioned by social contexts and reader responses (1992: 14, 30-31).

Cognitive research does not support this relativization of intentions. Readers of literary texts are tied to authors by many mutual assumptions that "constrain how the meanings of texts are defined" (Gibbs 1994: 73). If intentionality is not located in the textual meaning, it would imply that both the author and the reader would be divorced from the text, which "then remains an inert, self-contained artifact." Meaning is always construed both from knowledge of the culture and from inferences of human intentions.[35]

32. To create a literary world as writer or reader "is closely related to that of setting up conditions for the proper use of language" (Mey 1993: 280), just as when people interact to make up "a conversational world."

33. According to Mey, "the ways textual and dialogical constraints are manipulated depend entirely on the contemporary conditions . . . redefined by each new generation" (1993: 281).

34. Intention can surely be distributed through interactive turns, i.e., negotiated in multiturn sequences and thus across turns (Goodwin and Duranti 1992: 18-19); but does not this call intentions into question? And if readers have the power to "determine what act an utterance will be officially heard to constitute" (1992: 18), interpretation is just an act of power. Yet conversation is intentional, even if the outcome cannot be planned in advance (Clark 1996: 319, 331). Searle (1992) suggests that intention in conversation is shared between two language users.

35. Gibbs admits that each reading may lead to a "multiplicity of meanings" (1994: 74), but it is still the text that gives "enduring opportunities for readers to construct meaning within a . . . context" (1994: 74).

This particular meaning can be recovered by cognitive and linguistic processes that are similar to interpretation in everyday discourse. Experiments support the view that people understand written text by presupposing that texts are composed by intentional human beings.[36] This is clear evidence for the importance of pragmatic information and "the powerful role of authorial intentions in people's understanding of isolated written expressions" (1994: 75). In cognitive terms we can say that pragmatic intentionality includes contextual clarity. In passing it may also be pointed out that these cognitive facts effectively assure that readers can figure out the intended effects and even operationalize this understanding in a notational apparatus like the rhetorical structure theory.[37]

The relation between speaker, hearer, and meaning in context can be further explained by Goffmann's (1981: 226) proposal that *the speaker role* subsumes three different agents that may or may not coincide:[38] (1) the *animator,* or the *inscriber/vocalizer* who transmits the message as preacher, writer, or manuscript editor; (2) the *author,* or the *formulator* who is the real author, who in narrative fiction often has to share his credits with an implied author like the narrator; (3) the *principal,* "the party to whose position, stand, and belief the words attest" and who is ultimately responsible for the meaning of the communication. Outside conversation these roles often get "decoupled" (Clark 1996: 21).

This model of different speaker roles can help us to explain important aspects of the communicative situation in the case of anonymous authorship. The following discussion will eventually be summarized in the table of story worlds in the book of Judges below. The book was written by a writer who never identified himself as author but chose the role of narrator, most likely in order to let the narrated events and worlds be directly reflected in the story. Only from his work can we construe the intentions of this implied writer. His dominant goal was evidently to write a work of art on the relationship between the God of Israel and the nation or individuals in the early period of the Judges. The writer probably also meant to write historical canonical liter-

36. People found unusual metaphorical expressions more meaningful when told that they were written by a famous contemporary poet than by a computer program (Gibbs 1994: 74).

37. See the pragmatic analysis of rhetorical relations proposed in Winther-Nielsen (1995: 87-96) and applied to the entire book of Joshua.

38. The glosses *inscriber/vocalizer* and *formulator* are from Clark (1996: 20); other terms are *transmitter, composer,* and *motivator* (Levinson 1983) or *Spkr1* and *Spkr2* for the first two distinctions (Hanks); see conveniently Miller (1996: 100 n. 12).

ature for future generations of readers.[39] Yet he clearly did not point directly to the significance of his own situation, which must surely imply that readers are not meant to focus exclusively on historical authorship in the way suggested by Hardmeier (1990). One may dispense with the reasons for text production or its authorial background, but the text is of no use if it does not influence the reader to action (Widdowson 1992: ix).

However, we may perhaps not be left completely in the dark with regard to the specific details of the book's production as a communicative event. Possibly we can trace an implied contemporary audience through an *addressee hypothesis*, along the lines suggested by Hardmeier (1990), if we follow the seminal work of O'Connell (1996).

O'Connell (1996) studies the ideological purpose or agenda of the compiler/redactor of Judges with respect to his implied readers. He looks at plot-development rather than scenes or episodes as well as at characterization to find clues to the rhetorical concerns of the writer or the compiler/redactor (1996: 1, 5 *et passim*). He believes that the writer portrayed non-Judahite deliverers and foreign kings with traits foreshadowing the failure of Saul, the first king of Israel (1996: 309), while Judah is idealized as the divinely appointed leader of Israel in order to foreshadow implicitly the new king David chosen from the tribe of Judah. It is also significant that the book ends in a gloomy picture of tribe-wide cultic apostasy and social disintegration (1996: 315). The monarchical refrain of 17:6, 18:1, 19:1, and 21:25 serves as a rhetorical clue to endorsing a divinely appointed Judahite king at the time of David. The effect is that tribal hero stories are rhetorically recontextualized in order to show some higher standards of leadership (1996: 315-18). There is at the same time an intentional reticence in implicating any individual hero of Judah among the judges (1996: 321). Throughout, the book also serves to persuade the recipients to maintain inter-tribal loyalty to Yahweh by warning against improper cultic actions and violations of social justice (1996: 322-24) and by pointing to the role of divine empowering and favor (1996: 326-29).

O'Connell suggests that this compositional form of the book will allow us to infer an ostensible rhetorical situation "implied within the world(s) of the texts" (1996: 306), though not the actual historical situation (1996: 310 n. 16 and 329).[40] This ostensible situation is inferred from references to inci-

---

39. Judges seems to be intended to function independently of the other books of the former prophets, but it is still part of this canonical contextualization (O'Connell 1996: 307).

40. For a survey of other proposals on the situation of compilation/redaction, ranging from 1053 BC to about 350 BC, see O'Connell (1996: 305-6 and 345-68). O'Connell assumes that the book was compiled from originally separate tribal traditions (1996: 347) and follows Stone's proposal for a coherent final redaction: the final stage comprises theo-

dents in Gibeah and Bethlehem, the birthplaces of Saul and David (1996: 308), and in particular from the religious-political situation of the early years of King David's reign in 2 Samuel 1–4. David had not yet conquered Jerusalem, defeated the Philistines, or brought the ark to Jerusalem (1996: 311, 314-20), but he was still reigning in Hebron as the legitimate heir to the city of Caleb (1:14-15), who was also a former giant-slayer (1 Samuel 17; 1996: 313). O'Connell even assumes that the frequent references to Ephraim in Judges indicates that they, as representatives of northern Israel, are the implied audience addressed in the Israelite civil strife of 2 Samuel 2:8–4:12, encouraged to "sway their allegiance from the Benjaminite dynasty of Saul (under Ish-Bosheth) to the Judahite monarchy of David" (1996: 314).[41] In support of this rhetorical situation O'Connell also points to an implied recency in chronological references and historical situation (1996: 329-42).

O'Connell's addressee hypothesis makes an impressive case for the early relevance of the present book in the time of David. The tribe of Judah has a prominent role in the similarly worded contrast between the original ideal of an obedient Israel in 1:1-3 and the violation of the divine directive in 20:18-28. Other details may be more open to discussion, and their value for a reconstruction of an implied audience considerably less.[42] It is, for instance, quite clear that the future capital of Jerusalem fares quite well in 19:10-14, while the Judahite father-in-law of the Levite in 19:3-10 carries the major blame for the intoxication and fatal delay of the Levite. Nor did it have a clear positive effect on the personality of Micah's Levite to have once lived in Bethlehem in Judah (17:7). The direction of influence could actually be from Judges to Samuel, as admitted even by O'Connell (1996: 310).

However, even if we assume that the implied rhetorical situation is the early reign of David in Hebron, we still do not have the final clues as to the book's production as a communicative event. *The Judges writer* made every effort to avoid any concrete biographical references, and only lends his voice

---

logical material (1:1–2:5; 3:31; 6:7-10; 10:10-14; *8:22-35) as well as chap. 9, the minor judges and Othniel (3:7-11), and chaps. 17-21 (1996: 365-66 and 368).

41. The old order loyalists had to be convinced that David was no usurper (9:56-57; O'Connell 1996: 324), but they honored those who were loyal to the old dynasty, as in the case of Jabesh-Gilead in 21:8-14, 1 Sam 10:27–11:11, 31:11-13, 2 Sam 2:4-6, and 21:12b (1996: 326).

42. Note that Othniel has connections with Debir rather than with Hebron (1:10-15 and 3:7-11), and is in great need of water. The blame on the Benjaminite Ehud is insignificant if at all present (contrast O'Connell 1996: 99-100), and the situational parallels between the cult abuse by Micah and the Danites and the situations in 1 Samuel 13 and 15 are extremely general (contrast 1996: 309). Phrases like "was with Judah/David" in 1:19(22) and in 1 Sam 16:13 and 18:12 (1996: 312) are too general to prove anything.

in full to the speaking actors and God of a world of the Judges that he believed existed in the past. He had the *actors* speak directly in their conversational encounters, and he sketched the historical contexts of their conversations. The anonymous writer narrated the stories in his own words with the appropriate dramatization and commentary. He had everything lead up to a climax in the last great judge, Samson, and his double prayers in his agony of victorious death (16:28 and 30).

He was consciously aware of the presence and principal role of *a divine speaker* who spoke through his angels (2:1-3; 6:11-24; 13:2-23), his prophet (6:7-10), or his priests (1:1-2; 20:18, 23, 28). The writer believed he knew exactly how God thought about the sad times (2:20-23). He was convinced that he spoke for the divine principal through his story and that his conclusions reflected the divine perspective especially in his explanatory introductory discourse (2:6–3:6). Occasionally he expressed this belief through direct comments on Yahweh's help (e.g., 1:4 and 18) or his criticism of wayward Israel's doing what was evil (2:11; 3:7, etc., and 17:6 etc.). In Widdowson's (1992: x) terms, we have an *author/formulator* who assumes limited initiatives but acts on dictates of some other authority, being personally responsible for the wording yet dependent on this other principal for the ideas expressed.

Goffmann's distinctions for speaker roles can also help us to explain different *hearer roles*. Widdowson (1992) uses these distinctions in order to clarify the role of the reader in a practical stylistics of poetry in terms of "the reception end of the communication process" (1992: x). A *reader-animator* will choose to attend to the words simply to "activate meanings deemed to be in the text" (1992: x).[43] A *reader-author* will make an effort to identify their current meaning in an attempt to "engage creatively with the text and so act as author of personal reaction." Widdowson recommends this reader-author role because he will justify his "own judgment by making as precise reference to the text as possible" (1992: xii).[44] This is in clear contrast to the practice of reader-response criticism, which turns the *reader-principal* into someone "asserting an interpretation on the readers'

---

43. Widdowson (1992: xi) considers Bible interpretation "an élite and privileged activity, reserved for such people as scholars and priests," but this is mostly true for the older kind of traditional academic theology.

44. In practical stylistics the autonomy of the text is usually combined with the authority of the critic, "each a guarantee of the other" (1992: xi). Precision is required in identifying "what it is in the poetic text which induces us to read a particular meaning into it" (Widdowson 1992: xii), i.e., in "identifying cause in the text, but not in describing the effect on the reader."

own authority . . . authorizing *any* meaning no matter how idiosyncratic" (1992: xi).[45]

Pragmatic constraints also have a bearing on reading because they imply that the reader is totally dependent on the author, yet he must choose voluntarily to accept the author's world (Mey 1993: 281). For this reason, discourse is purposeful as an intentional and controlled human activity, in contrast to its effects on the recipient, which are not controllable (van Dijk 1997b: 8-9).[46] It is for the reader as interpreter to decide whether or not he believes that the biblical narrative is a true and accurate description of events with a valuable message for the present. Pratt (1990: 122-24), who has taken pragmatic concerns seriously in his proposal for interpreting Hebrew narrative, has suggested that an "Authority-Dialogue" model best fits the communicative interaction between the authors and readers of Hebrew narrative. In interaction with a superior, on the one hand "we come with our own expectations and questions that prepare us for meaningful dialogue. On the other hand, we come fully yearning for understanding beyond our own ideas" (1990: 32).

To sum up, then, the pragmatic constraints on communication imply that it is the speaker as the responsible principal who has the privilege of meaning something for the addressee. The message of Judges was perhaps particularly relevant to a public audience in the early years of the reign of King David over Judah, yet we cannot be sure that this was the actual audience. From the book we get the impression that the actual world of a past historical situation received the sole and unique emphasis. As hearers or readers of written narrative communication we have to identify the meaning intended by the implied writer and the named speakers, and we also have to understand and respond to the principal's meaning.

The following table summarizes most of the discussion thus far. The speaker roles are associated with the layers to be discussed in the following section. The inscriber and formulater roles are served by the writer/formu-

45. Reader-response criticism's only solution to this "interpretative promiscuity" (Widdowson 1992: xi) is to focus on "the socialized reader acting as principal and representative of some ideologically informed interpretative community" and sharing "the significance assigned to the text."

46. It may depend on whether we adopt the speaker's or the recipient's perspective: "For the recipients what count are what is said and its social consequences, that is, what is being *heard* or *interpreted* as (intentional) action" (van Dijk 1997b: 9). Recipients ascribe intentions, and this defines them as social actors: it becomes socially "real" if it has real social consequences. As readers of Holy Scripture we even carry an additional responsibility to attend to the text as a unique and authoritative inscribing formulation by a divine principal, if its claims are to be accepted at face value.

lator, who is conscious of speaking for other principals, the speaking actors in the stories, and the divine voice. The historical fix point — that is, the time of the original rhetorical situation — may or may not be the early years of David's rule in Hebron.

Table 1:
Layers, Speaker-Roles, and Historical Contexts in the Book of Judges

Layer	Speaker Role	Served by	Historical Context
Current	⇑	Translator, editor, etc.	Later contextualization
Delivery/Writing	*inscriber/vocalizer*	⎫ Writer/Narrator	ca. 1000 BC (?)
Story world	*formulator*	⎭	
Conversation	*principal*	Speakers	Time of the Judges
Divine messages	⇓	God	

6. The Coherence Principle:
Contexts, Layers, and Settings of Language Use

In the test of a pragmatic case for communication in Hebrew narrative we may now move from the speaker's intention to the second major issue, the problem of reference to the world through language. This is the point of the coherence principle, which, according to Mey (1993: 237, 246-49), explains how sequences of utterances in conversation and text can form meaningful communication.[47] Words are anchored in worlds by the will of the writer. In the following we will discuss how meaningfulness in some world is a matter of using language in a context, of organizing worlds and words into well-defined layers, and of situating language within its proper settings or arenas of language use.

Halpern wants to prove historiographic factuality by the following criterion: Hebrew history-writing was not produced by writers who were "unconstrained by the credence of contemporaries, without loyalty to fact or common knowledge" (1988: 27). This clearly shows that he is aware of contex-

---

47. Note similarly Blum-Kulka's discourse-pragmatic view that conversational implicatures may "serve as bridges of coherence: one turn of talk may be linked to the previous one not through direct linguistic means, but rather through an inference with regard to indirect meaning" (1997: 59).

tual features in his case for Hebrew narrative. But if the case is stated solely in terms of evidence from hypothetical sources, it is extremely vulnerable. Others may view the evidence differently, doubt the logic of the deductions, or attack the whole enterprise of historical-critical reconstruction. It is, however, possible to restate Halpern's case in terms of a modern pragmatic view of contextual coherence.

The pragmatic *coherence principle* can be thought of as the fact that we can usually understand how a discourse functions only if we understand that language is used in actual situations and for specific effects in a certain context. Speakers and writers can achieve their communicative goals only "on the basis of social and cultural knowledge, and other beliefs, with various aims, purposes and results" (van Dijk 1997b: 3). Discourse studies from their early beginning focused on meaningful, coherent, and acceptable talk and text (1997a: 5) and soon focused on how to connect "texts to discourse participants' knowledge of world and society" (de Beaugrande 1997: 53). Coherence was defined as what hearers or readers are bringing about when they apply their knowledge of the world to the text (Renkema 1993: 35, 37).[48] Discourse signals such contextual features; they are indexed in talk and text.

The coherence principle first of all explains how *meaning in a contextual sense* is solidly anchored in situations without being completely relative or polyvalent. The contextually determined nature of meaning is forcefully argued by cognitive research carried out within a pragmatic framework. It is clear that meaning emerges only through discourse and is "always relative to context and situated in social relations" (Palmer 1996: 38). Yet the notion of *emergent meaning* should not be carried to the extreme because that would have the absurd implication that "language and culture would not exist" (1996: 39).[49] It is far more realistic to assume that conventional meaning interacts with conventional situations in *situated meaning* "to frame meanings that are both conventional and relative to various situations" (1996: 39).[50] There is no need artificially to separate the pragmatic meaning from the referential meaning because we would lose the ability to communicate and understand stable meanings (1996: 40).

48. "The attribution of coherence is, therefore, partially dependent on the disposition of the receiver" (Renkema 1993: 32).

49. Otherwise the "stable, consensual meanings and patterns evident in cultures, traditions, and natural languages would never come into play" (Palmer 1996: 39). This is an important *caveat* to Vanhoozer's (1998: 249) discussion of the concept of emergence as supervenience.

50. We have access to "an epistemological context of shared knowledge and conventions" (Gibbs 1994: 74).

Palmer (1996: 40), like anybody else, rejects the suggestion that we can view meaning simply as some sort of discrete, stable object that somehow gets moved from the mind of a speaker over into the mind of a hearer by using language as a *conduit*. The cognitive linguists Tomlin, Forrest, Pu, and Kim (1997: 64-65) helpfully replace the conduit metaphor with a *blueprint* metaphor. The speaker's conceptual representation of objects in his mind is much too complex to be grasped fully in a text. Instead, the speaker becomes the architect of his text who guides his listener in constructing a conceptual edifice based on his own conceptual representation of events and ideas. The speaker as the architect and the hearer as the constructor must both construe a coherent text through their integration of knowledge and management of information. The hearer makes pragmatic implicatures from the contextual situation and builds cognitive inferences from the text and the world knowledge he shares with the speaker (1997: 72-73). In this dynamic view of communication the speaker directs his listener's attention to information and knowledge through grammar and text (1997: 103-5).[51]

The contextual significance of the coherence principle can also explain how narrative is pragmatically constrained in context. To make up a literary world is similar to using language to form a conversational world (Mey 1993: 280). Both an author and an interlocutor have to keep the constraints on their world "constant and consistent," especially those "relating that universe to language, and vice versa." Otherwise both will become unintelligible and lose their readers or interlocutors, their "potential collaborators in the literary or conversational effort" (1993: 281).[52]

Discourse studies at present focus on interaction and storytelling in conversations in order to understand how stories relate to other kinds of discourse and to locate the social, cultural, and other contextual clues in stories. Ochs's (1997: 185) survey of current research first focuses on how interlocutors coauthor oral stories by their questions, comments, and other responses contributing to the coherence of an evolving tale.[53] But narrative is found in many other popular

---

51. The function of grammar is this: "morpho-syntactic cues reveal the memorial and attentional characteristics of the speaker's conceptual representation and direct those of the listener to conform to the speaker's conceptual representation" (Tomlin, Forrest, Pu, and Kim 1997: 104).

52. The reader and the interlocutor are therefore part of a constrained world of constancy and consistency that "guarantee a consistent and well-functioning mechanism of discourse" (Mey 1993: 280), and "the literary constraints function as necessary and sufficient conditions on our reading; by extension, they can be interpreted as pragmatic constraints on our use of language" (1993: 280).

53. Interactional narration influences the way we think and interact: mutual relationships are formed by "the message content of jointly told narratives and the experience of working together to construct a coherent narrative" (Ochs 1997: 185).

and artistic forms, and in different modes as spoken, written, visual, or musical representations (1997: 185-86). Furthermore, narrative both embeds various kinds of discourse forms by blending oral and written modes and is itself embedded in other discourse forms and situations.[54] In this way narrative texts are embedded in social and historical dialogues and reflect cultural systems of knowledge, belief, values, ideologies, action, emotion, and other dimensions of social order (1997: 188-89). Narrative is thus a natural form of everyday communication and can be explained in terms of more general communicative processes. Coherence anchors the language of narrative in contexts.

Second, the principle of coherence can also explain how text and talk in narrative are organized into *layers* to ease understanding and to increase involvement. Clark in particular has emphasized that people regularly create layers to tell jokes or stories and to quote one of their characters. On top of the primary layer of a conversation they build one or more story layers, each specified by its "domain or world — by who or what is in it" (1996: 16), and each new layer has other agents in an independent place, time, and role (1996: 15). The first layer is the actual world, and the second layer built on it is a temporary stage where characters perform their actions in full view of the audience, the participants of the first layer (1996: 16 and 355).

Clark uses stories in conversation as the default to explain how a speaker invites a hearer to join him in imagining a second domain as an actual happening and often introduces a third domain in a direct quotation (1996: 361). Halpern, however, makes a sharp distinction between the two former layers and the latter and assumes that reported events may very well be factual, but reported speech is fictitious.[55] The Hebrew historian, much like Thucydides and other ancient authors, "supplied speeches for their characters" (1988: 9). The modern reader is expected to know such conventions for effective presentation and infer that "*in this case* no claim as to the accuracy of the particular" was made.

However, from a pragmatic perspective it is hardly the case that direct speech is used primarily to signal fancy. Ochs views direct speech as a way to

54. Narrative not only "plays host to a range of genres" (Ochs 1997: 187) and "house[s] other language activities," as when speakers embed an argument or gossip, but narrative "can itself be incorporated into a larger genre or activity" and become part of a dispute or prayer as stylized and strategic issues to questions posed by a situation (1997: 188). Note also Goodwin and Duranti's (1992: 3) discussion of Bauman's evidence for prose narration framing verse within a story, and talk between teller and recipient framing the story as an event. Talk within the story (prose frame) creates context for other talk (verse).

55. Halpern (1988: 9) believes that ancient authors made an explicit qualification for the truth value of speeches that proves that they worked as historians.

evoke one of the "communicative modalities" (1997: 187). A narrator shifts from prose narration to direct quotation to imply a shift to speech and "transform the reader into an (over)hearer as well."[56] Quoted speech can even be viewed as an effective form of demonstration (Clark 1996: 187, 242).[57] The contextualizing power of reported speech is also shown by the way that utterance, text, and story can juxtapose language from different cultural, social, and linguistic home environments (Goodwin and Duranti 1992: 19).

The evidence on reported speech in Judges is very rich. It begins immediately in the opening of the book, which quotes Israel's question for divine direction by lot on who should open the battle of Canaan (1:1-2). It continues with Judah's invitation to Simeon to participate in their battle (1:3), and with a quotation of a confession by the first subdued enemy, Adonizedek (1:7). Some quotations contain embedded quotes (2:1-3 and the last quote in 21:23), and occasionally a quotation is retold with minor pragmatic changes (13:6-7). It even appears that simple dialogue exchanges predominate in the main body of the book, while conversations become gradually more frequent toward the end of the book. There are numerous conversations in the Samson story in chaps. 13–15, in the story of Micah, the Levite, and the Danite spies in chaps. 17–18, and in the first half of the Gibeah story from 19:1 to 20:28. The book then abruptly ends with narration (20:29-48) and a number of detached monologues in chap. 21, perhaps underpinning the fragmentation and confusion ending the sad times of the Judges. Sometimes speakers tell their own stories, as when Jephthah does a political review of Israel's early history (11:12-28), the Levite gives his testimony on the Gibeah incident (20:4-7), or speakers tell about their lives (17:9; 19:18-19) or report their findings (18:9-10).

These encounters are of course not live recordings, but reported versions that have been carefully planned and condensed to look like communication in ideal delivery (Clark 1996: 255).[58] This does not necessarily detract from their value as evidence of oral interaction because even written transcripts of face-to-face conversations or telephone calls are no more than approxima-

---

56. When this device is refined in novels, the "play of communicative channels weaves a complex relationship between author, character, and reader/(over)hearer. If well wrought, such complexity yields meanings that render the author an artist and the product a work of art" (Ochs 1997: 187).

57. Narrators use reported speech to "communicate, often dramatically, a sense of being in the same context as the utterance" (Clark 1996: 16).

58. Miller (1996) shows convincingly how oral conversation and written reported speech in Hebrew share interactional features and other pragmatic functions, but notes also that all reported speech (whether oral or written) necessarily involves a reshaping and reinterpretation of the original locution.

tions to real-time data. Yet Clark unfortunately assumes that all layering involves joint pretense and pure imagination.[59] Nevertheless, many jokes are told to reflect a live experience, and their content is not necessarily "an assertion that is true only in the hypothetical world of the joke" (1996: 16).[60] Layers and fictionality are two entirely different and unrelated issues, and layers do not entail unreliability.[61] Perdue (1994: 263-72) helpfully distinguishes between common, creative, and religious imagination, and stresses that imagination "resists any equation with fantasy" (1994: 264).

The same point can be nicely illustrated by examples from Judges. People may lie and deceive in face-to-face conversations as Samson did to Delilah (16:7, 11 and 13), or they may tell the truth reliably in reported quotations of an angel (2:1-3) or share their true experiences as Jephthah did (12:2-3). These examples are much like the discussion on the *ipsissima verba* of Jesus. Some believe that later disciples invented virtually every reported saying, while others believe that the narrators expressed in their own words how the original speaker sounded to them in terms of their current context.

This also raises the question of the relation between modern fiction as a genre and Hebrew narrative. In Clark's view, stories in conversations are the foundation for other genres like novels, short stories, parodies, and satires (1996: 363).[62] A fictional novel differs from a conversational story in that utterances of the first layer (the real author) give way to utterances of the second layer (the implied author), and secondary layers can be recognized through the literary conventions for novels or on internal evidence. On this account Hebrew narrative does not count as modern fiction because there is no clear distinction between a real and an implied author. The format is usually that of the short story rather than of a lengthy novel.

Yet the real dilemma is that there are no irrefutable, factual, evidential, and totally objective criteria to distinguish a factual account from a fictional fancy in the Bible or elsewhere (Searle 1975). The difference is blurred because

59. This holds for novels that are real only in imagination and should be appreciated for what they are doing and why, for their rhetorical effect (Clark 1996: 367), but it is not clear that all layering is an acting *as if*, or a *non-serious* use of language (1996: 353), that speakers only *pretend* to assert something and act like playing make-believe (1996: 354), in a game of imagination (1996: 355).

60. Even Clark mentions a restriction: "Higher layers represent other domains, *often* hypothetical, that are created only for the moment" (1996: 17; my italics).

61. To use the word "pretense" is to settle the matter prematurely. Verbs like "pretend," "dream," and "imagine" in pragmatics count as nonfactitive presuppositions (Yule 1996: 29). A statement like "He pretends to be ill" entails that he was not ill at all.

62. Layering is found in jokes, novels, plays, stories, news stories, parables, and *what-if* narratives (Clark 1996: 17, 353, 362).

narrative is often fictional, fiction imitates history, and both are preoccupied with humans in space and time.[63] Halpern (1988: 9) correctly points out that there is no formal difference in content and accuracy, but still believes that we can tell why Herodotus is a historian while Shakespeare is a dramatist (1988: 9). He believes that it is possible to decide between the two by a "judicious appreciation both of metaphoric, or fictitious, and of literal, or authoritative, discourse" (1988: 11). However, current research has shown that metaphorical language is in no way secondary or substandard in relation to literal language (Gibbs 1994: 59-61).[64] Figurative language is basic to our conceptualization of the external world because language and cognition are metaphorically structured (1994: 5). Metaphors constrain everyday and literary discourse as well as the way we actually think (1994: 7-8, 120-207).[65]

The real problem is thus that we have no formal criteria to help us decide why we cannot believe in a ghost story with a realistic and antiquarian description of its setting, but can believe in a summary description of a divine victory in a battle like that reported in Judges 4. Uglow (1988) points out that it is a hallmark of her collection of twentieth-century ghost stories by female writers to portray an accurate and authentic milieu for the appearances and to stress the veracity of the happening. If we know ghost stories as a genre, we are able to distance ourselves from its claims, but our worldview is also involved. If history and fiction can be distinguished only "on the basis of their overall purpose" (Long 1994: 66), the difference would be that the ghost story intends to describe extrasensory appearances, while Hebrew narrative purports to tell about historical events which were interpreted as divine intervention.[66]

63. Perdue (1994: 280-81) notes how Ricoeur emphasizes the similarities between narrative history and literary fiction.

64. Gibbs also points out that the definition of literal meaning will always depend on the context, yet an assumed literal content need not reflect "people's underlying mental representations of concepts or of the language we use to express our ideas" (Gibbs 1994: 78). Gibbs's approach is not "nonfoundationalist," but rather a more realistic view of cognition as "grounded in everyday bodily and perceptual experiences that form the nonmetaphorical part of thought and language" (1994: 79).

65. Note the excellent discussion of Ricoeur and Derrida in relation to hermeneutics by Vanhoozer (1998: 126-32 and 139-40).

66. Ultimately I must confess that my worldview does not contain belief in ghosts or the gods of the ancient Near East, but it does contain belief in the Israelite God being active in history as claimed by the narratives. Historian Ben Carter in personal communication has pointed out that there is a "metaphysical [or psychological?] criterion" to distinguish between the two kinds of narration: the plausibility of a ghost is rooted in its metaphysical credibility, which we as hearers are invited "to apply in a somewhat uncritical way (suspended disbelief)."

The question of the fact or fancy of stories therefore ultimately boils down to the communication partners' coordination of intentions and beliefs along the lines suggested by the Gricean cooperative principle. In the end I have to decide that the Israelite writers are credible and valuable communication partners. I know that authors may invent and recontextualize, but also that these are only some of the possibilities when stories look historical. Halpern would never state his case in this way, but these are to some degree the pragmatic facts of the matter. It is in line with Coady's (1992) study of how "believing in other persons, in authors and testimony, is an essential part of the act of communicating (as irreducible as promises)," how trust in others is basic to serious cognitive activity (cf. Long 1994: 177-80). In general, humans believe in speakers who, they assume, vouch for the evidence (1992: 43). In the light of speech act theory it is possible to point out that reporting is the dominant form of assertion (1992: 154) and that it builds on some degree of shared outlook (1992: 153). Humans rely on an integration of memory, perception, testimony, and inference in their normal use of language, and learn by trusting (1992: 169-170), which of course also gives them the ability to be trained to distrust some sources of information. But it is a standard mistake to assume that "lack of evidence, that is our ignorance, shows indeterminacy or undecidability in principle" (Searle 1994: 648).

Third and finally, however, the principle of coherence may after all explain how the language use in these narratives reflects *real-world life situations*. Hebrew narrative refers to a rich variety of spoken settings of language use that can be categorized according to the situation of language use and the spoken or written mode (Clark 1996: 4-8). We have already seen how interpersonal conversation abounds in stories of encounters throughout the entire book of Judges. Other spoken settings are less spontaneous and more formal.[67] Institutional settings are found in the story of Jotham's political speech from a mountain in Shechem (9:7-21) and in a court session, or hearing, followed by military demands for surrender (20:1-13). A religious institution is reflected in the wording of the question and answer in the priestly procedure for acquiring a divine decision by lot (1:1-2 and 20:18-28). Another type of spoken setting is mediated by a spokesperson when Jephthah negotiates with Ammon through messengers bringing accusations back and forth between the two countries (11:12-28). More often, somebody speaks as or in the name

---

67. The modern examples of spoken settings are the institutional setting like the news conference and interrogations in court and marriage ceremonies as prescriptive subsets of institutional talk. Other spoken settings are mediated by spokespersons, and plays are nonpersonal representations of others' intentions (Clark 1996: 5-6).

of Yahweh himself (2:1-3; 6:7-10; chap. 13). The only fictional setting is found in Jotham's fable of the talking trees (9:8-15).

These spoken settings reflect various social aspects of language use in ancient Israel. Niditch (1997) has shown convincingly that orality and literacy must have existed side by side in ancient Israel, but her views are influenced by Yugoslavian evidence on storytelling. Bailey (1995a, b), who since the 1950s has studied the traditional village culture of Arab villages in the Middle East, may have a preferable model of how villagers recounted their identity-forming stories in conversational interactions. Stories on important events and persons and their significant and very remarkable sayings have always been told in a memorized form that was controlled by the community. Village memory can guarantee reliable oral reporting across centuries, and written versions serve only to retain the stories in a more stabilized form that may be consulted, while the conversational recounting continues in the interest of continuously preserving the identity of the community over passing generations. The case Bailey has made for the oral transmission of the Gospel narratives may in principle be made for the important highlights and memorable words of great leaders in any period of history, and thus also for the centuries of the Judges period. Given the cultural continuity in the Middle East, this new model offers promising prospects for analysis of conversational communication in traditional historical societies.

If we then look at the written settings for a work like the book of Judges, it therefore, without any doubt, represents a mediated setting in the form of recorded oral tales and it probably also functions in an institutional setting as a national-religious story of past history, but it does not really exhibit the fictional elements characteristic of a work of "pure" literature.[68] The discourse types include not only narrative but also lists, reports, and expository discourses. The book opens with a few selected incidents and lists on settlement history in chap. 1 and continues with explanatory discourse of a theological nature in 2:1–3:6. The report-like account of Othniel in 3:7-11 is followed by the first of several short stories that unfold toward a culminating masterful poem in ancient language in chap. 5. Afterward follow quite extensive accounts of Gideon, Jephthah, Samson, the Danite migration, and the events leading up to and following the Benjaminite war. These stories report a lot of live communication in spoken settings.

---

68. The written "nonpersonal" settings are institutional (reporting news stories, writing essays or textbooks or making laws), mediate (writing speeches for other persons as secretaries or recording folktales), fictitional (an author writing for an audience), and private (writing diary)(Clark 1996: 6-8). On the concept of "pure" vs. "utilitarian" literature, see Long 1994: 152-53.

This varied use of different oral settings and various written discourse types makes the book of Judges resemble everyday language in conversations, exposition, listing, and storytelling much more than the prototypical form of fiction as a genre that focuses on fewer and often heroic persons, a more singular or unified and entertaining plot, and a central and unifying form. The genre of this kind of much more diversified Hebrew narrative is perhaps best characterized as a reporting on past history, no doubt selected for its ideological significance for the Israelite community. This assertion seems to support Halpern's claim that Hebrew narrative presents a stripped-down text that adheres to the meaning of reported events rather than a free fancy, fabricating intimate details of personal life (1988: 10, 12).

The only positive line of evidence may then turn out to be that Hebrew narrative reports on a great number of very different historical contexts from everyday life and not just some narrow poetic world. This is no final, absolute proof of the author's historical intentions, but it does provide some actual evidence of what he accomplished: portraying significant aspects of an intellectual-religious past along with a strong persuasive address to future generations. This kind of narration does not in any significant way diverge from the kind of conversational storytelling to which most of us are accustomed in our daily lives, which gets reflected in texts from our culture.

To summarize, then, the principle of coherence in pragmatics and discourse studies offers a possibility to account for the contextual aspects of meaning, the layering of words in worlds in talk and text, and the portrait of a wide diversity of everyday situations in a broad spectrum of discourse types. The diverse spoken settings and written discourse types may provide some of the corroborative evidence on historiographical intentionality that Halpern was looking for and is therefore the best, and maybe the only, evidence to support his case, or at least to tip the balance. In the final analysis, however, all current and past history writing will call on our hermeneutical trust, and the days of confessionalist, positivist, or minimalist absolute "proof" are gone forever.

7. Conclusions

The pragmatic evidence discussed in this paper cannot prove whether or not the fictional elements of Judges, its artistry in design and rhetoric, are integrated in a historically true portrait or grand story of the the period or not, not least because a final and absolute proof cannot be given and should not be hoped for since history is in the past. No method can ever give final verified and absolute proof of what was designed to be available as a testimony to be believed in the form in which it was given.

Yet rather than simply choosing presuppositions from reader-response or historical-approach minimalism (the verificational ideology) we might consider once more the case for history once launched by Baruch Halpern's innovative study *The First Historians* (1988), but not really developed very far in that study, and focus on the role of language and its actual use in contexts as evidence of speakers' pragmatic intentions and socio-historical situations. Pragmatics in a broad sense as the study of language use can explain communicative action in oral, everyday encounters and in written communication within a society like ancient Israel.

We have argued that Halpern's one-sided historical approach is problematic because it does not properly address the issues and insights in literary approaches (section 1). Much can be gained by a three-pronged literary, historical, and theological approach, yet a more useful and pragmatically oriented approach will have to work from the language and text of a narrative book like Judges and only then, in a second stage, explore the wider historical and theological dimensions of the book, much as Sternberg and Hardmeier have done (section 2).

We have therefore first introduced pragmatics as a new perspective on how actual language is used intentionally to communicate with interlocutors in interaction (section 3). The first step of analysis was to look for concrete evidence on intentional communication and discuss the relations between oral and written communication and the roles of speaker and hearer within the world of Judges, as well as the role of writer and reader in ancient and contemporary contexts. Different speaker and hearer roles can clarify the functions of the writer/narrator and the human and divine actors and speakers (section 4). The second step of analysis was to explore aspects of coherence in order to clarify how speakers use the actual context in interaction and communication. This kind of pragmatic evidence again allowed us to draw parallels between language use in the situations recorded in the Bible and in any other everyday situation. It may be argued that Judges is a record of language use and situations in a real past world rather than in a totally fictionalized world.

None of the evidence on language use can prove conclusively whether the Bible is fact or fancy because this is a decision that depends on the speaker's intentions and involves the hearer's trust, and no comparative evidence can establish the details conclusively. However, pragmatic evidence may tip the balance toward historical fact in the sense that both the reported interaction and the contexts resemble the realities of natural, everyday communicative action.

Even if not conclusive, this kind of evidence rests on known modern contexts of language use and communicative action, is informed by the analysis of a wide variety of contemporary cultures, and is in this respect arguably stronger than the mute evidence of chance finds from ancient times. However, to be carried any further, this case would have to be argued in much more detail in all narratives in Judges, which is far beyond the confines of this proposal.

8. References

Austin, J. L.

1962   *How to Do Things with Words.* Cambridge, Mass.: Harvard University Press (2nd ed. 1975).

Bailey, Kenneth E.

1995a   "Informal Controlled Oral Tradition and the Synoptic Gospels." *Themelios* 20: 4-11.

1995b   "Middle Eastern Oral Tradition and the Synoptic Gospels." *ExpTim* 106: 363-67.

Beaugrande, Robert de

1997   "The Story of Discourse Analysis." In Teun A. van Dijk, ed., *Discourse as Structure and Process.* Discourse Studies, vol. 1. London: Sage, 35-62.

Berkhofer, Robert

1997   *Beyond the Great Story: History as Text and Discourse* (1st ed. 1995; 2d printing, first paperback 1997). Cambridge, Mass.: The Belknap Press of Harvard University.

Blum-Kulka, Shoshana

1997   In Teun A. van Dijk, ed., *Discourse as Social Interaction.* Discourse Studies, vol. 2. London: Sage, 38-63.

Brettler, Mark Z.

1995   *The Creation of History in Ancient Israel.* London and New York: Routledge.

Bunimovitz, Shlomo

1995   "How Mute Stones Speak: Interpreting What We Dig Up." *BARev* 21/2: 58-67, 96, 98-100.

Clark, Herbert

1996   *Using Language.* Cambridge and New York: Cambridge University Press.

Coady, C. A. J.

1992   *Testimony: A Philosophical Study.* Oxford: Clarendon; New York: Oxford University Press.

Coulthard, Malcolm, ed.

1994   *Advances in Written Text Analysis.* London and New York: Routledge.

Davies, Philip R.

1997   "Whose History? Whose Israel? Whose Bible? Biblical Histories, Ancient and Modern." In L. L. Grabbe, ed., *Can a 'History of Israel' Be Written?* JSOTS 245. Sheffield: Sheffield Academic Press, 1997, 104-22.

Gibbs, Raymond W.

1994   *The Poetics of the Mind: Figurative Thought, Language, and Understanding.* Cambridge and New York: Cambridge University Press.

Goffmann, Erving

1981   "Radio Talk." In Erving Goffman, ed., *Forms of Talk.* Oxford: Blackwell; Philadelphia: University of Pennsylvania, 197-327.

Goodwin, Charles, and Alessandro Duranti

1992   "Rethinking Context: An Introduction." In Alessandro Duranti and Charles Goodwin, eds., *Rethinking Context: Language as an Interactive Phenomenon.* Cambridge: Cambridge University Press, 1-42.

Green, Georgia M.

1996   *Pragmatics and Natural Language Understanding.* Second Edition. Mahwah, N.J.: Erlbaum.

Grice, H. P.

1957   "Meaning." *Philosophical Review* 66: 377-88.

Gunn, David M., and Danna Nolan Fewell

1993   *Narrative in the Hebrew Bible.* Oxford and New York: Oxford University Press.

Halpern, Baruch

1988   *The First Historians: The Hebrew Bible and History.* San Francisco: Harper & Row.

Hardmeier, Christof

1990   *Prophetie im Streit vor dem Untergang Judas: Erzählkommunikative Studien zur Entstehungssituation der Jesaja- und Jeremiaerzählungen in II Reg 18–20 und Jer 37–40.* BZAW 187. Berlin and New York: de Gruyter.

Lemche, Niels Peter

1998   *Prelude to Israel's Past: Background and Beginnings of Israelite History and Ideology.* Peabody, Mass.: Hendrickson.

Levinson, Stephen C.

1983   *Pragmatics.* Cambridge and New York: Cambridge University Press.

Long, Burke O.

1991   "The 'New' Biblical Poetics of Alter and Sternberg." *JSOT* 51: 71-84.

Long, V. Philips

1994   *The Art of Biblical History.* Foundations of Contemporary Interpretation, vol. 5. Leicester: Apollos; Grand Rapids: Zondervan.

Mey, Jacob

1993   *Pragmatics: An Introduction.* Oxford and Cambridge, Mass.: Blackwell.

Millard, Alan R.

1994   "Story, History, and Theology." In Alan R. Millard et al., eds., *Faith, Tradition, and History: Old Testament Historiography in Its Near Eastern Context.* Winona Lake, Ind.: Eisenbrauns, 37-64.

Miller, Cynthia L.

1996   *The Representation of Speech in Biblical Hebrew Narrative: A Linguistic Analysis.* Harvard Semitic Museum Monographs 55. Atlanta: Scholars Press.

Niditch, Susan

1997   *Oral World and Written Word: Orality and Literacy in Ancient Israel.* London: SPCK; Louisville: Westminster/John Knox; subtitled *Ancient Israelite Literature.*

Ochs, Ellinor

1997   "Narrative." In Teun A. van Dijk, ed., *Discourse as Structure and Process.* Discourse Studies, vol. 1. London: Sage, 185-207.

O'Connell, Robert H.

1996   *The Rhetoric of the Book of Judges.* VTS 63. Leiden: E. J. Brill.

Palmer, Gary B.

1996   *Toward a Theory of Cultural Linguistics.* Austin: University of Texas Press.

Perdue, Leo G.

1994   *The Collapse of History: Reconstructing Old Testament Theology.* OBT. Minneapolis: Fortress.

Pratt, Richard L.

1990   *He Gave Us Stories: The Bible Student's Guide to Interpreting Old Testament Narratives.* Brentwood, Tenn.: Wohlgemut & Hyatt.

Provan, Iain W.

1995   "Ideologies, Literary and Critical: Reflections on Recent Writing on the History of Israel." *JBL* 114: 585-606.

1997   *1 and 2 Kings.* OTG. Sheffield: Sheffield Academic Press.

Renkema, Jan

1993   *Discourse Studies: An Introductory Textbook.* Amsterdam and Philadelphia: John Benjamins.

Schiffrin, Deborah

1994   *Approaches to Discourse.* Oxford, U.K. and Cambridge, Mass.: Blackwell.

Searle, John R.

1969   *Speech Acts.* London: Cambridge University Press.

1975   "The Logical Status of Fictional Discourse." *New Literary History* 6: 319-32.

1992   "Conversation." In John Searle et al. (compiled and introduced by Herman Parret and Jef Verschueren), *(On) Searle on Conversation.* Pragmatics and Beyond New Series 21. Amsterdam and Philadelphia: John Benjamins.

1994   "Literary Theory and Its Discontents." *New Literary History* 25: 637-67.

Sternberg, Meir.

1985   *The Poetics of Biblical Narrative: Ideological Literature and the Drama of Reading.* Bloomington: Indiana University Press.

Tomlin, Russell S., Linda Forrest, Ming Ming Pu, and Myung Hee Kim

1997   "Discourse Semantics." In Teun A. van Dijk, ed., *Discourse as Structure and Process.* Discourse Studies, vol. 1. London: Sage, 63-111.

Uglow, Jennifer

1988   "Introduction." In Richard Dalby, ed., *The Virago Book of Ghost Stories: The Twentieth Century.* London: Virago Press, 1988, ix-xvi.

Vanhoozer, Kevin J.

1998   *Is There a Meaning in This Text? The Bible, the Reader, and the Morality of Literary Knowledge.* Grand Rapids: Zondervan.

van Dijk, Teun A.

1997a   "The Study of Discourse." In Teun A. van Dijk, ed., *Discourse as Structure and Process.* Discourse Studies, vol. 1. London: Sage, 1-34.

1997b   "Discourse as Interaction in Society." In Teun A. van Dijk, ed., *Discourse as Social Interaction.* Discourse Studies, vol. 2. London: Sage, 1-37.

Watson, Francis

1997   *Text and Truth: Redefining Biblical Theology.* Grand Rapids: Eerdmans.

Widdowson, Herbert G.

1992   *Practical Stylistics: An Approach to Poetry.* Oxford: Oxford University Press.

Winther-Nielsen, Nicolai

1995   *A Functional Discourse Grammar of Joshua: A Computer-assisted Rhetorical Structure Analysis.* Coniectanea biblica: Old Testament Series 40. Stockholm: Almqvist & Wiksell.

Yule, George

1996   *Pragmatics.* Oxford: Oxford University Press.

Literacy in Iron Age Israel

RICHARD S. HESS

In a recent article Ian Young (1998a) argues that neither the biblical text nor the epigraphic witness is a reliable indicator for assessing the extent of literacy in Iron Age Israel. Judges 8:14 attests that a young man (Heb. *naʿar*) of Sukkoth was able to write. However, Young argues that this gives no clue as to how many young men in Israel could write. Nor is the increasingly large number of Iron Age inscriptions helpful. This is because a few people can produce a large number of inscriptions. Young suggests that the only way in which literacy can be judged to be widespread is if a vast number of inexpensive texts is present. These texts can be produced only by the printing press and dispersed through an extensive school system. Since the former was not present in ancient Israel, and the existence of the latter is disputed, by definition the presence of mass literacy is excluded. Young (1998a: 244-53) collects the biblical and epigraphic evidence of all those who are said to have been able to write or read. He suggests that even in these cases it was not unusual to have a professional scribe do the physical task of writing and yet to have the text attribute "writing" to the author, who merely spoke the words to the scribe.

In a second article Young (1998b) summarizes the biblical and epigraphic evidence as demonstrating that scribes, administrators, and priests were those who could read and write. He argues that Lachish letter 3 is best understood as suggesting that literacy was a matter of high social standing. Literacy is attested most frequently in the area of administration and the making of lists. Even the Siloam Tomb or Royal Steward inscription from 700 BC, which warns individuals to avoid the tomb and not to attempt to rob it, is not evidence that ordinary people could read. Rather, "it was normal practice in antiquity for people to read out loud, and hence interested

82

but illiterate bystanders would be able to obtain the information presented in the text."

The question of literacy in ancient Israel received a renewed interest in the past decade with the 1991 publication by Jamieson-Drake of *Scribes and Schools in Monarchic Judah: A Socio-Archeological Approach*. In this monograph the author presents a case that the inscriptional and other evidence from Iron Age Israel suggested the absence of writing in that region until after the eighth century BC. This conclusion was developed by others who went on to argue that writing in the sense of literature and especially of biblical literature was unknown until the formation of professional groups in the Hellenistic period. More recently, Susan Niditch (1996) has contended that all writing in ancient Israel was in the context of an "oral mentality." It was therefore either limited to specific military and commercial purposes, as in the cases of the Samaria ostraca and the Lachish and Arad ostraca, or it was iconic and not really intended for reading, as in the case of the Siloam inscription and Mesha stele.

The question of the degree to which literacy can be assumed or dismissed in ancient Israel is one that has no direct answer. We cannot assume one conclusion or the other. Nor is the comparison of other societies necessarily helpful. Except for contemporary societies in the ancient Near East, assumptions about religious, political, economic, and cultural motivations in other societies, whether preliterate or literate, cannot be transferred directly to Israel. If one brackets out the biblical text as a potentially later and unreliable source, there remains little evidence of societal features, and therefore the application of models from other societies becomes highly speculative.

This leads to the need to survey the extrabiblical evidence that does exist and to comment on what it may suggest about this question. In so doing, we will review two areas of evidence: the evidence from pre-Israelite Canaan, and the evidence from Iron Age Israel along with the Iron Age evidence from the regions surrounding Palestine.

I. Pre-Israelite Canaan

This evidence is indirect, but it is important for laying to rest several unwarranted assumptions. First, there is the attestation of various archives in the West Semitic world, such as those found at Alalakh, Emar, and Ugarit. Each of these contained hundreds of documents, and in the case of Ugarit the number reaches into the thousands. These major collections match the sophistication of their contemporary counterparts in Babylon and Assyria. They thus demonstrate the presence of writing on a wide scale throughout population centers of the Levant.

In addition, more than three hundred letters from the Amarna archive in Egypt attest to active correspondence with most of the population centers of Late Bronze Age Canaan. These include places such as Hazor, Megiddo, Gezer, Beth Shan, Pella, Shechem, Gaza, and Jerusalem. Scribes wrote on behalf of rulers at each of these sites. They sent letters to the pharaoh in Egypt. Therefore, there existed a tradition of writing that included even such small, relatively isolated sites as Jerusalem. For this reason, the size of a town is not an automatic criterion for excluding literacy. It could be argued that these letters demonstrate that Jerusalem was part of a larger administrative apparatus and that this would not have been the case during the Iron Age. In other words, the argument goes, although it was not necessary for the small, independent kingdom of Jerusalem to use writing, it was important for Late Bronze Age Jerusalem to use it since it was part of a larger empire.

However, the Amarna texts from Egypt are not the only texts to originate from Bronze Age Canaan. At sites such as Hazor (Horowitz 1996b; 1997), Megiddo, Taanach, Aphek, Bethshan (Horowitz 1996a), Kumidi (Huehnergard 1996), and Tell el-Hesi (EA 333) cuneiform texts have been found dating from the Bronze Age. The presence of scribal and lexical texts at Hazor, Megiddo, and perhaps Aphek suggests that the study of writing went on as well as the art of writing itself. Further, the discovery of a cuneiform text at Tell er-Rumeidah, very likely the site of ancient Hebron, attests to the presence of literacy in one of the more isolated regions of the southern hill country (Anbar and Na'aman 1986-87). This text is not a letter, nor does it suggest that Hebron was part of a larger empire. It is an administrative tablet recording sacrifices. The implication is that even in relatively small and isolated towns in Palestine writing could and did occur. Thus it is not acceptable to argue a priori that dearth of population is a sufficient reason to discount the presence of literacy. If this is true in the second millennium BC, it remains possible in the first millennium as well.

It is helpful to return to the Amarna correspondence and examine some texts from Jerusalem and Shechem. These are especially interesting in that they exhibit a level of rhetorical skill not always present in the other letters. However, many of the same expressions and techniques are also found in the Psalms and other biblical literature (Hess 1989; 1993; 1998b). There occur examples of synonymous and contrasting parallelisms, ABA'B' alternating structures, threefold repetitions, and chiasms. In addition, phrases that refer to the strong arm or hand of the pharaoh and the name of the pharaoh extending over Jerusalem from the rising to the setting of the sun have their parallels with references to God's strong arm and the praise of his name in the Psalms (e.g., Pss 83:19; 89:11, 14). Thus there was a literary and perhaps scribal connection between the writings of Late Bronze Age Jerusalem and the Jerusalem that produced biblical texts such as the Psalms. The absence of this sort of concentration of forms and expressions anywhere else than in Jerusalem in the Late Bronze Age, and their presence later in biblical poetry, strongly suggests that there was a continuing presence of a scribal tradition in David's capital. If this is the case, it suggests the presence of literacy in Jerusalem in a continuous tradition from the Late Bronze Age through to its destruction in 586 BC. It is possible that some outside source, such as Egypt, might have preserved a tradition of these expressions and techniques, but it is not as simple an explanation as their continued presence in Jerusalem itself.

Further, the Jerusalem Amarna letters are unique for their inclusion of a codicil at the end of four of the five letters whose ending is preserved. That codicil addresses the scribe of the pharaoh and asks him to present eloquent words to the pharaoh. This additional note betrays a consciousness of, and interest in, the formulation of words and expressions that is not found in the other letters from Amarna Palestine. This same consciousness could have enabled a scribal tradition to remain strong in Jerusalem even as it changed hands between Canaanites and Israelites.

If this is the case, then all assumptions about illiteracy throughout Palestine for the thirteenth century as well as the early Iron Age (1200-1000 BC) must be questioned and reexamined. More than two decades ago Cross (1967: 10*) could identify four inscriptions and one seal from at least four different sites in thirteenth-century Palestine.[1] These were alphabetic and written in Phoenician characters identified as Proto-Canaanite.[2] Their similarity to the paleo-Hebrew script is widely attested and easily recognized. Their locations of discovery include the northern site of Hazor as well as the southern places of Lachish, Beth Shemesh, Tell el-Hesi, and the Soreq valley. An additional hieratic inscription with a *tau* or *yodh* in Canaanite script has been identified at Tell Haror (Goldwasser 1991).

Thus there was a wide distribution of writing in both the north and the south. Further, at least three of the sites were also associated with the Amarna letters of the fourteenth century. The tradition of writing seems to have continued beyond the period of the Amarna correspondence and, indeed, to have shifted from the lingua franca of Akkadian to the local scripts and languages of Palestine.

---

1. These include Lachish Bowl No. 1, Lachish Ewer, the Goetze Seal (Soreq valley), the Beth Shemesh Sherd, the Hazor Dipinto, and perhaps the Tell el-Hesi Sherd.

2. For the presence of alphabetic cuneiform scripts in the thirteenth century, see the example at Sarepta in Puech 1989.

II. Ancient Israel

A. *Twelfth and Eleventh Centuries* BC *(Iron I)*

The textual evidence from Iron I (1200-1000 BC) has not been collected or examined in a systematic fashion. However, there is evidence of writing during the traditional period of the biblical Judges. Cross (1967: 10*) lists the Tell eṣ-Ṣarem sherd and the "Abba" inscription from the twelfth century. From the eleventh century BC, the most important text is the Izbet Sartah inscription that was discovered during the excavation of the site by that name located east of Aphek and identified with the biblical site of Ebenezer (Kochavi 1977; Demsky 1977). The script of the ostracon is not unlike that of early Hebrew. The text includes an abecedary as well as a collection of letters that do not appear to describe anything decipherable. Although archaeologists such as William Dever (1998: 47-48) identify this site as Israelite, with its four-room houses, stone-lined silos, and collar-rimmed storage jars, there are those who dispute the presence of Israel at this time and in this place. However, as Demsky (1977: 21, 23-24) notes, the *pe-ayin* sequence of the abecedary here is found in Israelite biblical acrostics but not in Phoenician ones. Further, he suggests that the *aleph* is similar to that on the Khirbet Raddana jar handle. Thus the text resembles that of later Israelite acrostics and has a script similar to another, roughly contemporary text found in an area that would be identified as Israelite.

In fact, the Izbet Sartah inscription appears to be a practice exercise useful for learning the Canaanite/Hebrew alphabet and for practicing letters. If this is correct, then there is evidence of learning the alphabet and writing skills in a small village in the eleventh century BC within the area that the Bible designates as Israel during this time. This is a remarkable discovery because it suggests that "Israelite-type" people were learning to read and write. Not only that, but this was being done in the small villages as well as the capital and central cities. How widespread was this? It is not possible to say. The accidents of preservation and discovery have yielded only this single document as witness to this practice. There could have been more, and they could have perished. The only certainty is that a small, eleventh-century village in the hill country could and did have at least one person learning to read and write the alphabetic script of the region.

There are, of course, additional texts from this period. Indeed, Holladay (1995: 381) argues that the evidence indicates "intense scribal activity" in which the Phoenician script, as found on eleventh/tenth-century-BC sarcophagi at Byblos, emerged in contemporary inscriptions on the following: the arrowheads of military leaders found near Bethlehem, the Khirbet el-Raddana handle (Cross and Freedman 1971), and the Izbet Sartah inscription. The number of arrowheads with the names of their owners continues to grow with discoveries in and around Palestine (Cross 1992; 1993a; 1996).[3] Some of these names correspond to biblical characters known from the books of Judges and Samuel (Hess 1998a: 174). But is this enough to demonstrate the presence of a literate culture in eleventh- and tenth-century Palestine? Using comparative evidence from earlier and later Near Eastern sources, several scholars have argued that indeed this could represent a flourishing literate culture, despite the absence of a royal archive and other inscriptions.

Millard (1995: 215) has observed that the absence of inscriptions from otherwise well-known rulers is not unique to David and Solomon. Not a single monumental inscription has been found from the Hasmonean dynasty nor from Herod's kingdom during his reign. Knoppers (1997: 40-42) notes that it is methodologically incorrect to conclude an "impoverishment of culture" on the basis of an absence of archaeological evidence. On this basis the postexilic period should also be a time of cultural and textual absence. Yet this is the very time when most scholars date the major production of many of the biblical materials. The Amarna Age (fourteeth-century BC) was capable of producing written documents of a literary style, and there is no reason to assume that tenth-century Jerusalem was any less populated or likely to produce written texts. Nuzi, which has produced more than 6,500 texts from the Late Bronze Age, was a site whose population was estimated at 2,000; not much different from the size of Jerusalem.[4]

B. Tenth Century BC (Iron II)

The tenth century BC continues to attest to a few arrowheads. Cross (1996: 16*) lists three. However, during this century universally recognized Hebrew inscriptions begin to appear. A convenient source for these and those in the

---

3. Cross 1996: 14*-16* identifies 26 arrowheads with names written on them in alphabetic script. Five come from El-Ḥaḍr west of Bethlehem, and they are all dated paleographically to the early or mid-eleventh century BC. At least 17 of the remaining 21 come from the eleventh century. Of these, five are in private collections, four are in Israeli museums or collections, four are in Beirut, three are in Paris, and one is in the British Museum.

4. Na'aman (1996a; 1996b: 180-183; 1997) also offers comparative arguments for the presence of a scribal center in tenth-century Jerusalem. He compares private libraries in Egypt and Assyria, and the work of the historians Manetho and Berossus. Na'aman concludes that Jerusalem could have preserved a similar library.

centuries that follow is the 1995 collection of Johannes Renz, which has so far appeared in three volumes. The volume on the seals has not yet appeared. For these it is necessary to consult the work of Avigad and Sass (1997), which deals with West Semitic stamp seals, and especially Davies (1991), who studies specifically Hebrew seals. He lists 900 seals and seal impressions from the time of the Israelite and Judean monarchies, though probably not all of these are Hebrew in origin. To these may be added 195 from more recent discoveries that have been published.[5]

Renz (1997 III: 3) lists four Hebrew inscriptions from the tenth century that have been discovered in the area occupied by ancient Israel. Of these the longest is the Gezer calendar. The others include about four identifiable letters each. In addition, one seal has been dated to the tenth century or the beginning of the ninth.[6]

This is not a great number of inscriptions, but the distribution is over a broad area: Tell el-Asi five kilometers west of Beth Shan, Tell Batashi, which is ancient Timnah, located eight kilometers northwest of Beth Shemesh, Khirbet Rosh Zayit[7] one and a half kilometers north of Kabul, and Tel Gezer. To these inscriptions may now be added a name carved onto a game board at Beth Shemesh.[8] This evidence includes areas in the northwest, northeast, and west/southwest of the country. Thus there would appear to have been writing going on in regions that complement the locations of the earlier inscriptions at Izbet Sartah in the west, eastward at Raddana, and near Bethlehem. These are all sites in the region of the central hill country both north and south of Jerusalem.

It may be of interest to note that at least some scholars would date a few Hebrew seals to this period. Thus the study of Ussishkin (1994) has identified the seal of Shema, servant of Jeroboam, as belonging to Jeroboam I rather than Jeroboam II. This, and at least one or as many as three other seals from Megiddo, would then date to the end of the tenth/beginning of the ninth centuries BC.

---

5. Barkay 1993; Lemaire 1990 (two of those listed); 1993 (four of those listed); Mährer 1992; Overbeck 1993 (47 of those listed); Deutsch and Heltzer 1994 and 1995 (nos. 11-23, 26-27, 54-68, 75); and 109 in Deutsch 1997.

6. Deutsch and Heltzer 1994: 55-56 (no. 24); also listed in Overbeck 1993 (no. A 18).

7. Renz notes that this location may have been within the area controlled by Phoenicia and should perhaps be identified as a Phoenician inscription. See Gal 1990.

8. Bunimowitz and Lederman 1997: 48 note that the name, ḥnn, occurs on the twelfth-century Beth Shemesh sherd as well as on the contemporary tenth-century bowl fragment at Tel Batash/Timnah.

C. Ninth Century BC (Iron II)

For the ninth century Renz (1995 III: 3-4) identifies eighteen inscriptions. Two of these, both from Arad, have only a single letter, but ten others have more than one line of text. The majority of inscriptions are from Arad and Kuntillet Ajrud, five and ten respectively. The remaining three inscriptions were found at Khirbet el-'Oreimeh, which is biblical Kinneret on the northwestern shore of the Sea of Galilee, at Tell el-Hammeh in the Beth Shan Valley, and at es-Semû', which may be identified with biblical Eshtemoa fifteen kilometers south of Hebron. The inscriptions again reveal a wide distribution and one that highlights different areas than those of the previous centuries.

The overwhelming majority of the texts are found in the south. Kuntillet Ajrud and Arad form the two primary sources for ninth-century Hebrew inscriptions. The southern desert often preserves texts better than the moister areas of Palestine where papyrus documents deteriorate quickly. However, these ninth-century texts were not written on papyrus. Rather, the preservation at Kuntillet Ajrud is probably due to the absence of occupation in later periods. At Arad there was also absence of much occupation after the Iron Age. As has been noted, the inscriptions at Kuntillet Ajrud appear to have been written by travelers. Thus reference to "Yahweh of Samaria" (Renz 1995 III: 4 KAgr[9]:8, line 2) suggests that the writer may have been a traveler to or from that land, and implies the presence of individuals who could read and write in Samaria.

Two ninth-century inscriptions, although not Hebrew, are worthy of note in terms of literacy because of their proximity to the land of Israel. The Moabite stone, with its inscription of Mesha king of Moab, is significant for several reasons. It has long been agreed that the northern kingdom of Israel is mentioned on this inscription. Recently, Lemaire (1994a; 1994b) has confirmed his suggestion that the "house of David" appears on the ninth-century Moabite stele. In the text, King Mesha of Moab celebrates his victory over the northern kingdom of Israel and mentions the capture of Horonen, possessed by the house of David. This stele is written by a king of a kingdom that bordered both those of Israel and Judah. The Moabites were not more cultured or literate than Israel or Judah. They did not have greater material or population resources. Further, the Moabite script and language resembled Hebrew. Therefore, the ability of Mesha to have a victory stele composed allows for the possibility that such inscriptions could have been authored by kings in Israel and Judah during the ninth-century.

Even closer in proximity is the Tel Dan stele. The July 1993 discovery of part of an Aramaic text on a stele at the southern city gate at Dan has been dated to the mid-ninth century BC (Biran and Naveh 1993). Two additional fragments were found later (Biran and Naveh 1995). The stele's mention of the "house of David" provides the earliest reference to the Jerusalem dynasty outside the Bible, despite some arguments to the contrary.[9] It also mentions "Israel," and this can be understood as the northern kingdom. In any case, the existence of an Aramaic stele suggests that the king who had it erected used writing and either expected people at the city gate to be able to read it or to have someone explain it to them.

As noted above (Tenth Century BC) the seal evidence remains limited. However, there are sufficient texts from the ninth century BC to suggest that at least some people in Israel and Judah could read and write. Further, this skill was not limited to the capitals but was widespread in towns and villages.

D. Eighth Century BC (Iron II)

Renz (1995 III:4-19) identifies 217 Hebrew inscriptions from regions in and around Palestine.[10] These all date to the eighth century BC, with the majority

---

9. Thus Assyria later designates Ahab's Israel as the "house of Omri," the father and founder of Ahab's dynasty. The presence of *dwd* on the ninth-century-BC stele of Mesha of Moab may be a reference to David, but the context does not allow a definite conclusion. Cf. Kallai 1993. See also its recently recognized appearance in the Mesha inscription by Lemaire 1994a. The suggestion of Davies 1994 that *btdwd* should be read as a place name, similar to Ashdod, is less likely. The historical geography of the region is well known, but there is no place name resembling *btdwd*. On the other hand, it fits perfectly with the biblical expression, "house of David." Lemche and Thompson 1994 have argued that *btdwd* is a sanctuary at or near Dan dedicated to a god, *dwd*. But they do not address adequately the parallels of "house of X" meaning a dynasty as found elsewhere in the ancient Near East. Thompson 1995a; 1995b has further argued that both "house of David" and "house of Omri" use names of deities, not dynastic founders. In order to do this, he must maintain that the reference to Omri in the Mesha stele is to a deity, not to a historical ruler. The basis for this interpretation appears to be the parallelism of Omri to the deity Chemosh on the stele. However, it is not clear that this parallelism exists. Cryer 1995 criticizes scholars for not considering *dwd* in the light of Ethiopic and Palmyrene parallels. However, these seem farther removed from the stele than David of the Hebrew Bible. See also Ben Zvi 1994; Cryer 1994 ; Knauf, de Pury, and Römer 1994. Knoppers 1997: 38-39 notes that no place name or deity, David or Dod, has yet been identified. See further support from Schnie-dewind 1996 and Kitchen 1997.

10. He also notes five eighth-century Hebrew inscriptions from Nimrud and two from Susa.

coming from the last quarter of the century. The majority from the first half of the century are the 81 texts that constitute the Samaria ostraca, from the capital of the northern kingdom. For the whole century Renz counts 93 texts from Samaria, including a small fragment of a stele (Renz 1995 II: 135) that preserves only three letters, ʾšr. The second largest source for texts in this century is Arad in the south, with some 47. All in all, 24 different sites are represented from the Beqaʿ valley to the Negev and from the Mediterranean coast to the Jordan valley.

Deutsch and Heltzer (1994) list two additional inscriptions from this period in an edition of texts from private collections and other sources.[11]

Included among eighth-century Hebrew texts is the Siloam Inscription that describes how workers completed a tunnel beneath the City of David in order to channel water to a safe place. Most scholars date this text to the period when Hezekiah was attacked by Sennacherib. Despite some comments to the contrary (Rogerson and Davies 1996) the paleographical evidence (based on the form of the letters in the script) confirms an eighth-century-BC date rather than a date centuries later (Hendel 1996; see Norin 1998 for additional evidence).

Perhaps here also should be dated the Balaam plaster fragments from Tell Deir Alla in the Jordan valley (Hackett 1980).[12] These texts are not Hebrew, but the precise nature of their language has not been conclusively demonstrated. They represent a hybrid dialect using script not unlike that of contemporary Hebrew writings. The mention of Balaam son of Beor and the appearance of relatively long descriptions about the prophet on what may have been the walls of a small cult center all attest to the importance of writing for this period in the Jordan valley.

The eighth century is also the period when seals are first attested in large numbers. According to Davies (1991: 118-263), 98 seals and seal impressions can be dated to the eighth century. Another 15 are dated ca. 700 BC. There are many more seals that have not been dated with certainty or could have been created in the eighth or seventh centuries. Thus 98 is the lowest possible number, and the actual number of seals that have been discovered and dated from the eighth century is more likely closer to two or three hundred.[13] In addi-

---

11. Numbers 6, 7.

12. Dijkstra 1995: 45 would date the text ca. 800 BC. For three additional ninth-century inscriptions from this site see van der Kooij and Hoftijzer 1989.

13. Note that, in addition to Davies, there are 75 in Deutsch and Heltzer 1995, the seal of Hoshea, Israel's last king, in Lemaire 1995, an iconic seal in Aufrecht and Shury 1997, and 109 eighth- or seventh-century seals now published for the first time in Deutsch 1997.

tion, another 57 royal stamps have been identified,[14] as well as 47 stamped jar handles,[15] and one or more inscribed bronze weights.[16]

All these seals, seal impressions, and stamps have writing on them. The seals most often have two names, that of the person to whom the seal belongs and that of that individual's father (the patronym). For this reason many seals and seal impressions have as many as ten or twelve different Hebrew letters on them. This can come close to half of the Hebrew alphabet. Although possession of a seal with one's name on it does not prove the ability to read or write, it is remarkable that in a world where the norm was to have seals with distinctive pictures or other markings on them and the rarity was to have a seal with writing on it, in ancient Israel and Judah the picture is the opposite. There the norm was one in which seals with writing were carried by most people who had them. It is not possible to say how many people in the society possessed such seals. There is no evidence that they were restricted to one class and not available to another level of society. Rather, the implication to be drawn is that a wide variety of people in every part of the land possessed seals that imply that they could read and write their own names. Perhaps it also suggests that they expected that others could read the names their seals left with their impressions.

What is the reason for the large increase in attested inscriptions in the eighth century? As will be seen, this phenomenon continues into the seventh century as well. Some have argued that the size of the towns and states became large enough to support writing and reading. However, as has been argued, the many small villages that produced inscriptions in the earlier centuries would not support this suggestion. Others might suggest that the influence of Assyrian culture, with its many inscriptions, brought about this shift. The problem here is that the Persian Empire was just as literate and yet the presence of inscriptions in the late sixth, the fifth, and the fourth centuries drops considerably when compared with the earlier period. Perhaps the clue lies in a similar phenomenon noted by Holladay (1987: 275-80) regarding

14. For the first 20 from Judah, see Lemaire 1981; Davies 1991: 246-49. In addition, see Eshel 1989 for one; Wolff 1994 for two from Beth Shemesh; Deutsch and Heltzer 1994 for three (nos. 8, 9, and 10); Bunimowitz and Lederman 1997 add 13, of which three have the seal of a royal official; Ussishkin 1996 adds another 18 from Lachish discovered since 1983.

15. Barkay 1992 records 36; Wolff 1994 records one from Beth Shemesh; Deutsch and Heltzer add two (nos. 52 and 53); Ussisshkin 1996 adds another seven from Lachish discovered since 1983. One can add a different type of stamp on a jar handle from Dan (Biran 1988).

16. Deutsch and Heltzer 1994: 63-68 list no. 31 from the eighth century and nos. 28-30 and 32 from the eighth or seventh century.

the distribution of cultic materials found in domestic contexts during the Iron Age at Hazor and Tell Beit Mirsim. The quantity of materials dramatically increased in the north at Hazor in the eighth century, and the same thing happened in the south at Tell Beit Mirsim in the seventh century. Both the inscriptional and the domestic cultic evidence converge in suggesting that at the time of the worst destructions of the Iron Age, both the northern and southern kingdoms preserved the largest quantity of materials from that period or a generation or two before it. Could this have something to do with the Assyrian invasion and destruction in the north and the Babylonian invasion and destruction in the south? These destructions could have preserved the documents and cult objects, whereas in previous generations they would have been reused or destroyed when they had served their purposes.[17]

E. Seventh Century BC (Iron II)

Renz (1995 III: 19-26) identifies 167 inscriptions from the seventh century BC. They come from 24 different places. To these can be added texts dated to the seventh or early sixth centuries, including one from Ma'on in Judah,[18] one from a private collection that mentions Eltolad in the northern Negev (Avigad 1990), four more from private collections (Deutsch and Heltzer 1995: 76-79), and most of the 31 inscriptions found at Ḥorvat 'Uza in the northern Negev of which four Hebrew inscriptions have been published, including a literary text (Beit-Arieh 1985; 1986-87; 1993a; 1993b; Cross 1993b). Again, there is a wide distribution over the northern and southern parts of the country. The largest number come from Gibeon, where 62 brief jar handle inscriptions follow four patterns. Some 14 texts are found at Arad. This leaves 93 inscriptions scattered among at least 23 sites. Many small sites possessed one or several inscriptions, attesting to a broad distribution of texts around the country.

An interesting example is the small site of Mesad Hashevayahu along the Mediterranean coast south of Joppa. Fourteen lines of the text are preserved and describe the plea of someone to his superior for return of a cloak that was taken from him. Although the exact interpretation is disputed, the use of writing to describe such a plea from a small site far removed from the large population centers of Judah opens a window on the possibly widespread use of writing to deal with all sorts of concerns.

---

17. Something similar to this was suggested in a private communication from Alan Millard some years ago.

18. The text reads *gwr ḥpr* on a broken potsherd. See Amit and Ilan 1990.

A text not included in the survey of Renz but dating from the seventh century is the Philistine dedicatory inscription discovered at Tel Miqne/ Ekron (Gitin, Dothan, and Naveh 1997). It describes a temple built for a deity and asks for divine blessing upon the king of Ekron. Of course, it is Philistine and therefore does not belong among Hebrew texts. Nevertheless, like the Mesha inscription and the Tel Dan stele of two centuries earlier, this text bears witness to the widespread use of the same alphabet and a similar script as found among the Hebrew inscriptions. Also at Tel Miqne at least 17 additional seventh-century inscriptions have been found. These are mostly cult-related, but they also attest to the prevalence of the alphabetic script and its use in writing among Judah's neighbors (Dothan and Gitin 1994).

Davies lists 154 seals and seal impressions dated specifically to the seventh century BC and an additional two dated ca. 600 BC. Again, this does not include hundreds that cannot be so specifically dated or those dated eighth/seventh or seventh/sixth century BC. Of the latter, for example, there are 200 from Tell Beit Mirsim and 50 from Jerusalem.[19] Thus the numbers of inscriptions continue to increase as one comes closer to 586 BC and the destruction of Jerusalem by the Babylonians. Thirty additional Hebrew seals and seal impressions from the seventh century or slightly later are listed by Deutsch and Heltzer (1994;[20] 1995[21]).

F. Early Sixth Century BC (Iron II)

This short period of about eleven or twelve years has few inscriptions that can be securely dated within its time limits. It may be that some of the inscriptions dated in the seventh century BC were composed later. In fact, Renz (1995 III: 26-35) lists only the 38 ostraca from Arad and the 25 from Lachish that describe the final period of these two Judean outposts. He adds two inscriptions from Jerusalem, one of which has not yet been published. In addition, it may be best to include here the two silver amulets from Ketef Hinnom at Jerusalem. These refer to the Aaronic blessing of Numbers 6.

Davies assigns only three seals to the early sixth century BC Many more are dated more generally.

---

19. Add to these a stamped jar handle and a *pym* weight from Tell Haror (Oren, Yekutieli, Nahshoni, and Feinstein 1991).

20. Numbers 11-23 and 26-27.

21. Numbers 54-68; note that 64-68 have been dated between the eighth and sixth centuries.

Conclusions

The evidence of writing in ancient Israel from 1200 to 586 BC can be drawn together. There are widespread occurrences of writing in cities and villages throughout the entire Iron Age. In 1995, Millard (1995: 211-12) counted 485 texts from 47 sites within Israel and Judah during the monarchy, not including hundreds of seals and seal impressions, and weights. Israel, Judah, and their neighbors had many individuals who could write the simpler alphabetic script and did so for a variety of reasons and purposes. Although state, cultic, administrative, and military concerns do appear, the presence of seals and impressions, as well as texts from small sites, suggests that writing was used for a variety of purposes.

Thus the following conclusions may be suggested in light of the arguments advanced by Young and others:

First, writing occurs at all periods of the Iron Age in Palestine. Century after century, the evidence suggests that writing was in continuous use from the beginning to the end of this period.

Second, it is not possible to limit those who wrote and read to specific classes or places. No site was too small or too large to possess written texts. The absence of more detailed information regarding the authors of the hundreds of inscriptions and hundreds more of seals and seal impressions leaves open the question whether or not this was an elite group. There is no evidence from the epigraphy to assume that members of any class could not learn how to read and write.

Third, the question of how widespread literacy was cannot be answered on the basis of the present evidence. However, the existence of numerous, widespread inscriptions argues against views that Iron Age Palestine did not at any time possess a sufficient level of statecraft or administrative complexity to allow for the development of writing (cf. Mastin 1992). Indeed, the implication of the evidence is that such matters are not of great importance for writing to exist in a population center, regardless of its size.

In conclusion, it is the concern of this paper to witness to the evidence for writing and reading in ancient Israel. This evidence, rather than modern anthropological models or technological inventions such as the printing press, must bear the major weight in any discussions for or against the presence of literacy in Iron Age Palestine.

Bibliography

Amit, D., and Z. Ilan
1990   "The Ancient Synagogue at Ma'on in Judah." *Qadmoniot* 23: 115-25.

Anbar, M., and N. Na'aman
1986-87 "An Account Tablet of Sheep from Ancient Hebron." *Tel Aviv* 13-14: 3-12.

Aufrecht, W. E., and W. D. Shury
1997   "Three Iron Age Seals: Moabite, Aramaic and Hebrew," *IEJ* 47: 57-68.

Avigad, Nahman
1990   "Two Hebrew 'Fiscal Bullae.'" *IEJ* 40: 262-66.

Avigad, Nahman, and Benjamin Sass
1997   *Corpus of West Semitic Stamp Seals.* Jerusalem: Israel Exploration Society.

Ayalon, Etan
1995   "The Iron Age II Pottery Assemblage from Ḥorvat Teiman (Kuntillet 'Ajrud)." *Tel Aviv* 22: 141-205.

Barkay, G.
1992   "A Group of Stamped Handles from Judah." *Eretz Israel* 23: 113-28. Hebrew.
1993   "A Bulla of Ishmael, the King's Son." *BASOR* 290/91: 109-14.

Beit-Arieh, Itzhaq
1985   "The Ostracon of Aḥiqam from Ḥorvat 'Uza." *Eretz Israel* 18: 94-96. Hebrew.
1986-87 "The Ostracon of Aḥiqam from Ḥorvat 'Uza." *Tel Aviv* 13-14: 32-38.
1993a   "A Literary Ostracon from Ḥorvat 'Uza." *Tel Aviv* 20: 55-63.
1993b   "An Inscribed Jar from Ḥorvat 'Uza." *Eretz Israel* 24: 34-40.

Biran, Avraham
1988   "A Mace-Head and the Office of Amadiyo at Dan." *Qadmoniot* 21: 11-17. Hebrew.

Biran, A., and J. Naveh
1993   "An Aramaic Stele Fragment from Tel Dan." *IEJ* 43: 81-98.
1995   "The Tel Dan Inscription: A New Fragment." *IEJ* 45: 1-18.

Bunimowitz, Shlomo, and Zvi Lederman
1997   "Beth-Shemesh: Culture Conflicts on Judah's Frontier." *BARev* 23/1: 42-49, 75-77.

Cogan, M., and H. Tadmor
1988   *II Kings: A New Translation with Introduction and Commentary.* AB 11. Garden City, N.Y.: Doubleday.

Cross, Frank Moore, and David Noel Freedman
1971   "An Inscribed Jar Handle from Raddana." *BASOR* 201: 19-22.

Cross, Frank M.

1967   "The Early Evolution of the Alphabet." *Eretz-Israel* 8: 8*-24*.

1992   "An Inscribed Arrowhead of the Eleventh Century BCE in the Bible Lands Museum in Jerusalem." *Eretz Israel* 23: 21*-26*.

1993a   "Newly Discovered Arrowheads of the Eleventh Century BCE." In A. Biran and J. Aviram, eds., *Biblical Archaeology Today, 1990: Proceedings of the Second International Congress on Biblical Archaeology. Jerusalem, June-July 1990.* Jerusalem: Israel Exploration Society, 533-42.

1993b   "A Suggested Reading of the Ḥorvat 'Uza Ostracon." *Tel Aviv* 20: 64-65.

1996   "The Arrow of Suwar, Retainer of 'Abday." *Eretz Israel* 25: 9*-17*.

Cryer, Frederick H.

1995   "A 'Betdawd' Miscellany: *Dwd, Dwd'* or *Dwdh?*" *SJOT* 9: 52-58.

Davies, Graham I.

1991   *Ancient Hebrew Inscriptions: Corpus and Concordance.* Cambridge and New York: Cambridge University Press.

Davies, Philip R.

1992   *In Search of 'Ancient Israel'.* JSOTS 148. Sheffield: JSOT Press.

1994   "'House of David' Built on Sand: The Sins of the Biblical Maximizers," *BARev* 20/4: 54-55.

Demsky, Aaron

1977   "A Proto-Canaanite Abecedary Dating from the Period of the Judges and Its Implications for the History of the Alphabet." *Tel Aviv* 4: 14-27.

Deutsch, R.

1997   *Messages from the Past: Hebrew Bullae from the Time of Isaiah through the Destruction of the First Temple: Shlomo Moussaieff Collection and an Up-to-Date Corpus.* Tel Aviv–Jaffa: Archaeological Center Publication. Hebrew.

Deutsch, R., and M. Heltzer

1994   *Forty New Ancient West Semitic Inscriptions.* Tel Aviv–Jaffa: Archaeological Center Publication. Hebrew.

1995   *New Epigraphic Evidence from the Biblical Period.* Tel Aviv–Jaffa: Archaeological Center Publication. Hebrew.

Dever, W. G.

1998   "Archaeology, Ideology, and the Quest for an 'Ancient' or 'Biblical' Israel." *Near Eastern Archaeology* 61: 39-52.

Dijkstra, Meindert

1995   "Is Balaam Also among the Prophets?" *JBL* 114: 43-64.

Dothan, T., and S. Gitin

1994   "The Rise and Fall of a Philistine City." *Qadmoniot* 105-6: 2-28. Hebrew.

Edzard, Dietz Otto

1985   "Amarna und die Archive seiner Korrespondenten." In J. Amitai et al., eds., *Biblical Archaeology Today: Proceedings of the International Congress on Biblical Archaeology, Jerusalem, April 1984*. Jerusalem: Israel Exploration Society, 248-59.

Eshel, Hanan

1989   "A *lmlk* Stamp from Beth-El." *IEJ* 39: 60-62.

Gal, Zvi

1990   "Khirbet Roś Zayit — Biblical Cabul: A Historical-Geographical Case." *BA* 53: 88-97.

Gitin, Seymour, Trude Dothan, and Joseph Naveh

1997   "A Royal Dedicatory Inscription from Ekron." *IEJ* 47: 1-16.

Goldwasser, O.

1991   "A Fragment of an Hieratic Ostracon from Tell Haror." *Qadmoniot* 24: 19. Hebrew.

Hackett, Jo Ann

1980   *The Balaam Text from Deir ʿAllā*. HSM 31. Chico: Scholars Press.

Hauser, Alan J., and Russell Gregory

1990   *From Carmel to Horeb: Elijah in Crisis*. JSOTS 85. Bible and Literature Series 19. Sheffield: Almond.

Hendel, Ronald S.

1996   "The Date of the Siloam Inscription: A Rejoinder to Rogerson and Davies." *BA* 59: 233-37.

Hess Richard S.

1989   "Hebrew Psalms and Amarna Correspondence from Jerusalem: Some Comparisons and Implications." *ZAW* 101: 249-65.

1993   "Smitten Ant Bites Back: Rhetorical Forms in the Amarna Correspondence from Shechem." In J. C. de Moor and W. G. E. Watson, eds., *Verse in Ancient Near Eastern Prose*. AOAT 42. Kevelaer: Butzon & Bercker; Neukirchen-Vluyn: Neukirchener, 1993, 95-111.

1997   "The Form and Structure of the Solomonic District List in 1 Kings 4:7-19." In G. D. Young, M. W. Chavalas, and R. E. Averbeck, eds., *Crossing Boundaries and Linking Horizons: Studies in Honor of Michael C. Astour on His 80th Birthday*. Bethesda, Md.: CDL, 279-92.

1998a   "Issues in the Study of Personal Names in the Hebrew Bible." *Currents in Biblical Research* 6: 169-92.

1998b   "Rhetorical Forms in Joshua 10:4." In M. Dietrich and I. Kottsieper, eds., *"Und Moses schrieb dieses Lied auf": Studien zum Alten Testament und zum alten Orient. Festschrift für Oswald Loretz zur Vollendung seines 70. Lebensjahres mit*

Beiträgen von Freunden, Schülern und Kollegen. AOAT 250. Münster: Ugarit-Verlag, 363-67.

Holladay, J. S., Jr.

1987   "Religion in Israel and Judah under the Monarchy: An Explicitly Archaeo-logical Approach." In P. D. Miller, Jr., P. D. Hanson, and S. D. McBride, eds., *Ancient Israelite Religion: Essays in Honor of Frank Moore Cross, Jr.* Philadel-phia: Fortress, 249-99.

1990   "Red Slip, Burnish, and the Solomonic Gateway at Gezer." *BASOR* 277/78: 23-70.

1993   "The Use of Pottery and Other Diagnostic Criteria from the Solomonic Era to the Divided Kingdom." In A. Biran and J. Aviram, eds., *Biblical Archaeol-ogy Today, 1990: Proceedings of the Second International Congress on Biblical Archaeology, Jerusalem, June-July 1990.* Jerusalem: Israel Exploration Society, 86-101.

1995   "The Kingdoms of Israel and Judah: Political and Economic Centralization in the Iron IIA-B (ca. 1000-750 BCE)." In T. E. Levy, ed., *The Archaeology of Society in the Holy Land.* New York: Facts on File, 368-98.

Horowitz, Wayne

1996a   "An Inscribed Clay Cylinder from Amarna Age Beth Shean." *IEJ* 46: 208-18.

1996b   "The Cuneiform Tablets at Tel Hazor, 1996." *IEJ* 46: 268-69.

1997   "A Combined Multiplication Table on a Prism Fragment from Hazor." *IEJ* 47: 190-97.

Horowitz, Wayne, and Aaron Shaffer

1992a   "An Administrative Tablet from Hazor: A Preliminary Edition." *IEJ* 42: 21-33.

1992b   "A Fragment of a Letter from Hazor." *IEJ* 42: 165-66.

1993c   "Additions and Corrections to 'An Administrative Tablet from Hazor: A Pre-liminary Edition.'" *IEJ* 42: 165-67.

Huehnergard, John

1996   "A Byblos Letter, Probably from Kāmid el-Lōz," *ZA* 86: 97-113.

Jamieson-Drake, D. W.

1991   *Scribes and Schools in Monarchic Judah: A Socio-Archeological Approach.* JSOTS 109; Social World of Biblical Antiquity 9. Sheffield: Almond.

Kallai, Zecharia

1993   "The King of Israel and the House of David." *IEJ* 43: 248.

King, P. J.

1989a   "The Great Eighth Century." *Bible Review* 5/4: 22-33, 44.

1989b   "The Eighth, the Greatest of Centuries." *JBL* 108: 3-15.

Kitchen, Kenneth A.

1997 "A Possible Mention of David in the Late Tenth Century BCE, and Deity *Dod as Dead as the Dodo?" *JSOT* 76: 29-44.

Knauf, E. A., A. de Pury, and T. Römer

1994 *"Baytdawid* ou *Baytdod?* Une relecture de la nouvelle inscription de Tel Dan." *BN* 72: 60-69.

Knoppers, G. N.

1993 *Two Nations under God: The Deuteronomistic History of Solomon and the Dual Monarchies, Volume 1: The Reign of Solomon and the Rise of Jeroboam.* HSM 52. Atlanta: Scholars Press.

1995 "Prayer and Propaganda: Solomon's Dedication of the Temple and the Deuteronomist's Program." *CBQ* 57: 229-54.

1996 "Ancient Near Eastern Royal Grants and the Davidic Covenant: A Parallel?" *JAOS* 116: 670-97.

1997 "The Vanishing Solomon: The Disappearance of the United Monarchy from Recent Histories of Ancient Israel." *JBL* 116: 19-44.

Kochavi, Moshe

1977 "An Ostracon of the Period of the Judges from 'Izbet Ṣarṭah." *Tel Aviv* 4: 1-13.

Lemaire, Andre

1981 "Classification des estampilles royales Judéenes." *Eretz Israel* 15: 54*-60*.

1990 "Cinq nouveaux sceaux inscrits ouest-sémitiques." *Studi Epigraphici e Linguistici* 7: 97-109.

1993 "Sept nouveaux sceaux nord-ouest sémitiques inscrits." *Semitica* 41-42: 63-80.

1994a "'House of David': Restored in Moabite Inscription." *BARev* 20/3: 30-37.

1994b "La dynastie davidique *(byt dwd)* dans deux inscriptions ouest-sémitiques du IXe 5. av. J.C." *Studi Epigrafici e Linguistici* 11: 17-19.

1995 "Name of Israel's Last King Surfaces in a Private Collection." *BARev* 21/6: 49-52.

Lemche, N. P., and T. L. Thompson

1994 "Did Biran Kill David? The Bible in the Light of Archaeology." *JSOT* 64: 3-22.

Mährer, S.

1992 "Ein Namen- und Bildsiegel aus 'Ēn Šems (Beth Schemesch)," *ZDPV* 108: 68-81.

Mastin, B. A.

1992 Review of Jamieson-Drake 1991. In *JTS* 43: 145-47.

Millard, Alan R.

1995 "The Knowledge of Writing in Iron Age Palestine." *TynBul* 46: 207-17.

1997 "King Solomon in His Ancient Context." In L. K. Handy, ed., *The Age of Solomon: Scholarship at the Turn of the Millennium.* Studies in the History and Culture of the Ancient Near East 11. Leiden: Brill, 30-53.

1998a "The History of Israel against the Background of Ancient Near Eastern Religious History." In T. Eskola and E. Junkkaala, eds., *From the Ancient Sites of Israel: Essays on Archeology, History and Theology: In Memory of Aapeli Saarisalo (1896-1986)*. Justitia Supplement Series 1998. Helsinki: Theological Institute of Finland, 101-17.

1998b   Review of S. Niditch, *Oral World and Written Word: Orality and Literacy in Ancient Israel*. London: SPCK, 1997. In *JTS* n.s. 49: 699-705.

Na'aman, N.

1996a   "The Contribution of the Amarna Letters to the Debate on Jerusalem's Political Position in the Tenth Century B.C.E." *BASOR* 304: 17-27.

1996b   "Sources and Composition in the History of David." In V. Fritz and P. R. Davies, eds., *The Origins of the Ancient Israelite States*. JSOTS 228. Sheffield: Sheffield Academic Press, 170-86.

1997   "Cow Town or Royal Capital? Evidence for Iron Age Jerusalem." *BARev* 23/4: 43-47, 67.

Niditch, Susan

1996   *Oral World and Written Word: Ancient Israelite Literature*. Library of Ancient Israel. Louisville: Westminster John Knox.

Norin, S.

1998   "The Age of the Siloam Inscription and Hezekiah's Tunnel," *VT* 48: 37-48.

Oren, E., Y. Yekutieli, P. Nahshoni, and R. Feinstein

1991   "Tell Haror — After Six Seasons." *Qadmoniot* 24: 2-19. Hebrew.

Overbeck, Bernhard

1993   *Das heilige Land: Antike Münzen und Siegel aus einem Jahrtausend jüdischer Geschichte*. Munich: Staatliche Münzsammlung.

Puech, Emile

1989   "Nouvelle inscription en alphabet cunéiforme court à Sarepta." *RB* 96: 338-44.

Renz, Johannes

1995   *Die Althebräischen Inschriften, Band I, Teil 1: Text und Kommentar; Band II/1, Teil 2: Zusammenfassende Erörterungen Paläographie und Glossar; Band III, Text und Tafeln*. Handbuch der Althebräischen Epigraphik. Darmstadt: Wissenschaftliche Buchgesellschaft.

Rofé, A.

1988   *The Prophetical Stories: The Narratives about the Prophets in the Hebrew Bible, Their Literary Types and History*. Jerusalem: Magnes.

Rogerson, John, and Philip R. Davies

1996   "Was the Siloam Tunnel Built by Hezekiah?" *BA* 59/3: 138-49.

Schniedewind, William M.

1996   "Tel Dan Stela: New Light on Aramaic and Jehu's Revolt." *BASOR* 302: 75-90.

Smelik, K. A. D.

1991   *Writings from Ancient Israel: A Handbook of Historical and Religious Documents.* Edinburgh: T&T Clark; Louisville: Westminster/John Knox Press.

Thompson, Thomas L.

1995a   "Dissonance and Disconnections: Notes on the *bytdwd* and *hmlk.hdd* Fragments from Tel Dan." *SJOT* 9: 236-40.

1995b   " 'House of David': An Eponymic Referent to Yahweh as Godfather." *SJOT* 9: 59-74.

Ussishkin, David

1994   "Gate 1567 at Megiddo and the Seal of Shema, Servant of Jeroboam." In M. D. Coogan, J. C. Exum, and L. E. Stager, eds., *Scripture and Other Artifacts: Essays on the Bible and Archaeology in Honor of Philip J. King.* Louisville: Westminster/John Knox.

1996   "Excavations and Restoration Work at Tel Lachish 1985-1994: Third Preliminary Report." *Tel Aviv* 23: 3-60.

van der Kooij, G., and J. Hoftijzer

1989   "Inscriptions." In G. van der Kooij and M. M. Ibrahim, eds., *Picking Up the Threads . . . A Continuing Review of Excavations at Deir Alla, Jordan.* Leiden: Brill, 62-70 (and catalog 91-110).

Wolff, S. M.

1994   "Archaeology in Israel." *AJA* 98: 481-519.

Young, Ian M.

1998a   "Israelite Literacy: Interpreting the Evidence: Part I." *VT* 48: 239-53.

1998b   "Israelite Literacy: Interpreting the Evidence: Part II." *VT* 48: 408-22.

History and Legend in Early Babylonia

ALAN MILLARD

In reconstructing the history of ancient Israel we are hampered by the absence of any Hebrew records outside the Bible. As is well known, neither David nor Solomon, nor any of their successors on the thrones of Israel and Judah, has left original inscriptions or documents. The best that can be presented are seal impressions of Ahaz and Hezekiah.[1] The lack of texts is readily explained in archaeological terms; the principal sites, Jerusalem and Samaria, have been destroyed and rebuilt repeatedly, old inscriptions being smashed or used as building blocks. There are no grounds for supposing Israelite kings would have considered the erection of monuments in their own names to be immodest or blasphemous. The books of Samuel and Kings are the basis for our knowledge of the Israelite monarchy, and they reached their present form only after 562 BC, although they contain much older material. They are also supplemented by Chronicles. Attempts are made to assess in various ways the historical reliability of these accounts, current fashion being unwilling to accept anything not supported by independent witnesses, and even those sometimes seem to be discounted.[2]

Any objective evaluation of Hebrew history writing has to take account of the wider context of the ancient Near East and, perhaps, of Greece. That context does not offer any books like Samuel-Kings, but it does provide a va-

---

1. See R. Deutsch, *Messages from the Past: Hebrew Bullae from the Time of Isaiah through the Destruction of the First Temple: Shlomo Moussaieff Collection and an Up-to-Date Corpus* [in Hebrew] (Tel Aviv: Archaeological Center Publications, 1997), 35, no. 199; 49, no. 1.

2. J. M. Miller, "Separating the Solomon of History from the Solomon of Legend," in L. Handy, ed., *The Age of Solomon: Scholarship at the Turn of the Millennium*, Studies in the History and Culture of the Ancient Near East 11 (Leiden: Brill, 1997), 11-24.

riety of texts that can shed light on the way accounts of past events were created and transmitted. I attempted to demonstrate how closely some episodes in the Hebrew books correspond to Aramaic records of the period of the monarchy a few years ago.[3] The present paper examines a more remote analogy, but one that is productive, exploring Babylonian texts relating to the third millennium BC and concerning the dynasty of Akkad and its two most famous kings, Sargon and Naram-Sin. They ruled long before Israel came into existence, Sargon's reign currently set at 2340-2284 BC and Naram-Sin's at 2260-2223 BC. Lower dates, however, may be preferable, such as Sargon's at 2296-2240 BC and Naram-Sin's at 2213-2176 BC. Their fame endured for nearly two millennia in Babylonia, and reached the Hittites also. The recent publication of volumes containing their inscriptions and epic tales about them has facilitated this study.[4]

Sargon was the first "Semitic" emperor, the founder of the dynasty. Unlike King David, Sargon has only one surviving original inscription, so battered, alas, that little more than his name and title can be read.[5] However, there are a few administrative texts from his reign that carry dates. They are formulated in the style "Year Sargon destroyed the place Arawa," or "Year Mari was destroyed." Four years are labeled in this way, referring to the conquests of Uruk and other Sumerian towns, to Elam and a place in it, to Simurrum in western Iran, and to Mari on the mid-Euphrates.[6] Beside these sparse contemporary witnesses, we can set copies of Sargon's inscriptions made about 1800 to 1600 BC, possibly as writing or copying exercises in scribal training. Various aspects of script, spelling, and grammar convince Assyriologists who specialize in third-millennium history that they are faithful reproductions of the accounts of his accomplishments, which Sargon had inscribed upon monuments set up in the central Sumerian temple of Enlil, the Ekur at Nippur. The texts tell of Sargon's victories over Uruk and other Sumerian cities, of his control over shipping from the Gulf, and of how the god Dagan "gave to him the Upper Land: Mari, Iarmuti, and Ebla as far as the

---

3. "Israelite and Aramaean History in the Light of Inscriptions," *TynBul* 41 (1990): 261-75.

4. D. Frayne, *The Royal Inscriptions of Mesopotamia. Early Periods, 2: Sargonic and Gutian Periods (2334-2113 BC)* (Toronto: University of Toronto Press, 1993); I. J. Gelb and B. Kienast, *Die altakkadischen Königsinschriften des dritten Jahrtausends v. Chr.,* Freiburger altorientalische Studien 7 (Stuttgart: Steiner, 1990); and J. Goodnick Westenholz, *Legends of the Kings of Akkade: The Texts,* Mesopotamian Civilizations 7 (Winona Lake, Ind.: Eisenbrauns, 1997).

5. Frayne, *Royal Inscriptions of Mesopotamia* 26-27, E2.1.1.10.

6. Ibid., 8.

Cedar Forest and Silver Mountains."[7] These inscriptions are laconic. More detail is supplied by poems about Sargon written about 1800 BC, so far as modern knowledge can tell, and copied over the next thousand years or so. In these there are speeches, descriptions, and an intermingling of divine and human activities. They deal with Uruk and the Sumerian cities, with Simurrum, and, most notably, with Sargon's actions to the north, up the courses of the Tigris and the Euphrates. He reportedly overwhelmed a principality on the north Tigris at Mardaman, then led his troops to "the Cedar Mountain" across the Amanus. One poem, "The King of Battle," available to us only in a copy of the fourteenth century BC found in the El-Amarna archive and in later fragments, relates Sargon's most far-reaching adventure, when he answered a call for help from oppressed merchants at Purushkhanda in west-central Anatolia, making the long and difficult journey to relieve them.[8]

The reign of Sargon's grandson, Naram-Sin, is better supplied with contemporary documents. Statuary, votive notices, and brick stamps are to be added to several year-names. The last attest campaigns to Maridaban (probably the Mardaman of Sargon), to Upper Mesopotamia (Subartu), to three unknown places, and to a defeat of Uruk. One year was named for Naram-Sin's venture to the Cedar Forest and the Amanus Mountains.[9] As in the case of Sargon's texts, scribes centuries later made copies of now lost inscriptions that had been erected in Nippur, Ur, and perhaps other centers. They add much more information, telling of military activity in all directions, that up the Euphrates to the northwest receiving especial attention. There Naram-Sin claimed the conquest of Armanum (perhaps Aleppo) and Ebla, and of the Cedar Mountain, and that he reached the Mediterranean Sea. Like Sargon, he became the hero of epic poems preserved in later manuscripts. They do not duplicate the earlier king's feats, although one does tell of a campaign against Apishal somewhere in northwest Syria, and an attack on Talkhadum, perhaps Gaziantep, could be on the route Sargon took to Purushkhanda.

A comparison of the triumphs of Sargon and Naram-Sin is fruitful. Both kings had to crush rebellions within Babylonia, and both fought in Iran — a fragmentary Elamite version of a treaty between Naram-Sin and Khita of Awan in Elam was discovered at Susa — in the Gulf, and in the north. Since original monuments of Naram-Sin survive that attest some of these forays, they can be granted historical reality. An inscribed copper statue base is witness to his presence on the northernmost reaches of the Tigris within modern

---

7. Ibid., 28-31.
8. Goodnick Westenholz, *Legends of the Kings of Akkade,* 102-39.
9. Frayne, *Royal Inscriptions of Mesopotamia,* 85-87.

Iraq, bricks stamped with his name prove his power at Tell Brak, further west, and a broken stele from the Anatolian foothills near Diyarbekir marks the journey to the sources of the Tigris and Euphrates that a year-name records.[10] Some of Naram-Sin's victories are also attested by objects brought as spoil from conquered places. A marble lamp, a stone plaque, and a bronze bowl all bear his name and epithet, followed by the title "conqueror of Armanum and Ebla." Other stone bowls are marked with his name and the words "booty from Magan," a place in the Gulf often identified with Oman.

Lacking such witnesses for Sargon's distant campaigns, can we claim historical reality for them? A few years ago the eminent Italian historian Mario Liverani asserted that Sargon marched no further than Tuttul, now Tell Bi'a, where the Balikh flows into the Euphrates. "From Sargon's extant inscriptions (or copies) we know for sure that he never reached beyond Tuttul on the Middle Euphrates, and had only indirect or mediated contacts with the lands further away in the northwest."[11] Yet it is the very same copies made in the eighteenth or seventeenth centuries BC of Sargon's inscriptions recording his worship of the god Dagan in Tuttul that report his progress further northwest; so on what grounds are those statements dismissed? Three are offered by Liverani. First, Naram-Sin's northwestward expansion was, according to his own inscriptions, "a novelty": "Whereas, for all time since the creation of mankind, no king whosoever had destroyed Armanum and Ebla, the god Nergal, by means of (his) weapons, opened the way for Naram-Sin, the mighty, and gave him Armanum and Ebla."[12] If Naram-Sin was the first to destroy (šulputum) those places, Sargon could not have done it before him! Here attention to words is necessary, besides a recognition of the practicalities of ancient strategy. Sargon could have "conquered" the places, making their rulers subject, without destroying the towns; his texts do not claim destruction, simply that Dagan "gave" them to him, which could well imply their rulers recognizing him as overlord and paying tribute. After his death they probably ceased sending any tribute or acknowledging the suzerainty of Akkad, so they had to be resubjugated by a successor. "Destruction," the term used in Naram-Sin's texts, would be the punishment for rebel or antagonistic states. The scenario is commonplace. Sargon is proclaimed "conqueror of Elam and Parakhshum," his son Rimush (2284-2275/2239-2230 BC) claimed the same title, and among those he conquered was a general of Parakhshum

10. Ibid., 85.

11. M. Liverani, "Model and Actualization: The Kings of Akkad in the Historical Tradition," in M. Liverani, ed., *Akkad: The First World Empire: Structure, Ideology, Tradition* (Padova: Sargon, 1993), 41-67, quotation from 53.

12. Frayne's translation, *Royal Inscriptions of Mesopotamia*, 132-33.

whom his father had also conquered. It is unlikely that Rimush simply copied his father's inscription, for this general, Sidga'u, is the only one of four Elamite leaders named by Rimush who appears in Sargon's texts, which name eight. Both kings fought the same enemy, the son having to reassert Akkad's supremacy after his father's death. Naram-Sin, too, is titled "conqueror of Elam" and also defeated Parakhshum.[13]

The second reason given for doubting Sargon's claim is that he left no monument about it that later Babylonian scribes might copy, as they copied his others. Liverani wrote, "In case Sargon had arrived in central Anatolia, or had destroyed Ebla, he would obviously have erected a celebrative monument, this monument would have remained at sight in the Ekur, and the Old Babylonian scribes would have arranged copies of its inscriptions."[14] While it is true that we have no such texts, that does not mean that they did not exist. There is no certainty that there would have been a series of monuments recording every one of Sargon's campaigns in the temple at Nippur. Sargon built a new city at Akkad that has yet to be located. If it was completed by the time of the supposed Purushkhanda campaign, that might be the site preferred for the monumental record, rather than Nippur. There are two copies of inscriptions of Naram-Sin that once stood in Ur, one relating in some detail his campaign against Armanum and Ebla. They are not duplicated elsewhere, only references to the basic facts appearing in other texts.

The third reason produced is the lack of any archaeological mark. Here we have to ask what traces we might expect to find if a town opened its gates to an invader. The victorious soldiers might loot and rape, then leave a garrison within the walls. Material remains would hardly show any signs of that. Real proof of a conquest is attainable only if the conqueror's inscribed monument is found *in situ*, either in the reoccupied buildings or in his new structures. Liverani's objections to a possible campaign by Sargon beyond Tuttul into northwest Syria or beyond do not withstand scrutiny. Of course, it is not justifiable to affirm that Sargon did march that far; it is possible to argue that he did so.

Liverani argued that authors of the Old Babylonian period took the two famous Akkadian kings as models, using them to present their ideas on the basis of more or less the same information as is available today. Thus the epic of Sargon's adventure to the far northwest presents the king as "a model to be imitated, but the specific enterprise ascribed to him has been forged" to suit

13. Ibid., 22-26, 51-60, 130, and 167; note also 55 objects inscribed with dedications following Rimush's Elamite campaign, 60-67.

14. Liverani, "Model and Actualization," 50.

the situation of the writer's time.[15] If, as argued above, that campaign is historically possible, then the later writers may have been less inventive with regard to facts than Liverani supposed, but that does not alter his contention that their work had particular didactic purposes. In the case of Naram-Sin there is one epic poem that is sufficiently well preserved to show its purpose: it was written to advise future kings on right conduct. Naram-Sin faced a fearsome enemy, as we shall see shortly, and, as any good king would do — indeed, as David did (e.g., 2 Sam 5:17-25) — he consulted the oracle. But as the "Cuthean Legend" tells us, he decided not to follow the response, with disastrous results, only reversed after divine intervention. The tale ends with an exhortation to future rulers about their conduct.[16]

Why should biblical scholars find any relevance in these distant texts? There are two principal reasons. The first is the attitude of modern scholarship. Many historians of Babylonia have used the epic texts as sources of historical information, while recognizing the folkloristic traits they contain. Now, as we have seen, they are being treated as propaganda for rulers of the time when, it is assumed, they were written, long after the protagonists were dead, propaganda providing precedents for current policies, so their value for reconstructing earlier history is thought to be minimal. There is a closely similar attitude abroad in biblical studies concerning Israel's history.

The second reason flows from the first. As already explained, there is growing evidence for the occurrence of some of the events the epics celebrate in the reigns of Sargon and Naram-Sin, and, where direct evidence is absent, there are indications of the feasibility of basic aspects of the accounts. Notice the extent of the realm they supposedly ruled, from the Gulf to the Mediterranean, perhaps into Anatolia, an empire much greater in extent and over a thousand years earlier than the kingdom of David and Solomon, an empire that no Babylonian king rivaled until Nebuchadnezzar at the start of the sixth century BC. Without the sort of original testimonies I have described, that would be considered impossible on the criteria applied to the biblical narratives, and, indeed, has been so considered by some scholars. The progress of discovery changes the situation, with the advantage that cuneiform tablets survive much more readily than leather, papyrus, or wooden writing materials.

Monuments of the kings of Akkad were visible and legible centuries after their time, like monuments in our churches and cathedrals. Some scribes copied them directly; some scribes may have copied parts of one and parts of

15. Liverani, "Model and Actualization," 47; cf. S. Tinney, "A New Look at Naram-Sin and the 'Great Rebellion,'" *JCS* 47 (1995): 1-15.

16. Goodnick Westenholz, *Legends of the Kings of Akkade*, 263-331.

another. Did those scribes, or others, create the epics on the basis of those monuments, or were those epics the products of a long-standing tradition of lauding past heroes? When we read of two kings fighting the same enemy or campaigning in the same area, is one a copy of the other? In the epics there are echoes of the phraseology of the royal inscriptions, but they do not always knit easily with adjacent clauses. On the other hand, there is one fragment about Naram-Sin that dates from the time of his dynasty itself and that may contain a small part of an epic, although it is possible that it is part of a contemporary copy of a royal inscription.[17] Although crossed out and thrown onto a rubbish dump in the ancient town of Eshnunna, it could be evidence that there was at least one poem about that king circulating in or soon after his lifetime. It is important to remember that no royal archive or library or collection of school texts that might contain such compositions has been recovered from the capital or any other central town of Akkad.

The contrast between the epics and the biblical narratives, apart from the difference of poetry and prose, is strongest in the area of fantasy and magic. Some of the epics have little or none; some are heavily laden with it. Sargon faced 40,000 iron-clad warriors, according to an Old Babylonian poem,[18] the number surely an exaggeration, at least, and the extensive use of iron an anachronism. Naram-Sin, according to a Neo-Assyrian text, was harassed by 360,000 warriors with bodies of birds and raven faces, who ravaged the lands from Purushkhanda to Magan (i.e., from central Anatolia to the Gulf) except for Babylonia. The king sent a scout to prick them to ascertain whether they were supernatural or human beings — blood flowed, so they were deemed human.[19] The Hebrew histories are devoid of these paranormal elements, unless David's much more modest killing of the giant Goliath and of a lion and a bear are cast into the same category. The Hebrew histories are sober, unexciting by comparison with the Babylonian poems, and for that very reason may be deemed more credible.

If the Babylonians could preserve, in various ways, narratives and records about long-dead kings, why could not the Israelites? Foreign kings celebrated their conquests in Israel, as the fragment of Shishak's stele from Megiddo and of Sargon's stelae from Samaria, Ashdod, and an unknown site testify. If there were monuments in Jerusalem or other places commemorating David's de-

17. Ibid., 223-29; B. R. Foster, "Naram-Sin in Martu and Magan," *Annual Review of the Royal Inscriptions of Mesopotamia Project* 8 (1990): 25-44, n. 14, "a copy of a genuine Naram-Sin inscription"; D. Frayne, *Royal Inscriptions of Mesopotamia*, 108-9, "historical-literary text."

18. Goodnick Westenholz, *Legends of the Kings of Akkade*, 66-69.

19. Ibid., 308-15.

feat of Hadad-ezer or Solomon's marriage to the pharaoh's daughter, they could have served as sources for later history writers. If, as seems likely, there were written records, chronicles, of the reigns of those kings and their successors, there is no reason why copies may not have survived on papyrus or leather rolls or on wax-covered wooden writing tablets in the palaces of Jerusalem and Samaria and in the houses of priests, prophets, and other citizens. If Judeans taken captive by Sennacherib could leave their homes with bales of goods loaded on wagons, as shown in the "Lachish reliefs" from Nineveh, it is realistic to suppose that some could have taken such books with them. The normal ancient rolls were not large and cumbersome like the Torah rolls of modern synagogues; rather, they were only twenty-four to thirty centimeters high and, if rolled tightly, three or four centimeters thick. The compilers of Samuel and Kings, whenever and wherever they worked, could have had access to earlier reports and chronicles, found in those books, the works they cite as sources in their histories. Those compositions are impersonal and usually critical of the kings, in some ways like some of the Babylonian works that relate a king's downfall to his failure to respect the gods, as in the case of Naram-Sin cited above. In the light of such an ancient Near Eastern context, the Hebrew reports may be deemed to be valuable collections of historical information.

The Controlling Role of External Evidence in Assessing the Historical Status of the Israelite United Monarchy

KENNETH A. KITCHEN

Summary

Recent devaluation of the historicity of David and Solomon and the scope of the United Monarchy stems from (among other things) lack of knowledge of relevant data and of their significance. This paper exemplifies from positive data the ground rules for the use of evidence in the biblical world, including data very largely unknown to OT scholars.

Introduction

It is often remarked that, outside the pages of the Hebrew Bible, there is no continuity between the isolated mention of "Israel" on the victory stela of the pharaoh Merenptah in 1209 BC and the ninth-century "Divided Monarchy" of Israel and Judah,[1] when we find Ahab of Israel listed as one of many opponents by Shalmaneser III at the Battle of Qarqar in 853 BC. Therefore, it is al-

---

1. Cf., e.g., P. R. Davies, *In Search of 'Ancient Israel'*, JSOTS 148 (Sheffield: Sheffield Academic Press, 1992), 60, not understanding the Egyptian mention. On the textual state of Merenptah's stela, see now my strictly factual report, K. A. Kitchen, "The Physical Text of Merenptah's Victory Hymn (The 'Israel Stela')," *Journal of the Society for the Study of Egyptian Antiquities* [Toronto] 24 (1994/97): 71-76.

leged, we should treat Merenptah's Israel as merely a "proto-Israel" (W. G. Dever's currently favorite term),[2] rather than the real thing of the ninth century and later.

However, the lack of continuity does *not* reside in the history of early Israel itself, but in the failure in witness by external, nonbiblical sources, and for very specific reasons. After Merenptah, only one other pharaoh — Ramesses III, ca. 1184-1153 BC — was involved in the Levant until the mid-tenth century BC. Virtually all of the topographical lists from his reign are simply re-editions of those of earlier kings[3] and thus do not reflect peoples, places, or conditions of his own time. The same is true of the Syrian war reliefs in his temples at Karnak and Medinet Habu in Thebes. The only specific sources for his dealings with the Levant are (1) the texts and scenes of his conflict with the Sea Peoples (from Gaza to the Nile mouths) in his Year 8 (ca. 1177 BC)[4] and (2) the strictly historical summary in his testament in Papyrus Harris I.[5] This does at least add knowledge of his having chastised the inhabitants of Se'ir; but little else. One may add taxation ostraca from Tell Sera (Ziklag?) in southwest Canaan.[6] There was here no conflict with Israel up in the hills, and hence no occasion to mention them. And no pharaoh ever again went to war in Canaan until after ca. 970 BC (Siamun) and then in 925 BC as did Shoshenq I ("Shishak"), when specific peoples and states were not mentioned, only settlements (as is the norm in detailed topographical lists like his). Thereafter, all *specific* Egyptian records of wars in Palestine cease entirely. In parallel with this, after Tukulti-Ninurta I of Assyria (ca. 1244-1208

2. For example, most recently W. Dever, "Israelite Origins and the 'Nomadic Ideal': Can Archaeology Separate Fact from Fiction?" in S. Gitin, A. Mazar, and E. Stern, eds., *Mediterranean Peoples in Transition: Thirteenth to Early Tenth Centuries BCE: In Honor of Professor Trude Dothan* (Jerusalem: Israel Exploration Society, 1998), 222, 231.

3. Notably of Ramesses II and (partly through him) of Tuthmosis III still earlier; cf., e.g., Kitchen, *Ramesside Inscriptions, Translated and Annotated, Notes and Comments* (Oxford: Blackwell, 1999), 2:70, §78.

4. For full translations, see W. F. Edgerton and J. A. Wilson, *Historical Records of Ramses III: The Texts of Medinet Habu,* Studies in Ancient Oriental Civilization 12 (Chicago: University of Chicago Press, 1936), 49ff. and passim (place names not all correctly understood).

5. A brief English translation (re. Se'ir) is found in *ANET,* 262; full new edition of this document in P. Grandet, *Le Papyrus Harris I, BM9999* (Cairo: Institute français d'archéologie du Caire, 1994), vols. 1-2.

6. O. Goldwasser, "Hieratic Inscriptions from Tel Sera' in Southern Canaan," *Tel Aviv* 11 (1984): 77-93, pls. 4-7; Kitchen, *Ramesside Inscriptions* (Oxford, 1988), 7/9: 259-60, §252. On Tell Sera and its possible identifications, cf. E. D. Oren, in E. Stern et al., eds., *The New Encyclopedia of Archaeological Excavations in the Holy Land* (New York: Simon & Schuster, 1993), 4:1329-35.

BC), again, no Assyrian army even aspired to reach as far west as the North Mediterranean coast until Assurnasirpal II did so in 882 BC, with the brief exceptions of Tiglath-pileser I in about 1100 BC and Assur-bel-kala soon after. No Assyrian ruler whatsoever is known to have reached south Syria (let alone Palestine!) until Shalmaneser III from 853 BC onward. Therefore, precisely as with Egypt, no Assyrian king or chronicler had clear contact with, or had occasion to say anything about, peoples in Palestine during the 300/350 years between 1200 and 900/860 BC. And still less so Babylonia, caught up in purely local rivalries with Assyria to her north and Elam to her southeast. In these circumstances of Great Power–eclipse, when often even internal records are sparse and wholly local and internal, it is a total waste of time to complain of no mentions of either early Israel consolidating in Canaan or a locally expanding Israel (David and Solomon) reaching into Transjordan and south or even central Syria. Such data never existed because there was no occasion for them; but Israel did exist, as the OT documentation makes clear, supported by relevant indirect data.

And what about Israel's closer neighbors in Phoenicia, Aram, or Transjordan? The facts are very simple. No archives of inscriptions have ever yet been found anywhere in Iron-Age Phoenicia (Tyre, Sidon, Arvad; barely half-a-dozen short texts on stone from Byblos). Nothing whatsoever has come from Damascus, the heart of central-Syrian Aram — totally rebuilt many times and fully built over down to now (cf. Jerusalem). And very few major Aramean inscriptions come from anywhere else, for example, Hazael, on scraps of ivory and horse harness; the recently published Tel Dan stela is the nearest geographically — and, significantly, is explicit about Israel and Judah. The Neo-Hittite hieroglyphic inscriptions are too far north to be concerned with Israel far south and are mainly building texts of purely local interest; very few people can read them. They will, however, be of indirect help.

The Twelfth to Tenth centuries BC — Epoch of "Mini-empires"

It is precisely from the Neo-Hittite hieroglyphic texts, and traces of or about the Arameans, that we can begin to see a wider historical profile for this period.

1. Let us look very briefly first at the transmitted image of the realm of David and Solomon. *Phase 1.* After seven years' rule in highland Judah only (at Hebron, 2 Sam 2:11), David became ruler of all Israel (2 Sam 5:1-5) and took over Jerusalem as capital (2 Sam 5:6-10). To the southwest he checked the Philistines (2 Sam 5:17-25; 8:1). Beyond Judah and Israel, conflict brought expansion to the east and north.

Phase 2. Eastward, directly adjoining Gad and East Manasseh and having taken over Reuben's terrain, Moab probably fell first to David's ambition (brief note only, 2 Sam 8:2). Perhaps Edom fell next, and lost its kingship for a generation (2 Sam 8:13-14 and note 1 Kings 11:14-22).[7] Thus, when embroiled in conflict with David (2 Sam 10; summary 8:5), Ammon could not call upon Moab and Edom if already tributary, under David's control. Instead, Ammon had to appeal northward, to their other neighbors Maacah and Tob, and to bigger Aram-Zobah (2 Sam 10). They survived defeat one year, as did their Aramean ally Hadadezer (2 Sam 10:9-14; then 10:15-19). But next year and season, Ammon too was vanquished.

Phase 3. Then David deemed it politic to settle accounts with Hadadezer of Aram-Zobah, striking from behind when Hadadezer had gone north to quell revolt on his Euphrates border (2 Sam 8:3), the result of his humiliating defeat by David previously, when some (southern) vassals had already consequently sided with David (2 Sam 10:19). In this second Israel-Zobah clash, the latter drew in Aram-Damascus; both were defeated and became tributary (2 Sam 8:5-7).

Phase 4. This last triumph in Syria brought David a subject ally: Toi or Tou, king of Hamath, who, liberated from Aramean attacks (if not control), threw in his lot with David (2 Sam 8:9-10). The adherence of this subject-ally meant that David's realm then reached indeed to the river Euphrates — as later Hamathite Hittite hieroglyphic texts may show that Hamath's own authority reached to the Euphrates and across it into Laqe. Moreover, there was no other intervening kingdom, parallel to Zobah — the oft-cited land of Hatarikka was part of Hamath, and *not* an independent state. Success gained David another, but independent, ally in the last decade of his reign — Hiram I of Tyre (cf. 2 Sam 5:11, following a summary statement of his power).

All this threefold mini-empire came into the possession of Solomon, at least for the first part of his reign. We may intelligently distinguish between (1) subject-ally (Hamath), (2) tributary lands as vassals (Aram-Zobah, Aram-Damascus; Moab; probably Ammon) and annexed areas (Edom), and (3) home territories (Judah, Israel). The Philistines (hostile) and the Phoenician ports from Tyre northward (friendly) remained independent.

It all began to drop to bits later on. References to activities in passing (hence, not ideological!), possibly to Tadmor (precursor of Palmyra) and cer-

---

7. On this aspect see K. A. Kitchen, *Third Intermediate Period in Egypt,* 2d ed., augmented reprint (Warminster: Aris & Phillips, 1996), 273-74 and n. 186; more fully covered in my yet-unpublished *Hittite Hieroglyphs, Arameans and Hebrew Traditions,* Table IV, Commentary, §4, latter part.

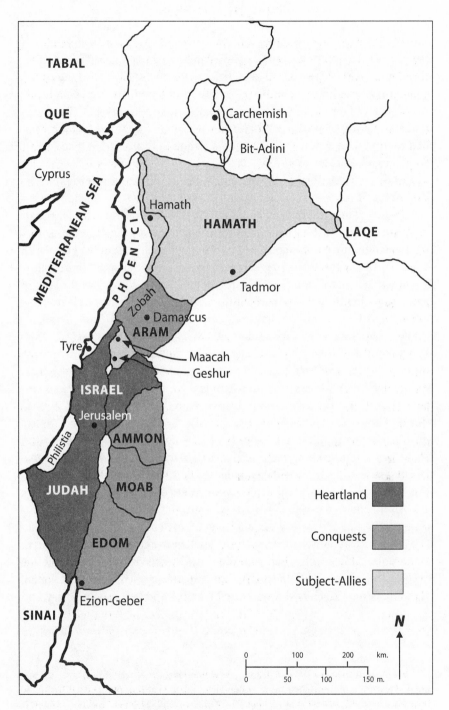

TABAL

QUE

Cyprus

MEDITERRANEAN SEA

PHOENICIA

Carchemish

Bit-Adini

Hamath

HAMATH

LAQE

Tadmor

Zobah

Damascus

ARAM

Tyre

Maacah

Geshur

ISRAEL

Jerusalem

AMMON

Philistia

JUDAH

MOAB

EDOM

Ezion-Geber

SINAI

Heartland

Conquests

Subject-Allies

N

0		100		200	km.
0	50		100		150 m.

Mini-Empires: David and Solomon

tainly to Lebanon (1 Kings 9:18-19), illustrate Solomon's initial hold on the Davidic inheritance. Its eventual collapse later in his reign is indicated by the successful return of Prince Hadad (1 Kings 11:14-22) from Egypt to Edom (removing southern Transjordan from Israelite rule), and the successful rebellion by the veteran Rezon (1 Kings 11:23-25), taking over Aram-Damascus, which — at a stroke — also cut off both Aram-Zobah and Hamath from Israelite overlordship. Doubtless, Moab and Ammon duly seceded in turn; but we are given no record of this.

2. Let us move north, into Syria, to examine the next mini-empire — Aram. From Aram itself (either -Damascus or -Zobah), we do not possess even *one* narrative inscription; there is only the fragmentary Tel Dan stela found in Israelite territory, and rare mentions of rulers by the Assyrians (ninth century and following). So, apart from a few fragments, we are thrown back on the OT narratives for Aram, precisely as for Israel. (Curiously, the "minimalist" movement seems to have forgotten to rubbish Aram along with Israel.) If, again, we patiently analyze these, a little can be gained. Hadadezer's realm of (Aram-)Zobah (cf. 2 Sam 8:3, 5, 12; 10:8), for example, was also known as Beth-Rehob (2 Sam 10:6; both terms conjoined), or "House of Rehob," just like Beyt-Dawid, "House of David."[8] Hadadezer is called "son of Rehob" (2 Sam 8:3, 12), which may well have been true if Rehob had been his father and immediate predecessor. But in the Assyrian sources, it is also a way of referring to a successor of a dynastic founder (direct or otherwise, related or otherwise). Witness the well-known example of Shalmaneser III's reference to "Jehu son of Omri," which is simply an idiom for "Jehu (ruler) of Beth-Omri" (*Bit-Khumri in Akkadian), as pointed out long ago.[9] So, Hadadezer "son" of Rehob could possibly be a substitute for Hadadezer (ruler) of Beth-Rehob, at some interval after the time of Rehob. Clearly, the Aramean realm of Hadadezer consisted of a heartland, Zobah, centered on his patrimony of Beth-Rehob (cf. Israel and Judah under David and Solomon), and then of an "empire" of tributary lesser states and chiefdoms, whom Hadadezer (and Rehob before him?) had brought under political control (again, as did David with Transjordan, and the Arameans also). This is reflected in the two passages, 2 Sam 10:19, citing Hadadezer's vassals (on his south?), local "kings," who fell away to David, and

8. Listed in good measure in K. A. Kitchen, "A Possible Mention of David in the Late Tenth Century BCE, and Deity *Dod as Dead as the Dodo?" *JSOT* 76 (1997): 38-39, with a map (p. 37) of locations of "Beth-" kingdoms.

9. By B. Landsberger, *Sam'al I: Studien zur Entdeckung der Reinenstätte Karatepe* (Ankara: Drückerei der Türkischen historischen Gesellschaft, 1948), 19 with n. 37; this basic point was entirely missed by T. Schneider, "Did King Jehu Kill His Own Family?" *BARev* 21/1 (1995): 26-33, 80, passim, through her not knowing the key reference on this matter.

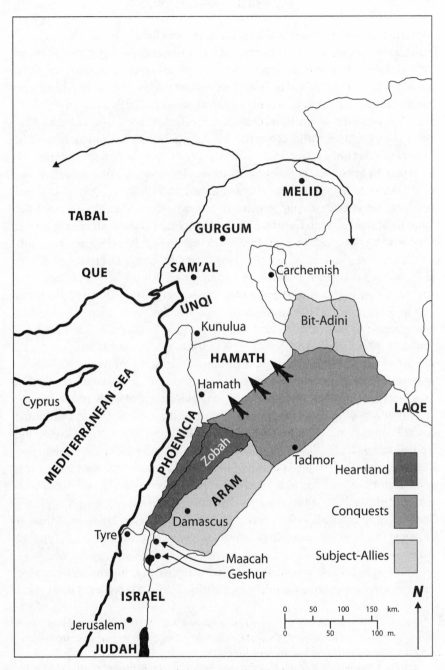

TABAL

MELID

GURGUM

QUE

SAM'AL

Carchemish

UNQI

Bit-Adini

Kunulua

HAMATH

Hamath

LAQE

Cyprus

MEDITERRANEAN SEA

PHOENICIA

Zobah

Tadmor

Heartland

ARAM

Conquests

Damascus

Tyre

Subject-Allies

Maacah

Geshur

ISRAEL

Jerusalem

JUDAH

N

| 0 | 50 | 100 | 150 | km. |
| 0 | | 50 | | 100 | m. |

Mini-Empires: Hadadezer of Aram

implicitly 2 Sam 8:3, when Hadadezer deemed it vital to "restore his control" near the Euphrates, and thus over local rulers there. These petty kinglets were rulers of what the anthropologists would call "chiefdoms," a much overworked term. We find them in Aram-Damascus also, at a later date, in the thirty-two "kings" who supported Ben-Hadad against Israel (1 Kings 20:1). Zobah is at times located west or north of Damascus. It is probably at least a part of the Beqaʿ valley, between the Lebanon and Anti-Lebanon mountain ranges. In Gen 22:24, the line of Nahor via Reumah ran to Tebah, Gaham (unknown), Tahash, and Maacah. These form a north-south sequence: Tebah, the Tubikhi of the Amarna Letters;[10] then Tahash, equivalent to Takhsi in Egyptian lists[11] (in Upe, from Qadesh-on-Orontes southward), then Maacah, east of lakes Huleh and Galilee, with Geshur. This Tebah/Tubikhi is probably identical with the Tebah/Betah of 2 Sam 8:8 (cf. 1 Chron 18:8). Thus, it lay parallel to Aram-Damascus, based on the oasis-area of the town of Damascus. From east of earlier Qadesh-on-Orontes, Hadadezer had imposed his rule up to the Euphrates (perhaps via Tadmor), reducing urban and tribal entities to vassaldom, and exercised influence on the Arameans living north within the great west bend of that river (as at Bit-Adini), whence he summoned forces (cf. 2 Sam 10:16). So, probably because it overawed both Aram-Damascus to his southeast and Hamath to his north, we can see the outlines of the mini-empire of Hadadezer as it was before David's intervention: (1) a "homeland" area in the Beqaʿ valley, based on the enclave of Beth-Rehob (Hadadezer's dynasty's home patch); (2) conquests of lesser chiefdoms northeast to the Euphrates and southward toward Maacah and Geshur; and (3) subject-allies in Aram-Damascus to the immediate east (cf. 2 Sam 8:5) and in Hamath (unwillingly) in the north. David's irruption broke this up. Geshur allied itself with Israel (cf. 2 Sam 3:3, 5; 13:37-39, for Geshur); Maacah may have become his vassal. Hamath sided with the new power Israel (and remained independent from Solomon's day until Assyrian dominance); Zobah was broken up, and from Solomon's time it (Zobah) was wholly replaced as an Aramean power by Damascus (Rezon and his successors).

3. Now, at last, we can move still further north, into north Syria, the west bend of the Euphrates, and southeast Anatolia. Until soon after 1200 BC, that

---

10. In EA179, trans. W. L. Moran, *The Amarna Letters* (Baltimore/London: Johns Hopkins University Press, 1992), 262; note its author's concern with Amurru, which occupied the Lebanon range along the west of the Beqaʿ valley.

11. As earlier suggested by A. H. Gardiner, *Ancient Egyptian Onomastica* (Oxford: Oxford University Press, 1947), 1:150*f. Takhsi, in Amarna Letters, no. 189: verso 9-12 (Moran, *Amarna Letters*, 270). In Egyptian sources, Kitchen, *Ramesside Inscriptions, Translated and Annotated: Notes and Comments*, 1:37, §68.

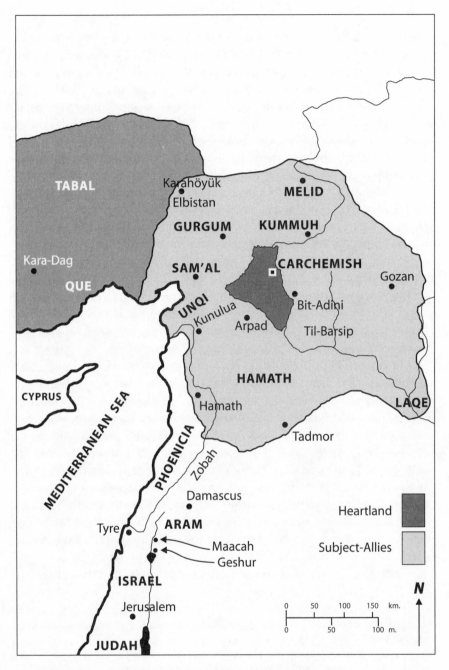

TABAL

Karahöyük
Elbistan

MELID

GURGUM

KUMMUH

Kara-Dag

SAM'AL

CARCHEMISH

QUE

UNQI

Gozan

Kunulua

Bit-Adini

Arpad

Til-Barsip

CYPRUS

HAMATH

LAQE

Hamath

Tadmor

MEDITERRANEAN SEA

PHOENICIA

Zobah

Damascus

Tyre

ARAM

Maacah
Geshur

ISRAEL

Jerusalem

JUDAH

Heartland

Subject-Allies

N

| 0 | 50 | 100 | 150 | km. |
| 0 | | 50 | | 100 | m. |

Mini-Empires: Carchemish and Tabal

area was part of the Hittite Empire, with satellite states in north Syria as its vassals. A branch of the Hittite royal house reigned in Carchemish, situated on the west bank of the Euphrates, on one of the routes from Mesopotamia over into Syria and Anatolia. During the thirteenth century BC, these Hittite kings of Carchemish had become *de facto* and then *de jure* viceroys over Syria for their imperial cousins ruling in central Anatolia. By the eighth year of Ramesses III, about 1177 BC, the "Sea Peoples" and other land-based move-ments had destroyed the Anatolian home area of the Hittite power and moved through Syria south to the borders of Egypt, where the pharaoh re-pulsed them. In his words, "No land could resist their arms, beginning from Hatti-Qode [= Cilicia], Carchemish, Arzawa [southwest Anatolia] and Alasia [Cyprus(?)], cut off in one place [*or* time]. Camp was pitched in one place, within Amurru [= Lebanon Mountains and coast strip]; they devastated its people and its land, like what had never existed."[12] The old series of Late-Bronze-Age city-states was indeed largely upset, and many were swept away. But the pharaoh's words are in some measure rhetorical. In central Syria, at least a small rump-kingdom of Amurru may have lasted into the eleventh century BC, before being absorbed by the Arameans, if one may so date two inscribed arrowheads of "Zakar-baal, King of Amurru."[13]

Much more important, Carchemish the fortress-city clearly lived to see another day, after 1180 BC. Until recently, the last-known king there before ca. 1200 BC was Talmi-Tesup, contemporary of the last Hittite emperor, Suppiluliuma II.[14] But he was succeeded by his son, Kuzi-Tesup, who may have been king in Carchemish when the empire fell, and survived the brush with the "Sea Peoples" as they turned back south to Amurru and then to Canaan and Egypt's border. As the brief chaos subsided, leaving a power vac-uum in northern Syria and southeast Anatolia, Kuzi-Tesup may have seized the opportunity to renew control by Carchemish in both zones — and to strike a blow at the old enemy Assyria (now under weaker rulers) by annexing terrain east of the Euphrates. Later Hittite-Hieroglyphic texts from Melid (Malatya) trace the line of Melidian kings back to a Kuzi-Tesup, Great King of Carchemish — a title ("Great King") *only* to be borne by effective rulers over

---

12. Text of the Year 8, lines 16ff.; translation mine; hieroglyphics text, K. A. Kitchen, *Ramesside Inscriptions* 5/1 (1970): 39-40; published translation, J. A. Wilson in J. B. Prit-chard, ed., *ANET*, 262.

13. One, J. Starcky, in *Archéologie au Levant: Recueil R. Saidah* (Paris: Lyon, 1982), 178-86; the other, R. Deutsch and M. Heltzer, *Forty New Ancient West Semitic Inscriptions* (Tel Aviv–Jaffa: Archaeological Center Publication, 1994), 12-13, fig. 1.

14. For sources, cf. J. D. Hawkins, in D. O. Edzard et al., eds., *Reallexikon der Assyriologie und Vorderasiatischen Archäologie* (Berlin: de Gruyter, 1980), 5:433-34.

subordinate territories and who had shown their mettle, in Late-Bronze-Age usage. Hitherto, this later reference has been identified with the ruler mentioned above, that is, Kuzi-Tesup son of Talmi-Tesup, of ca. 1170 BC. But this solution creates serious difficulties in dating the later monuments and kings of Melid.[15] Therefore, it may be wiser to distinguish between a Kuzi-Tesup I (son of Talmi-Tesup), of ca. 1170 BC — who may well have made himself the first "Great King" of Carchemish — and a later Kuzi-Tesup II at about 1070 BC, also a "Great King," as ancestors of the later kings of Melid; then the chronological problem disappears. Such repetition in royal names is common in the Neo-Hittite world.[16] Thus, extending from Hamath in the south, up to Gurgum, Melid, and even (modern) Elbistan in the north, west to the Mediterranean and eastward to Gozan, the realm of Carchemish formed at first a considerable mini-empire, well worthy of assumption of the title "Great King" by its rulers. After Kuzi-Tesup I, one may theoretically place a Great King Ir-Tesup, known for his intervention in Elbistan, beyond Melid/Malatya, and a Great King Tudkhalia, from the Carchemish inscription A16c.[17] By 1100 BC, Tiglath Pileser I of Assyria was strong enough to march west to Syria, eventually taking tribute from both Allumari of Melid and Ini-Tesup II, King of Hatti, almost certainly located at Carchemish (as Ini-Tesup I had been).[18] Soon thereafter, we may then insert Kuzi-Tesup II, as Carchemishian "Great King" (ca. 1070 BC) who then strengthened his hold on Melid by installing one of his own sons, Runtiyas, there as ruler. Between his time and roughly 1000 BC, further Great Kings of Carchemish included [xx]pa-ziti and his son and successor, Ura-Tarkhuns (Carchemish text A4b).

But then came a change. The next ruler of Carchemish, Suhis I, and all his successors bore the simpler title "King of Carchemish." The epithet "Great"

15. See data and full discussion by J. D. Hawkins, "Kuzi-Teshub and the 'Great Kings' of Karkamish," *Anatolian Studies* 38 (1988): 99-108.

16. For example, Ini-Tesup I and II and Suhis I and II at Carchemish; Arnuwantis I and II, and PUGNUS-mili I, II, and III at Melid; etc.

17. The Carchemish Hieroglyphic-Hittite inscriptions are published in the "A" series of plates, in D. G. Hogarth, C. L. Woolley, and R. D. Barnett, *Carchemish*, vols. 1-3 (London: British Museum, 1912, 1921, 1952). A new corpus of all such inscriptions, by J. D. Hawkins, is in press.

18. Modern translations; for Tiglath-Pileser I, see A. K. Grayson, *Assyrian Royal Inscriptions* (Wiesbaden: Harrassowitz, 1976), 2:23 §82, 27 §§95-96; and A. K. Grayson, *Assyrian Rulers of the Early First Millennium BC, I (1114-859 BC)* (Toronto: University of Toronto Press, 1991 [Royal Inscriptions of Mesopotamia. Assyrian Period 2]), 37:26-28 and 42-43:24-33. These correct the version in *ANET*, 275. For Assur-bel-kala in the West, cf. Grayson, *Assyrian Royal Inscriptions*, 52, §234, ii:19, 55, §248, iv:1ff.; Grayson, *Assyrian Rulers of the Early First Millennium BC, I (1114-859 BC)*, 101, ii:19b-24, and 103-4, iv:1-34a.

disappeared forever. Given the special significance of the higher title, sufficiently far-reaching changes must have occurred to produce this one. Several factors emerge to mark the end of Carchemish's two centuries of mini-empire. One was the increasing dominance of new Aramean local dynasties, replacing or breaking up the Neo-Hittite dominance. With this went the emergence of the newer "mini-empire" of Aram-Zobah under Hadadezer, noted above. And concurrently we find a greater independence among Neo-Hittite city-states, whose rulers began to set up their own hieroglyphic inscriptions at palaces and temples.

The sequence of the breakup might be provisionally sketched as follows: *First phase (ca. 1000 BC, and following): A. South and East:* Hadadezer of Aram-Zobah probably usurped the overlordship of Hamath ruled by Toi (thus losing Carchemish, its southernmost outlier), and extended his rule to the southwest part of the great bend of the Euphrates. There he supported local Aramean chiefs in founding new kingdoms — Adin in Til-Barsip, founding Bit-Adini, and Bakhian in Gozan, founding Bit-Bakhiani, thus ending all supremacy of Carchemish east of the Euphrates. David's defeat of Aram-Zobah (and Aram-Damascus) had no effect across the Euphrates, but Toi and Hamath became his subject-ally and did not return to the fold of Carchemish. *B. North and West:* In the northwest Gurgum launched out under a series of independent rulers from the early tenth century BC, their earliest kings being attested in a long Hittite-hieroglyphic genealogy left by a ninth/eighth-century king, Halparutas III.

Second phase (ca. 950-900 BC): By at least 920 BC, the Arameans had set up the small, independent kingdom of Sam'al or Ya'udi. Thereby, the "Empire" of Carchemish had lost everything to its south and east, and most of what lay to its northwest. Then, probably about this time, a little before our existing records, the Arameans took over Arpad, and (A)gus founded Bit-(A)gusi, not later than ca. 880 BC.[19] This cut off Unqi further west, which has independently attested rulers (in Assyrian texts) from about this time also. At this juncture, Kummukh, just northeast of Carchemish, is listed under its own kings. Thereby, Carchemish lost every last vassal or tributary, being reduced henceforth to a territorially limited city-state, albeit a prosperous one, sited by an important river crossing on main routes. These striking political changes, from mini-empire to local city-state, would have fallen mainly dur-

---

19. On the Aramean states (Gozan, Bit-Adini, Bit-Agusi, Sam'al, and Aram-Damascus) plus Hamath, cf. latterly H. S. Sader, *Les états araméens de Syrie depuis leur fondation jusqu'à leur transformation en provinces assyriennes* (Wiesbaden/Beirut, Franz Steiner, 1987); for Damascus, monographs by M. F. Unger, *Israel and the Aramaeans of Damascus* (Grand Rapids: Zondervan, 1957), and by W. T. Pitard, *Ancient Damascus* (Winona Lake, Ind.: Eisenbrauns, 1987).

ing the reign of the last "Great King," Ura-Tarkhuns, such that his successor Suhis I would have inherited (outside Carchemish) only Arpad and Unqi westward and Kummukh northeastward, and the zone of Sam'al. Melid had been long under largely independent but allied rulers, proud of their family link with Carchemish.

4. Last among our mini-empires (and more briefly) is one in southeast Anatolia, to the northwest of Carchemish's sphere of influence. During the last reigns of the Hittite Empire, rulers of the realm of Tarkhuntassa had sought equal rank with Carchemish, as its western pendant (so to speak). Just as the successor-kings in Carchemish carved out a sizeable realm for two centuries in the southeast, so such a ruler as Hartapus, son of a Mursilis (a pure Hittite "imperial" name!), may be ranked within ca. 1200-1000 BC as overlord of a further mini-empire in the southeast corner of the Anatolian high plateau; some centuries later he had moral (and probably territorial) successors in the "Great Kings" of Tabal, with their vassals (listed as twenty-four "kings" by Shalmaneser III of Assyria in ca. 837 BC).[20]

*   *   *

It is now time to sum up the changing sequence of ephemeral "great mini-powers" in the twelfth to tenth centuries BC. Before the "Sea Peoples" irruption into the Levant c. 1180 BC, that area was effectively divided into the spheres of the Egyptian Empire, holding Canaan, southern Phoenicia, and southern Syria (Upe) south of Qadesh, and of the Hittite Empire, extending from southeast Anatolia to cover all Syria (including the Mt. Lebanon state of Amurru) east to Emar and south to just beyond Qadesh. The Hittite area was controlled by the kings of Carchemish as viceroys for their cousins, the kings of Hatti reigning in central Anatolia at Hattusas. After the irruption, in which most of the former lesser states disappeared (e.g., Emar, Niya, Nuhasse, Ugarit, Qadesh, and Amurru except for an enclave mini-state), leaving in the north few political survivors other than Carchemish and the Phoenician ports (Arvad, Byblos, Sidon, and Tyre), northern Syria/southeast Anatolia was occupied by the displaced Luvian-speaking population from further north and northwest, and by incoming Arameans (already beginning to be present in south-central Syria in the fourteenth/thirteenth centuries BC). New entities were founded.

But from ca. 1170 BC, the political vacuum was promptly filled by the en-

20. Cf. J. D. Hawkins, "Kuzi-Teshub and the 'Great Kings,'" *Anatolian Studies* 38 (1988): 106-8.

terprising kings of Carchemish, who reimposed their former overlordship on Syria and the southeast margins of Anatolia. As the successors of the "Great Kings" of the now-deceased Hittite Empire, they adopted that title to signify their dominion. Further west in Anatolia, the heirs of the realm of Tarkhuntassa did likewise. Neighbors of the newly established Phrygians, they continued polity in Tabal of a paramount ruler over local chiefs down to the eighth century BC. In the southeast, the mini-empire of Carchemish lasted somewhat less than 200 years, down to about 1000-950 BC in round figures. Then the rise to power of new Aramean states (Zobah, etc.) amputated Carchemishian holdings to the south (Hamath) and east (Bit-Adini, Gozan), and new Aramean regimes at Arpad (Bit-Agusi) and Ya'udi/Sam'al cut Carchemish off from her western seaboard and from Unqi. North-placed Gurgum went independent, and long-loyal Melid fully so. Since it was left as a simple city-state, the kings of Carchemish (Suhis I onward) dropped the epithet "Great" from their title, permanently.

At some point in time not long before ca. 1000 BC, a third mini-empire arose when one Rehob set up his kingship in Zobah (Beqa' valley), and his probable immediate successor Hadadezer expanded the realm of Beth-Rehob/Zobah northward, attempting to turn Hamath into an Aramean vassal instead of a Neo-Hittite one, and pushed up to the Euphrates, where in the time of the lesser Assyrian king Assur-rabi II (ca. 1013-973 BC) the fords of the Euphrates at Pitru (Pethor) and Mutkinu were taken by a king of Aram.[21] At this time new Aramean dynasties in Til-Barsip (as Bit-Adini) and Gozan (as Bit-Bakhiani), allies of Hadadezer, arose, since he could call on forces from "beyond the River" (2 Sam 10:16). In the south, Zobah's ascendancy may have included Aram-Damascus as subject-ally (cf. 2 Sam 8:5), and for a time Geshur and Maacah. But Hadadezer's extensive mini-empire was not destined to last long (a decade or two at most). Conflict with David, in the latter's last two decades (i.e., within ca. 990-970 BC), destroyed it. Out of the ruins, the trans-Euphratean states of Bit-Adini and Gozan went their own way until the Assyrians took them over in the ninth century BC. Hamath (reaching from the Orontes to the southwest Euphrates) now became David's subject-ally, extending his sphere that far. Zobah sank into insignificance, while Aram-Damascus became a vassal of the Hebrew kingdom into Solomon's reign (after which it became the main central-Syrian power).

21. So, according to Shalmaneser III, Kurkh monolith inscription, ii:35b-38; D. D. Luckenbill, *Ancient Records of Assyria and Babylonia* (Chicago: University of Chicago Press, 1926), 1:218, §603; now, A. K. Grayson, *Assyrian Rulers of the Early First Millennium BC, II (858-745 BC)* (Toronto: University of Toronto Press, 1996 [Royal Inscription of Mesopotamia. Assyrian Period 3]), 18-19.

David's realm thus embraced (1) the heartlands of Judah and Israel (but not Philistia), (2) the conquered Transjordanian kingdoms of Edom, Moab, and Ammon, plus Aram-Damascus and Zobah as tributary vassals, and (3) Hamath (up to the Euphrates) as a subject-ally. This fourth mini-empire was not destined to last too long, either: a maximum of fifteen to twenty years under David (founded in his last two decades) and probably not much more than forty to fifty years at its full extent. It fell apart by the last decades of Solomon's reign (Hadad in Edom, Rezon in Damascus [cutting off access to Hamath], etc.). Thereafter, the age of mini-empires in the Levant was over. For the century ca. 950-850 BC, nobody local was supreme in the Levant, although Aram-Damascus tried its hand repeatedly; from 850 BC onward, growing Assyrian control from Mesopotamia effectively put a practical stop to all but the most local aspirations. They and the Neo-Babylonians eventually eliminated not only the aspirations but nearly all of the local kingdoms themselves.

Fantasy versus Cold Reality

So, if the available data is consulted, both outside the Hebrew Bible and within its pages, we can see that, politically, the twelfth to tenth centuries BC were *not* a blank; the political absence of the former great powers — Hatti, Egypt, and Assyria — left an arena in which several others (Tabal, Carchemish, Aram-Zobah, and Israel) could try their hand, *and did so.*

In a recent collective volume, J. Maxwell Miller expresses himself thus:

> The opening centuries of the Iron Age (from approximately the beginning of the 12th century well into the 9th century BCE) seems to have been a kind of "dark age" throughout the ancient world. The Bronze Age empires had collapsed, peoples were on the move, and localized socio-political structures apparently were the order of the day. A 10th-century, Palestinian-based empire of the territorial extent, opulence and international influence envisioned by the biblical writers would have been out of keeping with these general circumstances of the times. One can argue that it was precisely the lack of political and commercial competition during the 10th century, the power-vacuum which characterized the day, which enabled David and Solomon to create such an empire. The other possibility, however, which seems more likely when the three arguments are taken into account, is that the Solomonic empire envisioned by the biblical writers was anachronistic as well as idealized. Influenced by what would have been for them the more recent memory of the As-

syrian, Babylonian and Persian empires, they imagined an empire of equal magnitude for Solomon, the builder of the Jerusalem temple.[22]

Sadly, one hardly knows where to begin in "deconstructing" all this non-historical fantasy. (1) The twelfth to early ninth centuries BC were not a "'dark age' throughout the ancient world." We have a close, precise sequence of kings and dynasties in Egypt at that time (twentieth–twenty-first), with records of wars at the beginning and much internal information on Thebes, if little else-where, throughout. In Assyria, again, there was a precise sequence of closely dated rulers, the wars of Tiglath Pileser I and Assur-bel-kala, and some inter-nal archives at intervals. In Babylon the story was the same, even if some reg-nal dates are less complete. (And, if one allows essential historicity in the books of Judges and Samuel, we have something for Palestine too.) (2) The Bronze Age empires had not "collapsed." The Assyrians shrank to within their homeland territory; the Egyptians continued (after defeating the Sea Peoples) to rule in the coastlands of Canaan into the mid-twelfth century BC (to Ramesses IV and VI) and then withdrew (but did not "collapse"!). Only the Hittite Empire disappeared, because it was destroyed from without. (3) That "some peoples were on the move" is true — the "Sea Peoples" are (for us) the most noticeable, from the Aegean to Cyprus and northern Syria, then south through the Levant and Canaan to the borders of Egypt; then the Arameans, reinforcing an early presence in central Syria already, and setting up king-doms from Damascus in the south to Sam'al and Arpad up north, and Bit-Adini and Gozan in the northeast. To these may be added the Israelite tribal group from Egypt via Transjordan into Canaan, an altogether more modest affair, which — very curiously! — our ignorant and inconsistent, min-imalizing "biblical scholars" will too often not even consider seriously, along-side Aramean and Sea People parallels. (4) That localized socio-political structures were "the order of the day" is only partly true. They are not the sole type of organization to be found. The mini-empires of Tabal and of Car-chemish come to us from nonbiblical, firsthand, verifiable evidence and can-not be wished away; neither should the Aram-Zobah enterprise of Had-adezer, the probable reality behind the King of Aram reported for Assur-rabi II's time in our external sources. A tenth-century Palestine-based "empire" of the territorial scope given us is *not* "out of keeping with these general circum-stances of the times"! Exactly the opposite is true. We have the Tabal power

22. J. M. Miller, "Separating the Solomon of History from the Solomon of Legend: Response to Millard," in L. Handy, ed., *The Age of Solomon: Scholarship at the Turn of the Millennium,* Studies in the History and Culture of the Ancient Near East 11 (Leiden: Brill, 1997), 13-14.

that began in the twelfth century and probably survived to the eighth. We certainly (in Syria itself) have firsthand witness in Hittite hieroglyphic texts to a similar mini-empire of "Great Kings" of Carchemish, whose successors relinquished that title precisely when other Neo-Hittite and Aramean states appear independently (tenth/early ninth centuries BC), leaving Carchemish reduced to a city-state in itself, after nearly 200 years of "imperium." And there is the parallel to David and Solomon's short-lived dominion in that (equally ephemeral, and quite extensive) of Hadadezer of Aram-Zobah. In other words, the vacuum left by the absence of such powers as Hatti, Egypt, and Assyria *did* enable Tabal, Carchemish, and Aram-Zobah to expand into larger, complex states — so why not Israel, and almost as briefly as Aram-Zobah? On factual grounds, there is no fundamental problem here! None of Miller's three contrary reasons is valid. Absence of other empires did allow three lesser powers to flourish, so why not the fourth? People movements had largely ceased by the mid/later twelfth century BC, and failed to prevent establishment of three mini-empires, so why quibble over the fourth? Localized power structures were commonplace but — again, as Tabal, Carchemish, and Zobah demonstrate — could not exclude the imposition of larger structures at will. These three "arguments" are non-starters and must be rejected on factual grounds: we actually have three other mini-empires then. (5) The claim that the biblical account of the David/Solomon imperium was "anachronistic" is patently rubbish: we have three other such imperia of just the same type, before and down to their time. (6) That the writers of the accounts in 2 Samuel and 1 Kings were providing a Hebrew equivalent of the empires of Assyria, Babylon, and Persia is sheer, unsupported speculation. There is not one scintilla of hard, verifiable, independent evidence that the accounts of David and Solomon's reigns were invented in either the Neo-Babylonian or Achaemenid periods. This view is purely hypothetical, not based on fact, and hence inadmissible unless clear, independent facts can be produced to prove it. The morphology of the Davidic/Solomonic regime fits the model of Tabal, Carchemish, and Zobah for the twelfth-tenth centuries BC; it does not *remotely* resemble the huge dominions of Assyria or Babylon from the Gulf to the Nile, still less the all-embracing Persian Empire with its elaborate apparatus of satrapies, royal roads and post, and the rest of it. How careless can "biblical scholars" be?

Miller's essay is full of other blunders, non sequiturs, and contrary-to-fact statements for this epoch,[23] a characteristic shared by various of his col-

___

23. One should read the exchanges by J. M. Miller, "Separating the Solomon of History from the Solomon of Legend," and A. R. Millard, "Response [to Miller]: Assessing

leagues who are equally blind both to available facts and to real and realistic methods of historical assessment. They continually fail to weigh the *nature* of evidence, and not merely its quantity. And they continually set up "straw men" — erroneous ideas of what *they* think the biblical writers say (or should say . . .), which they then knock down, and (hey presto!) the Bible is wrong — but, alas, it is their *misrepresentation* that is proven wrong, and not necessarily the biblical text, into which the misinterpretation in question has been read.

In the light of what we have seen already, perhaps a few useful, fact-based principles can be stated. (1) *All* texts — including the biblical texts — should first be read *as they stand,* carefully and detachedly, to observe what they actually say or seem to say; alternative possibilities (in detail, or overall) should be noted down. (2) What the text itself claims to tell, or to be, or to achieve, should be noted, where stated. (3) In what category does the text itself appear to stand? (As myth, legend, stories about people; historical narration, i.e., happenings to humans in the past?) If our concern is with a biblical text, then (4) one must find out whether it belongs to a clear class of texts, and whether its contents have clear analogues, in the cultural context of the Near East. (5) Verification/falsification of a text, and of our possible views about it, must be sought from the independent, hence relatively objective platform provided by external sources. (6) The mute witness of uninscribed artifacts (whose interpretation is entirely at the whim of the observer) *cannot* be privileged over the explicit evidence of texts properly understood. The interrelationships (if any . . .) of texts and nontext artifacts have to be established with due respect to the relative weight-by-relevance of all the data.[24] Our contextual study (above) of mini-empires at the appropriate period, utilizing independent Hittite hieroglyphic and Mesopotamian cuneiform data illustrates all this in some measure. To work in a vacuum, solely by speculation determined by an a priori agenda, is not acceptable method, and can result only 95 percent of the time in self-deception. To put it a little brutally and inelegantly, one load of wholly imaginary codswallop is worth no more than any other, differing load of wholly imaginary codswallop, and without a satisfactory factual basis none is worth much, or perhaps anything at all.

Solomon: History or Legend" and "King Solomon in His Ancient Context," in Handy, ed., *The Age of Solomon,* 1-56.

24. See, for an exemplary study (relating to the thirteenth/twelfth centuries BC, through personal names), that by R. S. Hess, "Fallacies in the Study of Early Israel: An Onomastic Perspective," *TynBul* 45 (1994): 339-54.

Conclusion

Time and again, the merry-go-round of old, nineteenth-century-style literary and "historical" criticism of the biblical text in Samuel and Kings (as elsewhere) produces nothing but an indecisive babel of discordant opinions, none of which is ever able to establish itself as representing the truth about these texts, but merely as ephemeral "flavor of the month" (or year, or decade at most). The stubborn refusal to seek out a factual basis for assessing biblical texts, and to be willing to ditch personal prejudices and agendas when the facts point in other directions — this can only lead to stagnation and sterility, a situation already rapidly coming closer.

It takes much hard work and patience, as well as self-restraint, to ferret out the fullest possible facts about any given period or topic relevant to the biblical text. But there is no other way forward, if biblical studies are to be responsible and serious, rather than just parlor games to be played with.

As a result of such work scholars can come up with fresh insights into the structure and meaning of a text and the methods of the ancient writers. What we now know about ancient southwest and northwest Arabia indicates, for example, that queens could exercise definite political power down to 690 BC (Assyrian data), *but not later.* Thus, by her very gender the Queen of Sheba is of clearly predeuteronomic origin; other geopolitical aspects ring true also. The structure of the Sheba account in Kings indicates the interplay of wealth and personal royal roles.[25] The optimum dateline for composition of the wisdom work Proverbs 1–24 is undoubtedly ca. 1000 BC in round figures, since it is clearly transitional between known works elsewhere of the later second millennium BC and others of the full first millennium BC.[26] In the administrative sphere, concerning monthly palace supplies (1 Kings 4:7-19, 27-28), appeals to Egyptian "parallels" have proven superficial; as befits a Levantine ruler like Solomon, far better (and closer) antecedents for his arrangements

25. See K. A. Kitchen, "Sheba and Arabia," in Handy, ed., *The Age of Solomon,* 140-43, 152.

26. Basic factual evidence for this was clearly set out by K. A. Kitchen, "Proverbs and Wisdom Books of the Ancient Near East: The Factual History of a Literary Form," *TynBul* 28 (1977/78): 69-114, and in "The Basic Literary Forms and Formulations of Ancient Instructional Writings in Egypt and Western Asia," in E. Hornung and O. Keel, eds., *Studien zu altägyptischen Lebenslehren,* OBO 28 (Freiburg: Universitätsverlag; Göttingen: Vandenhoeck & Ruprecht, 1979), 235-82. The attempted critique of the Near Eastern material in an otherwise attractive book by S. Weeks, *Early Israelite Wisdom* (Oxford: Clarendon, 1994), is wholly vitiated by its author's lack of knowledge of the original data; see now K. A. Kitchen, "Biblical Instructional Wisdom: The Decisive Voice of the Ancient Near East," in M. Lubetski, C. Gottlieb, and S. Keller, eds., *Boundaries of the Ancient Near Eastern World: A Tribute to Cyrus H. Gordon,* JSOTS 273 (Sheffield: Sheffield Academic Press, 1998), 130-40.

can be found in the administrative records of palaces at Ugarit and Ebla, in Syria.[27] On the other hand, we should not lightly dismiss Egyptian and other data on use of gold by ancient rulers, and especially the totally unparalleled wealth spent by Osorkon I in Egypt within just four or five years of the death of his father Shoshenq I, the Shishak who reputedly had stripped Solomon's Jerusalem.[28] Solomon's temple at Jerusalem is not some fantasy structure, but both its general design and a variety of details find strictly realistic background in temple architecture and wealth of furnishings, both of his general time and from far earlier.[29] And much more could be said. Along these lines, one may reach definite results, factual in basis and effect, that can accurately refine our understanding of the biblical texts and their real milieus.

27. For convenient reference, see K. A. Kitchen, "Egypt and East Africa," in Handy, ed., *The Age of Solomon,* 121 nn. 27-28.

28. See, in accessible form, A. R. Millard, "Does the Bible Exaggerate King Solomon's Golden Wealth?" and K. A. Kitchen, 'Where Did Solomon's Gold Go?" and "Shishak's Military Campaign in Israel Confirmed," *BARev* 15/3 (1989): 20-34.

29. See, e.g., A. Mazar, in A. Kempinski et al., eds., *The Architecture of Ancient Israel: From the Prehistoric to the Persian Periods: In Memory of Immanuel (Munya) Danayevsky* (Jerusalem: Israel Exploration Society, 1992), 183-84, with 163 figs. 1-14 (overall, sketch); doors, A. R. Millard, in *Eretz-Israel* 20 (1989): 135*-39*; and on surrounding storerooms, Kitchen, in *Eretz-Israel* 20 (1989): 107*-12*. On its wealth, cf. n. 26.

Manasseh in the Books of Kings and Chronicles
(2 Kings 21:1-18; 2 Chron 33:1-20)

BRIAN KELLY

Summary

Over against the description in Kings, the Chronicler's account of Manasseh's reign is often considered to be a largely fictional report composed to serve the writer's theological outlook and purpose. This essay reviews the principal reasons for this judgment, notes the more positive view of the historical worth of Chronicles that is developing in some quarters, and argues for the complementarity (rather than opposition) of the two accounts.

I. Introduction

In his recent study of biblical historiography,[1] V. Philips Long develops the helpful analogy of history writing with representational portrait painting to explain the relationship between historical events and their creative presentation in biblical narratives. Long observes that artists who produce portraits of historical personages always employ some degree of license, adopting their own particular style and choice of materials. The final effect is only one glimpse onto a wider reality; nevertheless, it may be valid and true within its own terms.

1. V. P. Long, *The Art of Biblical History* (Grand Rapids: Zondervan; Leicester: Apollos, 1994).

131

In the same way, the historians of the Bible choose to present their subject matter from a particular perspective, using their own distinctive style and theological outlook. Like artists, the biblical historians use creative means for the representational end of depicting the past. Nevertheless, while they employ their literary ability to produce a consciously crafted narrative, if they are writing history (in a sense that we would recognize) rather than fiction they are constrained by the facts of the past as they are available to them. For a biblical writing to count as a reputable piece of historiography, the writer somehow must have had access to the past, which he intended to depict in his narrative, and he must have been reasonably competent in doing so.

In addition to the writers' purpose and ability, we must consider their working methods. The biblical historians, like their modern counterparts, are selective in the data they incorporate into their narratives. There is no question of providing a complete historical account, as if such a thing existed, or even of reproducing all the material found in a writer's sources. Instead, complex and diverse matters are simplified to highlight the major contours of the subject, and a choice is made between what is relevant and serves the writer's purpose and what runs counter to it. This is to say that interpretation is intrinsic to the task of writing history. The biblical historians are concerned to discern and represent the larger patterns and structures of meaning that lie behind particular events and circumstances. These patterns and structures may not have been evident to contemporaries of the period described; however, as Long comments, "historians standing at some remove from the subject are often in a favorable position to discern the major shapes and relations of the past,"[2] not least because they have the advantage of hindsight. For the biblical historians, of course, the interpretative frame is explicitly theological. There is no such thing as "secular" history in the Bible (nor, indeed, in the ancient Near East as a whole). Rather, the God of Israel is depicted as personally active in the history of his people, blessing or punishing them according to the terms of the Mosaic covenant, and to this end as well God exercises his sovereignty over Israel's neighbors.

It follows, therefore, that any evaluation of the biblical record must take into account the delicate interplay of referential, aesthetic, and ideological matters. We must be wary of too readily polarizing issues, for example, in contrasting "theology" to "history," or by concluding that the writer's creation of an aesthetically pleasing literary effect (e.g., through the use of typology or rhetorical language) precludes a serious historiographical purpose.[3]

2. Ibid., 73.

3. Long's book develops in a positive way some of the insights of Meir Sternberg's

II. The Historicity of Chronicles: Manasseh as a Test Case

Such caution is particularly apposite in the case of Chronicles, where the question of the character and historical reliability of the work has concerned scholars since the beginning of modern critical studies of the Bible. Most recently, William Johnstone has produced a very stimulating commentary on Chronicles,[4] in which he argues that the book is first and foremost a highly organized "theological essay" about Israel's vocation to holiness, that is, the responsibility of rendering to God all that is due to him, as laid down in the law of Moses. Johnstone believes that the Chronicler was outlining the way in which Israel could be restored under the tutelage of the Levites to its right relation to God. The theological and literary character of the work is therefore given the fullest exposition in this study, which is replete with illuminating comments. However, Johnstone denies that the author had historiographical aims, and he maintains that Chronicles contains numerous unhistorical episodes and details. But this is of no matter, says Johnstone, because the author was writing "theology" and not "history"; he wanted to draw theological lessons from his portrayal for the postexilic community. Johnstone sets out his approach in his Introduction, where he states: "To attempt to use C[hronicles] as a historical source, or even to defend the historicity of his work, is at best a distraction and, with no doubt the best of intentions, to run counter to the purpose of the work";[5] and he cites as examples the Chronicler's "invention of a repentance for Manasseh, 2 Chron. 33.12-17, [and] an exile for Jehoiakim, 2 Chron. 36.6-7."[6] Johnstone goes on to affirm that attempts to reconcile Chronicles with Kings are misguided:

---

work *The Poetics of Biblical Narrative: Ideological Literature and the Drama of Reading* (Bloomington: Indiana University Press, 1985). Sternberg comments (41), "Biblical narrative emerges as a complex, because multifunctional, discourse. Functionally speaking, it is regulated by a set of three principles: ideological, historiographic, and aesthetic. How they cooperate is a tricky question." From the field of comparative studies W. W. Hallo in W. W. Hallo and K. L. Younger Jr., eds., *The Context of Scripture: Canonical Composition from the Biblical World* (Leiden: Brill, 1997), vol. 1, makes the complementary observation that modern scholarship increasingly rejects "a hard-and-fast dichotomy between 'history' and 'literature' in favor of the recognition that, often enough, history is 'literature' and vice versa' (xxvii). A basic question in interpretation is of course the meaning that a passage would have held for its original readers.

4. W. Johnstone, *1 and 2 Chronicles*, JSOTS 253, 2 vols. (Sheffield: Sheffield Academic Press, 1997).

5. Ibid., 22.

6. Strictly speaking, however, the text does not state that Jehoiakim was taken to Babylon, only that Nebuchadnezzar intended to take him there.

The worst thing that one can do with a biblical text is — understandable though it may be and motivated with the highest of purposes — to propose a harmonizing reading. For in so doing, one may be destroying the very point that the respective writer is trying to make. Only by the willing suspension of historical considerations can one do justice to his intentions. . . . As for kind of writing, [the Chronicler's] must be termed a work of theology.[7]

On the other hand, at roughly the same time (and from the same publisher) a volume of essays has appeared exploring Chronicles as a historical document.[8] While the authors are by no means unanimous in their assessment of individual details, in general they affirm that the Chronicler did have historical aims and in a cautious, discerning way his work can be used, at least to some extent, in reconstructing the history of the monarchy.

This contrary judgment is a reflection of the changing perception of Chronicles in the research of the past generation or so. In addition to showing fresh appreciation of the literary artistry and theological message of the work, scholars have reevaluated its historical value. The line of criticism that took its rise from the pioneering studies of de Wette[9] and Wellhausen[10] was characterized by extreme skepticism about the historical value of Chronicles as a witness to the preexilic period. However, since the time of Martin Noth,[11] this has given way to a broadly more positive consensus, especially in Anglo-American and Israeli scholarship. It is more generally accepted now that the Chronicler did have access to a fair range of extrabiblical sources relating to

---

7. Johnstone, *1 and 2 Chronicles*, 22-23.

8. M. P. Graham, K. G. Hoglund, and S. L. McKenzie, eds., *The Chronicler as Historian*, JSOTS 238 (Sheffield: Sheffield Academic Press, 1997).

9. W. M. L. de Wette, *Kritischer Versuch über die Glaubwürdigkeit der Bücher der Chronik* (Halle, 1806).

10. Julius Wellhausen, *Prolegomena to the History of Israel* (Edinburgh: A. & C. Black, 1885; ET of German original, 1878), chap. 6. Wellhausen's discussion of the Chronicler's Manasseh reflects several of the arguments of K. H. Graf's seminal essay "Die Gefangenschaft und Bekehrung Manasses, 2 Chr. 33: Ein Beitrag zur Kritik der Chronik," *Theologische Studien und Kritiken* 32 (1859): 474-94. Graf believed that the Chronicler wrote in order to "correct" those things in Samuel and Kings that he found inconsistent with or offensive to his concept of God and his justice. The Chronicler's Manasseh was a parade example of the way the author "expanded, revised and embellished" the problematic historical traditions he had inherited, to make them accord better with his theological convictions and didactic purpose. Graf's essay anticipated and established the general lines of the broad critical approach to the Chronicler's presentation of Manasseh.

11. Martin Noth, *Überlieferungsgeschichtliche Studien: Die sammelnden und bearbeitenden Geschichtswerke im Alten Testament* (Darmstadt: Wissenschaftliche Buchgesellschaft, 1943).

the preexilic period, although there is no agreement as to the precise extent of these sources, or the degree to which they may have been rewritten by the Chronicler.

The changing contours of the critical assessment of Chronicles as historiography, from de Wette to the present, have now been surveyed in exhaustive detail by the Finnish scholar Kai Peltonen.[12] Roughly speaking, Peltonen characterizes this debate as follows: de Wette and Wellhausen established the thesis of Chronicles as historically unreliable; a conservative reaction in defense of its historicity then arose, but this did not prevail; then Noth's work appeared, representing a kind of synthesis between these opposed positions, using source criticism and archaeological discoveries to isolate genuine preexilic traditions in the Chronicler's work. Since Noth's time, there has been what Peltonen calls an "ascending line" of scholarship, supplementing and expanding Noth's list of historically reliable information in Chronicles.[13] So the debate proceeds case by case.

The Chronicler's portrayal of the reign of Manasseh is probably the most celebrated example of the historical problems in his work. In 2 Kings 21 Manasseh is presented as the worst ruler in Judah's history. He is the arch-apostate who undoes the work of his father Hezekiah and leads the nation into idolatry, such that a prophetic oracle is pronounced against him, declaring the inevitable destruction of Jerusalem and Judah. Manasseh is also accused of shedding innocent blood throughout the city.

In 2 Chronicles 33 the author basically follows his *Vorlage* up to v. 10, but then the two accounts diverge markedly. The oracle of destruction is omitted and a lengthy section, vv. 11-17, is interposed, recounting how Yahweh sends

---

12. Kai Peltonen, *History Debated: The Historical Reliability of Chronicles in Pre-Critical and Critical Research*, Publications of the Finnish Exegetical Society 64, 2 vols. (Helsinki: Finnish Exegetical Society; Göttingen: Vandenhoeck und Ruprecht, 1996).

13. Peltonen also discerns a "descending" or skeptical line, notably in P. Welten's monograph (see below) and R. North's essay "Does Archeology Prove Chronicles' Sources?" in H. N. Bream et al., eds., *A Light unto My Path: Old Testament Essays in Honor of Jacob M. Myers* (Philadelphia: Temple University Press, 1974), 375-401, directed against Noth's arguments. Noth had treated 2 Chron 32:30 and 35:20-24 as "bedrock cases" indicating the Chronicler's use of a now unknown source for at least these pieces of historical information, which archaeology (Hezekiah's tunnel; Nabopolassar's Chronicle) had confirmed. On the basis of historical analogy Noth believed that similar authentic material might be in the work. North, however, replied that in these cases there was no positive evidence that the Chronicler had used anything more than the "canonical Scripture," from which he had drawn "his own legitimate inference or paraphrase" (392). Similarly, there was no extrabiblical confirmation of Manasseh's captivity, which the author had deduced by "theological inference" rather than from any putative sources (383-86).

"commanders of the army of the king of Assyria" against Manasseh, who is bound in chains and taken to Babylon. In the distress of captivity the apostate king prays to God, who receives his entreaty and restores him to his kingdom. Once more in the land, the penitent king conducts building works in the city, stations army commanders in his fortified cities, and carries out some cult reform, removing idols from the temple and restoring its altar.

As noted above, the historical value of this account has been widely rejected, at least since the time of Graf (1859) and Wellhausen (1878).[14] The principal reasons for this conclusion are as follows.

1. Wellhausen (following Graf) believed that the account was theologically motivated and therefore historically suspect: it had been composed to explain why the worst king of Judah also enjoyed the longest reign, fifty-five years (697-642). Wellhausen read the account as teaching that Manasseh's exile was due retribution for his grievous sin of leading Judah into idolatry, while his restoration to the throne was on account of his repentance. This view is reflected most recently by J. A. Soggin, who describes it as "an edifying story,"[15] and by R. H. Lowery, who thinks it is an ideologically motivated creation.[16] Lowery argues — in an echo of nineteenth-century thinking — that where there is factual variance between Kings and Chronicles, historical proximity to events generally favors the earlier account. Lowery further affirms that "where a different Chronicles reading clearly fits a larger tendency of the book, the report is dubious. A different Chronicles account is most probable in terms of historicity when it fits no larger literary-theological pattern."[17]

2. The silence of the books of Kings is said to speak against the Chronicler's account, especially when the inclusion of such an incident might seem to serve quite well Kings' own theology of divine punishment for covenant-breaking. The portrayal of Manasseh as a penitent reformer of the cult is so much at odds with that given in Kings and amplified in near contemporary

---

14. Wellhausen, *Prolegomena*, 206-7.

15. J. A. Soggin, *Introduction to the Old Testament*, 3d ed. (London: SCM, 1984; Louisville: Westminster John Knox, 1989), 239.

16. R. H. Lowery, *The Reforming Kings* (Sheffield: Sheffield Academic Press, 1991), 185.

17. Ibid. G. W. Ahlström, *The History of Ancient Palestine from the Palaeolithic Period to Alexander's Conquest*, JSOTS 146 (Sheffield: Sheffield Academic Press, 1993), 737, follows P. Welten's understanding of the Chronicler's "theology of retribution" (see below). Ahlström thinks that the Chronicler invented Manasseh's imprisonment and "conversion" to account for his building works described in 2 Chron 33:14, "because in the Chronicler's theological historiography only a positively judged king is a builder." But Welten rejects the historical veracity of 2 Chron 33:14 or its dependence on sources, so it is not clear why the Chronicler should have linked these works with Manasseh if he was not dependent on an earlier tradition.

passages in Jeremiah (Jer 15:1-4) and Zephaniah (Zeph 1:4-10; 3:1-7) that it cannot be taken as historical.

3. There is no account of this event in Assyrian records. Instead of being a rebel, Manasseh features in the extant record as a loyal vassal: first, in the inscriptions of Esarhaddon, as one of twenty-two kings who were compelled to transport building materials to Nineveh for the Assyrian king,[18] and then in Ashurbanipal's similar list of rulers, which stated that Manasseh presented gifts to his overlord and then helped him to conquer Egypt, an event dated to 668/667.[19]

4. Imprisonment in Babylon seems most unlikely when the imperial capital is in Nineveh; the account appears, therefore, to be a literary device intended to foreshadow Judah's own experience of exile in Babylon and then its restoration; more particularly it anticipates the experience of Jehoiakim in 2 Chron 36:6, who is himself bound in bronze shackles by Nebuchadnezzar with the purpose of taking him to Babylon. The fact that there is a close verbal parallel between 2 Chron 33:11 and 36:6 leads commentators to suspect that a literary motif rather than a historical interest is controlling the report here.

5. The account is self-evidently in keeping with the theology and style of the Chronicler, especially the programmatic vocabulary of 2 Chron 7:14 (cf. niph. כנע; התפלל; שוב), which recurs throughout Chronistic *Sondergut* in 2 Chr 10–36.[20] These facts strengthen the impression that the passage did not depend on extrabiblical sources but was the writer's own imaginative composition.

The same may be said for the works undertaken by Manasseh after his restoration. P. Welten[21] argued, mainly on linguistic and thematic grounds,

18. R. Borger, *Die Inschriften Asarhaddons Königs von Assyrien,* Archiv für Orientforschung 9, (Graz: Ernst Weidner, 1956), 60, §27, Nin. A-F v 54-63. Manasseh's name occurs in line 55 in the copy dated 673 BC; however, a duplicate dated 676 has only "the twenty-two kings of Hatti-land" instead of the list of names; cf. A. K. Grayson, "Esarhaddon," in J. Boardman et al., eds., *The Cambridge Ancient History,* III.2: *The Assyrian and Babylonian Empires and Other States of the Near East, from the Eighth to the Sixth Centuries B.C.* (Cambridge: Cambridge University Press, 1991), 125.

19. Ashurbanipal's list is found on the so-called C Cylinder I, lines 24ff. (copied in 647 BC, several years after the event recorded); cf. J. B. Pritchard, ed., *Ancient Near Eastern Texts Relating to the Old Testament,* 3d ed. (Princeton: Princeton University Press, 1969), 294; R. Borger, *Beiträge zum Inschriftwerk Assurbanipals* (Wiesbaden: Harrassowitz, 1996), 18-19. Ashurbanipal's list records different names for the kings of Arvad and Ammon from those given in Esarhaddon's list, presumably because there had been changes of rulers.

20. Cf. 2 Chron 12:12; 15:4; 24:29; 30:6, 9, 11, 18; 32:20, 24; 34:27; 36:13.

21. P. Welten, *Geschichte und Geschichtsdarstellung in den Chronikbüchern,* Wissenschaftliche Monographien zum Alten und Neuen Testament 42 (Neukirchen-Vluyn: Neukirchener Verlag, 1973).

that stereotypical Chronistic theme passages or *topoi* detailing the building works, military organization, and battles of particular kings in 2 Chronicles 10–36 did not depend on extrabiblical or preexilic sources but were the "free parabolic" creation of the writer. Welten further suggested that the same could be shown of the *topos* of cult reform. He maintained that the Chronicler's point of including this fictional material was to advance his agenda of encouraging the community of Yehud, which was under threat from its neighbors in the Hellenistic period. Those kings of whom the Chronicler approved, at least in part, were rewarded by God for their piety with the means of national security, and the Chronicler's own (demilitarized) community should similarly conclude that their defense lay in trusting Yahweh.

III. A Response to Criticisms of the Chronicler's Account

Although these arguments are widely reflected in discussion of the Chronicles' historical value, each of them may be answered with varying degrees of cogency.

1. Against Wellhausen's view, it must be asserted that the Chronicler nowhere correlates the length of a king's reign with his piety. Neither is there any indication that Manasseh's imprisonment is intended to atone for his guilt or that of the people who shared in his idolatry. Sara Japhet observes in her commentary that "In view of the gross transgression of both Manasseh and his people, the exile of the king alone seems a rather mild divine response, which may be explained only on the assumption of its historicity."[22] It may be added that, contrary to a common view of the Chronicler's "doctrine of retribution," it is not the case that the writer rigidly confines the consequences of sin to the guilty party or generation. Manasseh may be forgiven his transgression and restored to his kingdom, but the repercussions of his earlier conduct may still be felt in the following generation, as part of the history of unfaithfulness that leads to exile.[23]

2. The fact that Kings has nothing to say about this incident is not as tell-

22. S. Japhet, *I and II Chronicles* (Louisville: Westminster/John Knox Press; London: SCM, 1993), 1003.

23. Cf. B. E. Kelly, *Retribution and Eschatology in Chronicles*, JSOTS 211 (Sheffield: Sheffield Academic Press, 1996), 106-10; contra S. Japhet, *The Ideology of the Book of Chronicles and Its Place in Biblical Thought*, Beiträge zur Erforschung des Alten Testament und des antiken Judentum (Frankfurt: Peter Lang, 1989), 156-65, who asserts that in the Chronicler's view the fall of Judah and Jerusalem is due solely to the sin of Zedekiah and his generation. However, 2 Chron 32:25-26 suggests that even so exemplary a king as Hezekiah contributed his share to Judah's downfall.

ing as it may first appear when it is recognized that Kings has its own *Tendenz* or point of view. It seems that an earlier period of criticism took a more positivist view of the historical value of Samuel and Kings. It was judged that because these books were closer in time to the period they described and were not influenced by the Priestly writing, they presented a more trustworthy picture. But the partiality or selectivity of Kings is obvious when its theological outlook is recognized. G. H. Jones notes that Kings was intended as a "thematic" or "theological" account of the monarchy: only those details were extracted from the sources that were considered necessary to demonstrate the theme, and many other details were left unrecorded.[24] This is most evident in the brief treatment of the reign of Omri in 1 Kings 16:21-28. While external sources testify to the political status and power of Omri, Kings mentions only his purchase of Samaria and includes a stereotypical condemnation of the northern monarchy (vv. 25-26). It seems that a theological judgment determined the selection of the sources, and thus an intentional suppression of important aspects of Omri's reign.[25] Jones applies this observation to the rather different portrayals in Chronicles and Kings of Abijah (or Abijam, as he is known in Kings). He suggests that Kings was not interested in Abijam, who is criticized for his lack of devotion to Yahweh (1 Kings 15:3). Kings does mention that there was war between Abijah and Jeroboam (v. 6), but it gives no information about the outcome of this war. By contrast, a more nuanced view of Abijah's reign is given in the much fuller report in 2 Chronicles 13, which details Judah's victory and the capture of Ephraimite territory.[26]

It may be suggested that, *mutatis mutandis,* something similar is happening in the contrasting presentations of Manasseh. It cannot be shown that the author of Kings knew of Manasseh's deportation, but if he did, it is under-

24. Similarly, M. Cogan and H. Tadmor, *II Kings,* AB (New York: Doubleday, 1988), 272, comment: ". . . the Chronicler's account of Manasseh . . . records two items which seem historically credible [*sc.* arrest and imprisonment; defensive works]. . . . These passages from Chronicles make it all the more evident that the Deuteronomistic historian focused solely upon one element, that of Manasseh's cultic offenses, which in his view determined Judah's future and which were expressly the object of Josiah's reform."

25. G. H. Jones, "From Abijam to Abijah," *ZAW* 106 (1994), 420-34, esp. 431-32. However, Omri is singled out in Kings as one who "sinned more than all those before him" (1 Kings 16:25), which may be an allusion to his marriage alliance with Ethbaal of Sidon (v. 31).

26. Jones overstates matters in following Welten's view that the Chronicler's portrayal of Abijah is unreservedly positive (427-29). D. G. Deboys' article "History and Theology in the Chronicler's Portrayal of Abijah," *Bib* 70 (1990): 48-62 (not cited by Jones) argues instead for a more complex and nuanced presentation in Chronicles that is less obviously contradictory to that given in Kings.

standable that such information should have been omitted. In the final form of Kings Manasseh's sin marks the breaking point of Yahweh's patience with Judah and makes the destruction and exile inevitable (2 Kings 21:10-15; 23:26-27; 24:3-4). From its exilic perspective, Kings underlines for its audience the awful consequences of idolatry, and it has been persuasively argued that part of the purpose of the work was to urge its exilic audience to look to the Lord with contrition and repentance.[27] To include an account of the punishment and restoration of Manasseh would certainly have diminished the rhetorical force of the work. There is a note of hope in Kings, but it is decidedly muted in the immediate aftermath of exile, where a summons to repentance is a more immediate concern. Chronicles, on the other hand, addresses a much later time and audience, and therefore draws a different (but complementary) lesson from the life of Manasseh, in emphasizing God's grace to a notorious sinner.

3. The absence of this incident from the Assyrian record may only be a reflection of how fragmentary that record is. Only two references to Manasseh are extant from a reign of fifty-five years, so we can only guess how much may have been recorded and then lost in the course of history — or, indeed, was never recorded in the first place. The Assyrian records were not comprehensive since they recounted only what the kings or their scribes thought posterity should know in order to praise the kings of the past. Since Manasseh was not an important king in the Assyrians' eyes, his situation may not have merited mention.

4. On the other hand, the surviving Assyrian record does provide us with a set of facts upon which tentative reconstructions of events have been proposed. In the Appendix to his recent monograph on the portrayal of Manasseh in Kings, Percy van Keulen notes a number of observations and suggestions that have been made on the relation of the Chronicler's account to the Assyrian records.[28]

The first point to note is that the Chronicler had no biblical model for his

27. See H. W. Wolff, "Das Kerygma des deuteronomistischen Geschichtswerks," *ZAW* 73 (1961): 171-86. According to a commonly accepted view, the books of Kings underwent an exilic redaction in which an original pro-Josianic document was expanded down to the redactor's period and the passages blaming Manasseh for the exile (2 Kings 21:11-16; 23:26-27) were interpolated as a *post factum* explanation of the fall. Whatever the truth of this claim, it is evident that the final author of Kings took a very negative view of Manasseh. Did, perhaps, one of his own ancestors fall victim to Manasseh's bloody outrages (2 Kings 21:16)?

28. P. van Keulen, *Manasseh through the Eyes of the Deuteronomists: The Manasseh Account (2 Kings 21:1-18) and the Final Chapters of the Deuteronomistic History,* Old Testament Studies 38 (Leiden: Brill, 1996), 212-22.

account, despite the claim that is sometimes made that he composed a "midrash" on Isaiah's words to Hezekiah in 2 Kings 20:18, "some of your descendants . . . will become eunuchs in the palace of the king of Babylon."[29] This hardly fits the context. Instead the Chronicler apparently attests to a surprising knowledge of the international political situation in an era perhaps three hundred years before his time. As van Keulen notes,[30] the Chronicler could not have derived this information from Kings because that book is silent about Assyrian interference with Judah after Hezekiah's time.

The second point of interest is the puzzling reference to Babylon in 2 Chron 33:11, instead of the Assyrian capital Nineveh. The Chronicler would have known from 2 Kings 19:36 that Nineveh was the residence of the Assyrian kings (although he omits reference to Nineveh in his rewritten parallel to this verse in 2 Chron 32:21). Many commentators have therefore suspected that Babylon is mentioned for typological and literary reasons rather than as a fact of history, so as to connect Manasseh's "exile and restoration" with Judah's subsequent experience.[31]

Attempts to correlate Chronicles with the turbulent international politics of the seventh century and the connection of the Assyrian kings with Babylon have led to a number of suggestions, including attempts to link it with Esarhaddon's punitive expedition to Egypt in 671 to 669,[32] Ashurbanipal's campaign against Egypt in 663,[33] and Ashurbanipal's capture of Ushu near Tyre in 645.[34] However, the most widely accepted proposal concerns the suppression of Shamash-shuma-ukin's rebellion.[35] In 652-648, as ruler of Babylon, Shamash-shuma-ukin led a revolt against his younger brother Ashurbanipal. The rebellion was centered in Babylon and Elam, but, as J. McKay

---

29. Thus B. Oded in J. H. Hayes and J. M. Miller, *Israelite and Judean History* (Philadelphia: Westminster; London: SCM, 1977), 454.

30. Van Keulen, *Manasseh*, 214.

31. Cf. R. Mosis, *Untersuchungen zur Theologie des chronistischen Geschichtswerkes*, Freiburger Theologische Studien 92 (Freiburg: Herder, 1973); P. Ackroyd, "The Chronicler as Exegete," *JSOT* (1977): 2-32.

32. Cf. M. Cogan, *Imperialism and Religion: Judah and Israel in the Eighth and Seventh Centuries B.C.E.*, SBLMS 19 (Missoula, Mont.: Scholars Press, 1974), 67-70.

33. Van Keulen, *Manasseh*, 215-17. Van Keulen notes that Esarhaddon had declared himself king of Babylon, and his presence there is attested on three occasions.

34. Cf. A. F. Rainey in Graham et al., *The Chronicler as Historian*, 54 n. 57.

35. Cf. E. L. Curtis, *The Books of Chronicles*, ICC (Edinburgh: T&T Clark, 1910), 498; W. Rudolph, *Chronikbücher*, Handbuch zum Alten Testament 21 (Tübingen: Mohr, 1955), 316-17; J. Bright, *A History of Israel*, 3d ed. (Philadelphia: Fortress; London: SCM, 1981); J. McKay, *Religion in Judah under the Assyrians 732-609 BC*, SBT second series 26 (London: SCM; Naperville: A. R. Allenson, 1973), 25-26; Japhet, *I and II Chronicles*, 1009.

notes, disaffection spread in Syria-Palestine and at the same time desert Arabs overran the Assyrian vassal states in Edom, Moab, and other lands in eastern Palestine and Syria.[36]

Ashurbanipal replied by crushing Babylon in 648 after a siege of two years. He then turned his attention to southeastern Babylonia and western Elam. After a number of campaigns, Elam was decimated, Susa was destroyed, and much of the Elamite population was deported. Finally, Ashurbanipal exacted revenge on the dissident Arab tribes in the western desert. Arab chieftains who had sided with Shamash-shuma-ukin were taken prisoner, and Assyrian hegemony was reasserted on the desert frontier.[37] It is not known whether or how long Ashurbanipal was resident in Babylon. Nor is it known whether Manasseh was involved in the rebellions or only suspected of being so. But since his father Hezekiah had rebelled against the Assyrian overlord, there would no doubt have been grounds for such a suspicion. There is good reason, then, for thinking that a rebellious or suspect vassal could have been brought before the Assyrian king in Babylon (rather than in Nineveh) around 648 or later, during Manasseh's reign.

Also of interest is the note in Ezra 4:10 relating to the much later Achaemenian period. Here it is recorded that Ashurbanipal (Aram. "Osnappar") had deported people from Babylon, Elamites from Susa, and other groups, and settled them in Samaria and "elsewhere in Abar Nahara" ("Trans-Euphrates," from a Mesopotamian point of view). Presumably these groups were composed of defeated rebels. If they were all moved on the one occasion, the most likely period would have been after the suppression of Shamash-shuma-ukin's revolt, while their displacement to Palestine may indicate that that area was subdued and intentionally resettled at that time.[38]

The pardoning and restoration of Manasseh also makes sense in the light of what we know of Assyrian practice. It is recorded that Ashurbanipal reinstated a previously rebellious vassal, Neco I, who was taken prisoner with other Egyptian rulers to Nineveh but then returned to his throne.[39] Ashurbanipal was also lenient toward Baal, the king of Tyre who had rebelled against him,[40] so it is understandable if similar treatment was meted out to Manasseh. Leniency to Manasseh would have served a good purpose. From around 655 Egypt under Psammetichus I had thrown off Assyrian suzerainty,

---

36. McKay, *Religion in Judah*, 25.

37. J. A. Brinkman, "The Great Rebellion (652-648 B.C.) and Its Aftermath: Ashurbanipal versus Shamash-shuma-ukin and His Allies," in *CAH* III.2: 53-60.

38. T. C. Mitchell, "The Reigns of Manasseh and Amon," *CAH* III.2: 382-83.

39. *ANET*, 246.

40. *ANET*, 296.

so it would have been to Assyria's benefit to have Judah as a buffer-state at the extreme south of the empire, with a strong wall around its capital and soldiers garrisoned in its fortified cities.[41]

5. Are there any indications that the cult reform and building works ascribed to Manasseh in 2 Chron 33:14-17 reflect a reliable tradition? We should note first that both McKay[42] and Mordechai Cogan[43] have concluded that the non-Yahwistic religion that Manasseh introduced to Judah was not an Assyrian import but native Canaanite cults; so the removal of these would not have counted as rebellion against the overlord. Second, it has been questioned whether there really was a reform since Amon is described as an idolater in the footsteps of his father (2 Kings 19:20; 2 Chron 33:22), and Josiah had a great deal to do with extirpating the foreign religions (cf. 2 Kings 23:4-14; 2 Chron 34:3-5). There is, at first sight, a tension between the Chronicler's claim that Manasseh removed the foreign gods and the image from the temple (33:15) and his subsequent comment that Amon "offered sacrifice and worship to all the idols his father Manasseh made" (33:22).

However, the Chronicler does not make major claims for Manasseh's reforms. His actions were confined to the removal of a few objects from the temple and a few altars from the city, and restoring the altar of the Lord and its sacrificial functions. The reform centered on the temple, and little if any of it extended beyond Jerusalem. While the Chronicler declares that Manasseh commanded Judah to serve Yahweh, it is unlikely that the command resulted in significant changes to religious practices outside Jerusalem.[44] Although the pagan cult objects were removed (וַיָּסַר, v. 15), it is not stated that they were destroyed, as happened in Josiah's reform (2 Chron 34:3-7). Presumably they were stored away in some repository from which they could have been returned to use under Amon without much difficulty.[45]

Where the building works are concerned, we have noted already Welten's claim that these are fictitious elements inserted to boost the portrayal of cer-

---

41. Cf. W. Rudolph, *Chronikbücher*, 315-17; E. L. Ehrlich, "Der Aufenthalt des Königs Manasse in Babylon," *Theologische Zeitschrift* 21 (1965): 281-86.

42. McKay, *Religion in Judah*, 20-27.

43. Cogan, *Imperialism and Religion*, 86-96.

44. C. D. Evans, "Manasseh," in *ABD* (New York: Doubleday, 1992), 4:496-99.

45. K. M. Kenyon, *Digging Up Jerusalem* (London: Benn; New York: Praeger, 1974), 135-43, reported the discovery of two caves cut into the eastern slope of the old city, which contained female and animal figurines, an incense burner, and other deposits of pottery. T. C. Mitchell, "The Reigns of Manasseh and Amon," *CAH* III.2: 374, supports a connection here with Manasseh and comments: "It is very probable that these caves were depositories for objects which had been used for some cultic purpose and could therefore not be returned to daily use."

tain kings. Welten rejects the historicity of 2 Chron 33:14, partly because he believes that language is Chronistic and is marked by Aramaisms or is attested only in late layers of the OT (especially ל + מערבה, "westward of," and חיצון, "outer").[46] But the latter term is attested in Ezekiel at least (cf. Ezek 10:5; 40:17, 20; 44:1), so it could have been current two hundred years or more before the Chronicler's time.[47]

Archaeological evidence has also been adduced in favor of the Chronicler's report. Kathleen Kenyon uncovered "a wall of substantial appearance" near the Gihon spring on the eastern slope of the hill of the city of David. Kenyon dated this wall to the eighth or seventh century and attributed it to Hezekiah,[48] but D. Bahat assigns it to Manasseh, arguing that the course of this wall follows the description in Chronicles.[49]

Against Welten's general thesis is the fact that there is no reference in the literature to refortification of Jerusalem under Josiah. If the Chronicler freely invented this material to enhance his portrayal of pious kings, it is strange that he should attribute such works to a figure as negative as Manasseh, while nothing comparable is said of the righteous Josiah. It seems more likely here that we are dealing with a historical tradition than with a (purely) "theological" *topos*.

If the above arguments are correct, this raises the question, In what form might such information have come down to the Chronicler? In principle this is not such a difficult issue, for if the Chronicler had extrabiblical sources relating to the earlier time of Abijah, then comparable material could also have been available from Manasseh's reign. While the source citations with which the Chronicler concludes each unit are often discounted as a fictional device, or treated as stylistic variations that essentially refer to Kings, the form of the citation in vv. 18-19 is quite unusual, especially in its length and in its specific reference to Manasseh's prayer. If the Chronicler did have such a written source at his disposal, did this give him the impetus for composing vv. 12-13 in particular? William Schniedewind argues that v. 18b preserves an original fragment of archival information preserved from a noncanonical source.[50] It

46. Welten, *Geschichte und Geschichtsdarstellung*, 31-34.

47. A. R. Millard comments (in a private communication): "Welten's argument from language carries no weight unless he can show that the Chronicler never uses 'late' Hebrew or 'Aramaisms' in any passage which has some historical reality; after all, the Chronicler was working when such elements had become part of Hebrew!"

48. Kenyon, *Digging Up Jerusalem*, 144-47.

49. D. Bahat, "The Wall of Manasseh in Jerusalem," *IEJ* 31(1981): 235-36.

50. Cf. W. Schniedewind, "The Source Citations of Manasseh: King Manasseh in History and Homily," *VT* 51 (1991): 450-61.

is interesting to observe here that the Chronicler did not attempt to supply the content of Manasseh's prayer (a deficit in the tradition that was subsequently filled by the apocryphal Prayer of Manasseh), although in other passages he recounted various royal prayers and speeches not given in Kings.[51]

IV. Concluding Reflections

Alluding to Long's book on biblical historiography, Iain Provan remarks that "The Book of Kings is only one portrait of Israel's past among the many which it might have been possible to paint."[52] Provan observes that it is a highly selective account, as the source citations themselves indicate; for Manasseh's fifty-five years are described in only eighteen verses (2 Kings 21:1-18), while forty-one verses are given to Josiah's reform in the eighteenth year of his reign. All that Kings wants to establish about Manasseh is that he is "Josiah's opposite — the worst Judean royal sinner of all, whose other achievements (alluded to in 2 Kgs 21.17) were irrelevant to the task in hand."[53] The implication is that much more could have been said, and, indeed, Chronicles takes up that task. In Long's terms, the Chronicler's account represents not an overpainting of Kings, and certainly not a whitewashing of Manasseh's reputation, but rather a second painting, a different perspective drawn from the materials available to the author. Writing for a much later situation and audience, the Chronicler presented traditions and materials that were considered appropriate for them, just as Kings had done; and the presence of *Tendenz* or bias in each presentation is not sufficient reason to consider them unhistorical.

How should we assess the arguments reviewed above? It may be readily conceded that there is no absolutely definitive evidence for these suggestions, and for that reason scholars like Simon De Vries ascribe the Chronicler's narrative to the writer's own imagination.[54] On the other hand, Japhet, along with a sizeable number of more recent commentators, is much more positive and concludes that it reflects an authentic historical tradition.[55] Our argument has been that a more accurate appreciation of the Chronicler's outlook and his working methods runs counter to the older assumption that he

---

51. Cf. 2 Chron 13:4-12; 20:6-12.

52. I. W. Provan, *I and 2 Kings*, OTG (Sheffield: Sheffield Academic Press, 1997), 53.

53. Ibid., 54.

54. S. J. De Vries, *1 and 2 Chronicles*, Forms of the Old Testament Literature 11 (Grand Rapids: Eerdmans, 1989), 400.

55. Japhet, *I and II Chronicles*, 1009.

idealized the past in an ahistorical way or created freely without the restraint of sources. Although the Chronicler's *primary* aim was certainly to address the concerns of his community (and to that end he gave his own distinctive portrayal of Manasseh), there are many indications that he relied on preexilic sources, and so acted (in some sense) as a historian and not simply a homilist. The three strands of history, theology, and literary concerns are manifestly intertwined throughout the work, and tracing their relationships is a matter of continual judgment and refinement. Knowledge of the extrabiblical context and a more precise grasp of the Chronicler's purposes and literary methods are essential elements in this task.[56]

56. I am grateful to Professor Alan Millard for reading an earlier draft of this essay and making numerous helpful suggestions.

Israel outside the Land:
The Transjordanian Tribes in 1 Chronicles 5

PETER J. WILLIAMS

Summary

1 Chronicles 5 can be shown to be an integral part of the Chronicler's work on linguistic, thematic, and theological grounds. Since the overwhelming majority of the material is exclusive to the Chronicler, the chapter may be used to test whether he had access to preexilic historical sources other than through existing biblical books. From a comparison of the information he gives with that of the rest of the OT and with the Mesha Stele it is clearly plausible that the Chronicler was able to obtain independent information from the early United Monarchy.

Introduction

Of all the books in the OT that purport to deal with the preexilic era at length, the one generally regarded as least likely to contain historically accurate information not otherwise attested in the biblical materials is the book of Chronicles. Generally when it exactly parallels Samuel and Kings, it is held to be as reliable or unreliable as they are. When it has pluses or changes in relation to their accounts, it has often been held to be unhistorical. This attitude has been exemplified by Wellhausen:

I am deeply grateful to Magnar Kartveit for his helpful comments on an earlier draft of this paper.

> Die Chronik hat für die vorexil.[ische] Zeit keine anderen Quellen zu benutzen gehabt als die auch uns im Kanon erhaltenen historischen Bücher.[1]

and,

> Von einer Tradition aus vorexilischer Zeit kann also in der Chronik nicht die Rede sein, weder in I.1-9 noch in I.10–II.36. Schon im Jahre 1806 hatte dies der damals 26 jährige de Wette bündig dargetan.[2]

A more moderate position is taken by Fohrer, who lists a few passages in Chronicles that seem to be based on reliable noncanonical, preexilic sources.[3] Even here the impression is given that these cases are rare. The consensus seems to be that Chronicles is best used as a witness to the history and ideology of the time of its composition, rather than as a witness to preexilic events.

It is exactly the issue of the value of Chronicles for history before the exile that is considered here. This is done on the basis of 1 Chronicles 5. This chapter is near the center of the genealogies of 1 Chronicles 1–9 and is generally without direct parallel within the OT. Its historical value can therefore be considered independently of any extant parallel such as Samuel or Kings. 1 Chronicles 5 also tells of the two and a half tribes on the east of the Jordan: Reuben, Gad, and half of Manasseh. These tribes, it is alleged, were an integral part of Israel in the preexilic period. Their history must therefore be considered part of a general description of this period. Investigation of preexilic Transjordanian history is considerably advanced by the Mesha Stele, which records the situation in the ninth century BC.

1 Chronicles 5 Considered More Closely

In 1 Chronicles 1–9 the history of the world is surveyed in names from Adam down to Shealtiel's descendants. 1 Chronicles 1 is based mainly on Genesis, while the remaining eight chapters focus largely on Judah (2:3–4:23), Levi (6), and Benjamin (parts of 8 and 9). The focus on these three tribes is in line with Chronicles' concentration on the southern kingdom, on the Davidic dynasty, and on matters associated with the temple. Other tribes receive less attention.

---

1. Julius Wellhausen, *Prolegomena zur Geschichte Israels,* 3d ed. (Berlin: G. Reimer, 1899), VII.

2. Wellhausen, *Prolegomena,* 229.

3. Georg Fohrer, *Introduction to the Old Testament,* trans. David Green (London: SPCK, 1970), 241-42.

Thus the two and a half Transjordanian tribes receive a mere twenty-six verses in chapter 5. The survey of the tribes from chapter 2 onward is arranged so that it begins with Judah, and then considers Simeon as connected with Judah in the south. The survey then crosses the Jordan and, beginning with the most southern Transjordanian tribe (Reuben), works northward via Gad and Manasseh, before crossing back over the Jordan.[4] For most of chapter 5 there is no agreed source within the OT. Thus Augustin says that vv. 4 to 10 are "Sondergut des Chronisten," or that vv. 23-24 are "ein reiner Sonderguttext."[5]

An obvious trait of 1 Chronicles 1–9 is the variety of forms in which lists appear. Adjacent lists often have quite different structures or different spellings for the names of the same individuals. This variety can be attributed to the sources of Chronicles (and therefore is used by some as an argument for Chronicles' faithfulness to its sources[6]), to problems in transmission,[7] or to redactors.[8] Some find considerable structure within 1 Chronicles 1–9. Oeming, for example, finds the primacy of the tribe of Judah (along with those of Levi and Benjamin) to be a uniting principle that shapes the whole.[9] The less connection with Judah a particular tribe has the less it will be mentioned. He believes the structures that show this are quite subtle at times.

4. Thus Sara Japhet, *1 and 2 Chronicles: A Commentary,* The Old Testament Library (Louisville: Westminster / John Knox Press, 1993), 130.

5. Matthias Augustin, "Neue territorialgeschichtliche Aspekte zu 1 Chronik 1–9 am Beispiel der Rubeniten," in H. Michael Niemann, Matthias Augustin, and Werner H. Schmidt, eds., *Nachdenken über Israel, Bibel und Theologie: Festschrift für Klaus-Dietrich Schunck zu seinem 65. Geburtstag,* Beiträge zur Erforschung des Alten Testaments und des antiken Judentums 37 (Frankfurt am Main: Peter Lang, 1994), 299-309; quotations from 299 and 301.

6. For example, Carl Friedrich Keil, *Chronik, Esra, Nehemia und Esther* (Leipzig: Dörffling und Franke, 1870), 33.

7. For example, Samuel Davidson, *The Text of the Old Testament Considered with a Treatise on Sacred Interpretation* (London: Longman, Brown, Green, Longmans, & Roberts, 1856), 767, "In different places the names vary from one another, owing probably to mistakes in transcription, as well as to other causes."

8. For example, Lucien Gautier, *Introduction à l'Ancien Testament, Tome II,* 2 ed. (Lausanne: Georges Bridel, 1914), 256, "Ces neuf chapitres renferment des répétitions, de véritables doublets, car certaines généalogies sont reproduites deux ou même trois fois. Sans doute le Chroniste en personne pourrait avoir intentionnellement enregistré bout à bout deux ou trois textes parallèles les uns aux autres. Mais il paraît plus naturel d'admettre que ces accumulations proviennent d'adjonctions faites après coup. Quelques-unes sont tellement tardives qu'elles ne figurent pas dans les Septante."

9. Manfred Oeming, *Das wahre Israel: Die 'genealogische Vorhalle' 1 Chronik 1–9,* Beiträge zur Wissenschaft vom Alten und Neuen Testament 128 (Stuttgart, Berlin, Köln: Kohlhammer, 1990), 208.

The Unity of 1 Chronicles 5

Within the section selected, vv. 23-26 have been regularly assigned to a redactor.[10] Kartveit regards five words in v. 26 as a chronistic interpolation.[11] Schorn takes all of vv. 18-26 as a redactional expansion.[12] The problem that causes scholars to assign vv. 23-26 to different hands is the structure of the chapter: Reuben is dealt with in vv. 1-10, and Gad in vv. 11-17. Then in vv. 18-22 there is an account of how the two and a half tribes fought against the Hagrites, among others. The tribes have then all been mentioned, and therefore the further account of the half-tribe of Manasseh in vv. 23-26 is judged to be secondary. However, there are good reasons for believing that both sections (vv. 18-22 and vv. 23-26) are integral to Chronicles, since they both display a number of features characteristic of the Chronicler.

A. Spelling

At the level of spelling we have תִּלְגַת פִּלְנֶסֶר for Tiglath Pileser in v. 26. This unusual spelling is similar to תִּלְגַת פִּלְנְאֶסֶר found in v. 6 and in 2 Chronicles 28:20.[13] We also have the unassimilated *nun* of מִן before a consonant (v. 18 as in v. 9, but contrast vv. 22, 23, 25), which is common in Chronicles. It should, however, be noted that Barr makes a good case that the spelling of books in the Masoretic Text does not necessarily reflect the spelling at the time of composition of the books.[14] Spelling therefore need not suggest literary unity, but perhaps in the case of a distinct spelling like תִּלְ גַת פִּלְנֶסֶר spelling carries more weight in indicating compositional unity.

---

10. H. G. M. Williamson, *1 and 2 Chronicles,* The New Century Bible Commentary (London: Marshall, Morgan & Scott; Grand Rapids: Eerdmans; 1982), 66-67.

11. Magnar Kartveit, *Motive und Schichten der Landtheologie in I Chronik 1–9,* Coniectanea Biblica: Old Testament Series 28 (Stockholm: Almquist & Wiksell International, 1989), 68-69.

12. Ulrike Schorn, *Ruben und das System der zwölf Stämme Israels,* BZAW 248 (Berlin and New York: Walter de Gruyter, 1997), 273.

13. On the form of the name see Alan R. Millard, "Assyrian Royal Names in Biblical Hebrew," *JSS* 21 (1976): 1-14, esp. 7.

14. James Barr, *The Variable Spellings of the Hebrew Bible,* The Schweich Lectures of the British Academy, 1986 (Oxford: Oxford University Press for the British Academy, 1989), 20.

B. Phraseology

At the level of phraseology these sections contain some formulae that are characteristic of Chronicles. These are as follows:

1. What may be called the "warrior formula," which contains up to four elements in varying order:

a. the tribe or group from which the warriors come
b. the arms of the warriors
c. the number of warriors
d. the readiness of the warriors for war

Such a formula occurs in v. 18:

a. בְּנֵי־רְאוּבֵן וְגָדִי וַחֲצִי שֵׁבֶט־מְנַשֶּׁה מִן־בְּנֵי־חַיִל
b. אֲנָשִׁים נֹשְׂאֵי מָגֵן וְחֶרֶב וְדֹרְכֵי קֶשֶׁת
d. וּלְמוּדֵי מִלְחָמָה
c. אַרְבָּעִים וְאַרְבָּעָה אֶלֶף וּשְׁבַע־מֵאוֹת וְשִׁשִּׁים
d. יֹצְאֵי צָבָא

This may be compared with another example of this formula in 1 Chronicles 12:9 (references are to the Hebrew text; English versification may vary, as here – i.e., v. 8):

a. וּמִן־הַגָּדִי . . . גִּבֹּרֵי הַחַיִל
d. אַנְשֵׁי צָבָא לַמִּלְחָמָה
b. עֹרְכֵי צִנָּה וָרֹמַח
c. the list in vv. 10-15

Further examples are in 1 Chron 12:25 (a., b., c., d.), 2 Chron 14:7a (b., a., c.), 14:7b (a., b., c., d.), 17:17 (a., b., c.), 17:18 (c., d.), and 25:5 (c., a., d., b.). The existence of this formula suggests that 1 Chron 5:18 is part of the Chronicler's work.

2. In v. 20 the niphal of עזר is used, which occurs only three times elsewhere (Ps 28:7; Dan 11:34; 2 Chron 26:15). The phrase here should also be compared with similar phrases within Chronicles (e.g., 1 Chron 12:20; 2 Chron 26:7, 13).

3. In v. 20 the niphal of עתר is used for God's response to prayer. This should be compared with 2 Chron 33:13, 19.

4. Large numbers occur in v. 21. Chronicles records more large numbers than most other books.

5. In v. 24 there is the phrase אַנְשֵׁי שֵׁמוֹת, which occurs elsewhere only in 1 Chron 12:31. The whole of the surrounding phrase is also like 1 Chron 12:31.

6. In v. 25 the verb מעל is used. Eleven of the thirty-five biblical occurrences of the verb מעל are in Chronicles. The phrase in which it occurs shows some similarity to 2 Chron 21:11 and 36:14.

7. The phrase "stirred up the spirit of Pul" (v. 26) is most similar to the phrase "stirred up the spirit of the Philistines" in 2 Chron 21:16.

Both vv. 18-22 and vv. 23-26 show several traits characteristic of the Chronicler. It seems right, therefore, to treat both sections as integral parts of the book. Thus, in evaluating Chronicles' account of the Transjordanian tribes the whole of vv. 1-26 will be considered.

Historical Debate about the Transjordanian Tribes

Many scholars are not very optimistic about being able to write a history of the preexilic period, particularly of the early monarchy. Recently Schorn has argued that the idea of a system of twelve genealogically related tribes developed only after the fall of the northern kingdom.[15] In particular she considers the case of Reuben. Various locations are mentioned as allotted to Reuben in Numbers 32. However, Schorn does not consider this allotment likely since, though these names occur on the Mesha Stele, they are claimed as belonging to Mesha "ohne den Hinweis auf eine frühere Zugehörigkeit zu Ruben."[16] But to argue that Reuben did not possess these territories at the stages stated by biblical texts merely on the basis of a brief account given by a propagandist monarch at a particular point in a much longer period seems to be an overinterpretation of the evidence. However, Schorn does grant that the nonmention of Reuben need not lead us to think that Reuben was not present in the Transjordan.[17] Likewise, Augustin,[18] following Oeming,[19] regards the material about Reuben as unhistorical, on the basis of the Mesha Stele.[20]

---

15. *Ruben und das System der zwölf Stämme Israels*, 282-87.

16. Ibid., 95.

17. Ibid., 202, though see 95.

18. "Neue territorialgeschichtliche Aspekte zu 1 Chronik 1–9," 304.

19. Oeming, *Das wahre Israel*, 140.

20. Interestingly, in Numbers 32, when Reuben and Gad ask for territory beyond the Jordan, six out of seven references (vv. 2, 6, 25, 29, 31, and 33 — all but v. 1) give the order Gad then Reuben rather than Reuben then Gad, which is the order of primogeniture followed elsewhere. This unusual order is also followed in Josh 18:7, which talks about the allotment of land across the Jordan. Could this indicate that Gad was the more prominent tribe and thus the one more likely to be mentioned in a source like the Mesha Stele?

In fact, the very existence of a tribe of Reuben is called into doubt by Augustin.[21]

A New Perspective

A. Historical Framework

One of the most striking things in the opening chapters of 1 Chronicles is the way pieces of information are not formally connected. This happens in the opening verses of the book, presumably because the connections between figures such as Adam, Seth, and Enosh were well known. It also happens in 1 Chronicles 5. Thus, after reading in v. 3 that Reuben had four sons, we are told in v. 4 about the sons of Joel. Nothing has been said about Joel before, and there is no indication whatsoever of his relationship with those preceding. Likewise, when in v. 11 we have been told of the location of the Gadites, in v. 12 we are told of another Joel and someone called Shapham. However, we are not told when they lived. We are informed in vv. 18-22 of a war that the two and a half tribes had with the Hagrites, yet nothing is explicitly said about when this took place except that it was before the exile.

Interspersed with these seemingly disconnected pieces of information are Tiglath Pileser's invasion (v. 6), a war with the Hagrites in the days of Saul (v. 10), the recording of genealogies in the days of Jotham and Jeroboam (v. 17), an exile (v. 22), and a deportation into exile by Tiglath Pileser (v. 26). It seems most natural to link the account of war with the Hagrites in v. 10 with that in vv. 18-22. It is also simplest to link the exile of v. 22 with that mentioned in v. 6 and v. 26.

When this is done and the events are linked with conventional dates, the following framework emerges:

i. Hagrite war	vv. 10, 18-22	ca. 1000 BC
ii. Census	v. 17	ca. 750 BC
iii. Exile	vv. 6, 22, 26	ca. 733-32 BC

We will now examine what happens when the other details in the passage are fitted into the framework provided by these events, and for the sake of argument we will treat the records as historical.

Joel's seventh descendant, Beerah, was taken captive by Tiglath Pileser (v. 6). At a stretch, if we suppose Joel to have been young at the time of the

21. Augustin, "Neue territorialgeschichtliche Aspekte zu 1 Chronik 1-9," 308.

Hagrite war, and Beerah to have been quite old when taken captive, these seven generations can span from the time of the war to the time of the deportation by Tiglath Pileser. Cogan, however, assigns Joel to the "latter half of the reign of Solomon."[22]

The Hagrite war resulted in territorial gains that lasted until the exile (v. 22). The Hagrites, however, were on the east of Gilead and may not have been sedentary (cf. "tents," v. 10).

1 Chronicles 5 states that the Reubenites covered Aroer, Nebo, Baal-meon, and up to the desert on the east, even reaching the Euphrates. They are said to have had large quantities of cattle in Gilead (possessed from the Hagrite war onward), and in relation to the account in Numbers 32 this may represent a shift toward the east.

The Gadites possessed Bashan as far as Salecah, Gilead, the pasturelands of Sharon, and Bashan and its villages (an unusual expression since "and its villages" normally occurs with the name of a town, and Bashan is normally an area). This would have been recorded around 750 BC, to judge by the kings named in v. 17, and thus after Mesha. From a comparison with Joshua 13 and Numbers 32 one might suppose that the area occupied by the Gadites has shifted northward under the influence of Mesha. East Manasseh possessed territory from Bashan as far as Baal-hermon, Senir, or Mt. Hermon. 1 Chronicles 5 omits references to well-known places like Dibon and Heshbon.[23] Thus the passage is not simply making extravagant claims about territory previously occupied by Israel.

What extrabiblical records would be expected to reflect these situations if they were real? Reubenite activity, possibly nomadic, in the area east of Gilead (v. 10) would naturally not be recorded by Mesha. Manasseh would also probably be too far north to be recorded by a Moabite king. Gad, on the other hand, is mentioned by Mesha as being in a location consistent with the picture given in 1 Chronicles 5.

B. Table of Stages

The table on p. 156 is a chart registering towns in the Transjordan occupied according to the various texts. The texts on which this chart is based are listed at the top from left to right in their *prima facie* chronological order. Thus within the

---

22. Mordechai Cogan, "The Men of Nebo — Repatriated Reubenites," *IEJ* 29 (1979): 37-39, esp. p. 37 n. 3.

23. Cf. Schorn, *Ruben und das System der zwölf Stämme Israels*, 277.

biblical narrative Numbers is set earlier than Isaiah and thus is to the left of it in the table. The column entitled "Bela" refers to 1 Chronicles 5 and to the figure in v. 8 who, assuming the genealogy is complete, is the great-grandson of Joel, who is assumed to be the same figure as the Joel of v. 4. If Joel was alive at the time of the Hagrite war, or even if his *floruit* was later, the date to be assigned to Bela probably still precedes the period recorded in the Mesha Stele.[24]

24. I take it that vv. 6-8 are not saying that Bela was a contemporary of Beerah. The "he" of v. 6 may refer to Joel.

The Shift of Transjordanian Territory from Israel to Moab
Based on the *Prima Facie* Order of the Texts

Town	Num 32	Joshua 13	Bela	Mesha Stele		Isaiah 15, 16	Jeremiah 48
Aroer	G 34	R 16 + מן, G 25 + עד	R 8	—	M26	—	M 6, 19
Ataroth	G 34	—	—	G 10	M 11	—	—
Baal-meon	R 38	R 17	R 8	—	M 9	—	M 23 (Beth-meon)
Beth-diblathaim	—	—	—	—	M 30	—	M 22
Dibon	G 34	R 17	—	M 28	M 28	M 15:2	M 18, 22
Elealeh	R 37	—	—	—	—	M 15:4; 16:9	M 34
Heshbon	R 37	R 17	—	—	—	M 15:4; 16:8, 9	M 2, 34, 45
Horonaim	—	—	—	—	M 31	M 15:5	M 3, 5, 34
Jahaz(ah)	—	R 18	—	I 19	M 19	M 15:4	M 21, 34
Jazer	G 35	G 25	—	—	—	M 16:8, 9	M 32
Luhith	—	—	—	—	—	M 15:5	M 5
Medeba	—	R + על 16	—	I 8	M 9	M 15:2	—
Mephaath	—	R 18	—	—	—	—	M 21 Qere
Nebo	R 38	—	R 8	I 14	M 14	M 15:2	M 1, 22
Nimrah/Nimrim	G 36	G 27 (Beth Nimrah)	—	—	—	M 15:6	M 34
Qir Hareset/Heres	—	—	—	—	—	M 16:7, 11	M 31, 36
Qiryathaim	R 37	R 19	—	—	M 10	—	M 1, 23
Sibmah	R 38	R 19	—	—	—	M 16:8, 9	M 32

This table is a record of place names in the key texts that deal with the Transjordan. Names are recorded in it only if they occur in more than two texts. Verse or line (or chapter and verse) numbers appear after the abbreviation for the group possessing the territory. The table seems to show a shift from Israelite to Moabite possession. Key: R = Reuben, G = Gad, I = Israel, M = Moab.

The columns on the left, that is, those that purport to tell of earlier events, generally record various towns as belonging to the Israelites. Those on the right, which purport to show later events, generally record towns as belonging to Moab. The table thus shows the change through time from Israelite to Moabite possession. However, it may show this too clearly. Because the passages in the left three columns are lists of Israelite territories, one would not expect explicit statements within them identifying Moabite towns. Likewise because the passages in Isaiah and Jeremiah are oracles about or laments for Moab, we would not expect them to identify Israelite territory. The topic in each case biases the listing. However, even given this bias, it is unlikely that Israel possessed significant territory in the Transjordan after the Assyrian invasions of the eighth century BC. If any correction were therefore to be introduced into the table, it might be possible to treat some of the unassigned locations in the lefthand columns as Moabite. In the table two columns occur under the heading of the Mesha Stele. This is to distinguish between the ownership of locations before and after Mesha's activities as reflected in the stele. Sometimes there are no indications of the ownership beforehand, and at other times there are clear indications of a shift of ownership under Mesha.

It might be argued that Numbers, Joshua, and Chronicles present later ideals about what Israel's borders had been, that they are postexilic and contain little that can be trusted historically. It is impossible in this essay to disprove such a model, but to take the sources in their *prima facie* order produces a model that seems to have several advantages over that one. The advantages are as follows:

1. It produces a neat arrangement in which the Moabite rebellion(s) recorded in 2 Kings 1:1 and 3:1-27 and the expansion of Moab under Mesha can be seen as key points in the transfer of territories from Israel to Moab. The model is attractive for its explanatory parsimony.

2. In one specific case, that of Ataroth, a detail from what is generally supposed to be a postexilic account in Numbers is confirmed. Numbers classes Ataroth as Gadite, and line 10 of the Mesha Stele states that the Gadites had dwelt there "from of old" (מעלם). Mesha then proceeds to relate how he conquered it. This territory at least changed hands under Mesha. If Numbers is merely a postexilic idealization of territorial boundaries, it is surprising that it managed to guess the correct tribe to record as having occupied Ataroth as confirmed by the Mesha Stele. It is unlikely that Numbers was influenced by the Mesha Stele — anyone supposing that it was would certainly be crediting the author with being a historian who went to considerable lengths to check his sources. Either way he has access to preexilic material. Thus it seems that

the account in Numbers has been confirmed in the instance of Ataroth, and its information should therefore be taken seriously in other cases.

3. The Mesha Stele suggests that Jahaz, Medeba, and Nebo came under Moabite rule during Mesha's time. This fits very well with the biblical information in the left-hand three columns of the table, which give them as Israelite. The terms used for Omri "inheriting" the land of Medeba (Mesha Stele, lines 7-8) and the king of Israel "building" Jahaz (lines 18-19) may suggest that at a yet earlier stage these territories did not belong to Israel. However, such a stage could easily still be posterior to the stage recorded in Joshua 13. Territorial disputes may have been long-standing.

4. The three towns mentioned in 1 Chron 5:8 as belonging to Reuben, namely Aroer, Nebo, and Baal-meon, fit very well between the *prima facie* earlier and *prima facie* later records. All three are recorded as Israelite in Numbers or Joshua, and all three are recorded as Moabite by the end of the events recorded in the Mesha Stele. It might be suggested that 1 Chronicles 5 has used Numbers or Joshua as its source, and has thus incidentally adopted historical information along with its source. However, neither is a likely source. Joshua 13 does not mention Nebo, and Numbers 32 mentions Aroer as Gadite in contrast to Chronicles, which assigns it to the Reubenites. One might suppose that the varying designations of Aroer as Reubenite and Gadite represent diachronic shift, or reflect a more complex historical situation. Either way, Chronicles has no known source at this point yet seems to contain plausible historical information.

C. Onomasticon

A further argument that suggests that in 1 Chronicles 5 we are dealing with authentic material from preexilic sources is the onomasticon that is used. The names in the list suit the context in which they are set. They suit the date, geography, and tribes to which they are assigned. It might be argued that what we have here is postexilic fiction, and that the author has carefully selected names that will suit the historical context he creates. However, if the author is supposed to be so good at this, one may at least ask why he was not equally capable of recording history. The case for the material being preexilic has several converging lines of evidence.

1. Verse 5 mentions Baal as a name for a Reubenite. Is such a name a likely postexilic creation? One could make an *ad hoc* argument to support its attribution to the postexilic period, but it is simpler to assume that it is preexilic, before Baal worship was purged from Israel. The name Baal is also interesting

because, to quote Dearman, "Place names compounded with *Ba'al* are only found in northern Moab in all of central and southern Transjordan."[25] That is, it fits the geographical region to which it is ascribed.

The following names suggest the widespread use of the name Baal in this area.

a. Bamoth Baal (Josh 13:17) is said to be in Reubenite territory.

b. Numbers 21:19-20 mentions a place called "Bamoth," which, when compared with Num 22:41, may be identified with "Bamoth Baal" mentioned there. This may be the same as Beth Bamoth (בת במה) mentioned in the Mesha Stele, line 27. Baal-meon is also in Reuben's territory (Josh 13:17; cf. Mesha Stele, lines 9 and 30), and Baal Peor (Num 25:3) is in the same area of the Transjordan. Thus Baal is a very suitable name for someone from Reuben in this area.

2. Cogan gives evidence that supports the names of the Reubenites as genuinely belonging to that tribe.[26] He notes that in the list of returnees from the exile in Ezra 2 and Nehemiah 7 are some names that seem to come from the Transjordan. The sons of Pahath-moab ("Governor of Moab," Ezra 2:6; Neh. 7:11) seem a clear example. Cogan argues that the men of Nebo (Ezra 2:29; Neh 7:33) are similarly Transjordanian (i.e., Nebo does not equal Nob), comparing Nebo in v. 8 of our passage. Transjordanians therefore return with the Judahites from the exile. Of particular interest to Cogan is Ezra 10:43, which lists those who agreed to divorce their non-Israelite wives. The verse reads:

Of the sons/men of Nebo, Jeiel (יעיאל), Mattithyah, Zabad, Zebina, Yaddai (Kethib: ידי), and Joel (יואל), Benaiah.

This has three names in common with the part of our passage about Reuben: Joel (vv. 4, 8), Jeiel (v. 7), and the location Nebo (v. 8). The name Jeiel further occurs in connection with the Transjordanian Aroer (also mentioned within our passage) in the list of David's mighty men (1 Chron 11:44).

Conclusion

While the argument laid out here is largely circumstantial, it at least shows that an elegant explanation of the passage and related biblical texts is to suppose that they present genuine preexilic data. The method used has been one

---

25. Andrew Dearman, *Studies in the Mesha Inscription and Moab*, Archaeology and Biblical Studies 2 (Atlanta: Scholars Press, 1989), 195-96.

26. Cogan, "The Men of Nebo — Repatriated Reubenites," 37-39.

of exposing the explanatory power of a particular position rather than of eliminating other possibilities. The historical development traced also fits well with the onomasticon, which independently seems to confirm the historical nature of the records. It has been shown, then, that there are good reasons to respect the historical information given in a passage in Chronicles for which there is little source material within the Bible. I began this study having selected the passage nearly at random, and with no idea what might be found, and have been surprised by the amount of material that has come to light. This suggests that other passages might profit from a similar examination.

It should be noted that this study has been done without extensive reference to questions of historical geography and the identification of locations. Such investigation would considerably lengthen this study, but it should be undertaken in order to verify the conclusions drawn here.

In the Stable with the Dwarves:
Testimony, Interpretation, Faith,
and the History of Israel

IAIN W. PROVAN

Introduction

The writer C. S. Lewis, near the end of the last of his children's stories known as the Narnia Chronicles,[1] pictures for us the eschatological end of everything, when the world of Narnia has been made new and the old things have passed away. Even though the new world clearly exists, there are nevertheless some — the dwarves — who refuse to acknowledge it. They have been let down earlier in the story, discovering that the god-figure whom they had been worshipping as Aslan the lion is in fact merely a donkey disguised as a lion. Having been taken in once, they are not about to be fooled a second time. Disappointment thus gives way to cynicism and self-interest; and that is why, as Aslan in reality appears, the dwarves are to be found huddled in an inward-looking group, in a stable that no longer really exists, complaining about the darkness and the smell. They are not about to be taken in again — not even by reality. And so all attempts at testimony to the reality outside the group founder on the rock of

---

1. C. S. Lewis, *The Last Battle* (Harmondsworth: Puffin, 1964), pp. 124-135.

Reprinted in A. Lemaire and M. Saebo, eds., *Congress Volume, Oslo* (Leiden: Brill, 2000), 281-319. Used with the permission of E. J. Brill, ©2000 Koninklijke Brill NV, Leiden, The Netherlands.

dwarvish solidarity, on the shared commitment to cynicism and scepticism. Even Aslan himself cannot shake their world-view. His low growl in their ears is interpreted simply as another attempt to trick them into faith; the glorious banquet he provides for them is experienced as animal fodder and dirty water. But in a curious way they are satisfied with their lot. "At any rate," they remind each other, "there's no Humbug here. We haven't let anyone take us in. The Dwarfs are for the Dwarfs."[2]

The story nicely illustrates the issues at the heart of the current debate over the Hebrew Bible and the history of Israel. For centuries the Bible has been widely held to define reality for its readers, including historical reality. It has more recently been discovered, to put this statement in its mildest form, that matters are a good deal more complex than hitherto suspected. This has led most readers of the Hebrew Bible, at least in the scholarly world (and that is all I am concerned about in this paper), to some degree of modification in their views about the relationship of the Bible to history. It has recently led significant numbers to doubt whether whole sections of the Bible give us access to history at all, and a few to the opinion that the Bible as a whole is more of an obstacle to the historian than an aid. So it is that we have journeyed from implicit trust in, to explicit distrust of, the Bible as providing access to Israel's past. Scholars that tend towards such principled distrust are apt to perceive themselves as the champions of truth and justice over against the forces of obscurantism and oppression. Their distrust is addressed not just towards the Bible, but often towards those who differ in their attitude to and use of the Bible, who are characterised as motivated more by religious or political commitments than by the pursuit of truth and justice. In brief, like the dwarves, these scholars are against humbug — historical humbug, whether found in the Bible or among the Bible's interpreters. They are determined not to be taken in; and so they take a maximally suspicious stance in respect of both. The dwarves are for the dwarves, and are most assuredly against anyone who is not to be found in their stable.

Is this attitude of principled suspicion toward the Hebrew Bible in particular, with regard to history, justified or indeed sensible? My own view, already expressed in my 1995 *JBL* article on this topic,[3] is that it is not at all justified or sensible. Clarifications are immediately in order at this point, given the misunderstandings that have arisen in some quarters about the argument of that essay.

2. Lewis, *The Last Battle*, p. 135.

3. I. W. Provan, "Ideologies, Literary and Critical: Reflections on Recent Writing on the History of Israel," *JBL* 114 (1995), pp. 585-606.

Clarifications

I have not taken my stand against some of the more recent developments in writing on the history of Israel primarily because of my theology. I do not in fact hold a view of the Bible as Scripture which requires me to defend its historicity against all-comers and in contradiction to what can otherwise be said to be facts. I do not hold a view of the Bible as Scripture which commits me to treating it, as an historical source, differently from any other historical source;[4] nor a view which commits me to what has been called "maximal conservatism" on historical matters.[5] I find it puzzling that my previous arguments in respect of the approach and attitude of some scholars writing recently on the history of Israel should have been read by some as implying such a view.[6] I should have thought it perfectly clear that I was mainly op-

4. P. R. Davies, "Method and madness: Some remarks on doing history with the Bible," *JBL* 114 (1995), pp. 699-705, on p. 700, is thus quite mistaken. My objection to his approach to the history of Israel does not stem from my regarding the Bible (because it is inspired Scripture) as a specially privileged source so far as historical reconstruction is concerned, but rather from the conviction that his approach is intellectually indefensible. This should have been clear to Davies from my original article, where I do in fact explain (contrary to his claim in "Method," pp. 699-700) what I mean by "positivism" and "materialism," focusing especially on verification (cf. "Ideologies," pp. 601-03). These labels were, incidentally, intended to be descriptive rather than pejorative (*contra* W. G. Dever, "Revisionist Israel revisited: A rejoinder to Niels Peter Lemche," *CR:BS* 4 [1996]: pp. 35-50, on p 41; R. P. Carroll, "Madonna of silences: Clio and the Bible," in L. L. Grabbe ed., *Can a 'History of Israel' be Written?* JSOTS 245 [Sheffield: Sheffield Academic Press, 1997], pp. 84-103, on p. 97, n. 28).

5. L. L. Grabbe, "Are historians of ancient Palestine fellow creatures — or different animals?" in Grabbe (ed.), *History*, pp. 19-36, on pp. 28-29, is apparently to be numbered among those who interpret my position as involving such a commitment, if juxtaposition of text and footnote 25 is any guide. It is not religious belief that drives such conservatism as I possess, however, but the kind of healthy regard for testimony in general (including biblical testimony) for which I shall argue below, in the course of outlining once again what I hold to be an entirely rational and critical approach to history. What I find reason to be "annoyed" about (p. 29) is precisely that scholars who happen to differ in their view of what is rational and critical should characterise such an approach as "naïve" (p. 28), "apologetic" (p. 28) and "insidious" (p. 29), when it is none of these. Why, exactly, should one go down any "road" (defined as "critical" or not) further than necessary? Is the demand for logic or for a blind faith-commitment?

6. It does serve to confirm me in my suspicion, however, that some of the scholars concerned are working with an exceptionally narrow vision of the world, in which there live in the end only two sorts of persons: the critical scholar (for which read "scholars who broadly agree with oneself") and the religious fundamentalist. To be perceived as not one is thus inevitably to be perceived as the other.

posing them on the grounds of epistemology and logic. I welcome, in any case, the opportunity to restate my position here in fuller terms, and to clear up any possible misunderstanding. I do not oppose the marginalisation of the Hebrew Bible in the task of writing the history of Israel because I am a Christian and revere these texts as part of Christian Scripture. I oppose this move on the grounds of epistemology and logic — because I do not regard the position adopted as well argued or, indeed, intellectually coherent.

Nor am I unaware, as some seem to imagine,[7] that in opposing this kind of position I am also raising questions about various aspects of Enlightenment historical method which have resulted by degrees in the position I am now criticising. I am perfectly aware of doing this, and happy to raise these questions for consideration. Nothing should be sacrosanct in the pursuit of truth — not even method. It is, in fact, the perceived sanctity of method that has for too long stifled debate in biblical studies (if not elsewhere) about the truly important question which should lie at the heart of any discussion about the history of Israel. How do we know what we claim to know about the reality of the past? It is a fundamental question, and yet often not articulated and itself debated by those writing about the history of Israel. All too often it is a question that in my view has been at least partially repressed and avoided for fear that it might complicate too greatly our ability to get on with our work. Here is the game known as historical enquiry. Here are the rules of the game. This is how one must play. If it is objected that perhaps some of the rules do not make particular sense, or that some aspects of the game are not worth playing, then the response is often, not debate on these points, but naked re-assertion. We have always played the game this way; at least we have done so since proper historical scholarship began in the 19th century. It is simply how modern scholarship is. If you do not like it, find a game of your own. In fact, if you do not like it, you are a fundamentalist, or some such undesirable.[8] So the game is saved, to be enjoyed by all its participants; but it is saved by avoiding fundamental questions about its viability.[9] The danger of

7. T. L. Thompson, "A neo-Albrightean school in history and biblical scholarship?" *JBL* 114 (1995), pp. 683-698, on p. 695 (beginning of second para.)-697 (end of first para.); Grabbe, "Creatures," p. 21, n. 6.

8. Thus Grabbe, "Creatures," p. 21, asserts rather than argues for the centrality of the "basic ground rules" of the game, moving seamlessly into a subsequent sentence about biblical fundamentalists which implies that only such people truly question these rules.

9. Thompson, e.g., apparently believes ("School," pp. 696-697, n. 37) that long footnotes indicating the company he allegedly keeps are any substitute for a rational and measured response to criticism of the general position that he adopts. The whole argument of his pp. 693-697 is in fact extraordinarily confused. He both denies that there is any broad

adopting this strategy is, of course, that a detachment from reality may begin to set in. The game goes on; but does anyone know any longer whether it has any connection with the world outside itself? The rules are upheld; but are they rules that allow or prohibit us from seeing reality more broadly? Are they rules, in fact, that in the end simply leave us in epistemological darkness, beyond the reach of any evidence itself that might invade our comfort zone, unsettle our ideology, spoil the game?

This leads on to a third initial clarification that I feel necessary to make, which will lead on to the substance of this current paper. For reasons that are again not entirely clear to me, I have been perceived as giving "the impression that the biblical text is unproblematic"[10] with regard to the history of Israel. This is again certainly not my position. My position is, rather, that the Hebrew Bible is indeed problematic for the historian, but that it is no more essentially problematic as a window into the past than any other kinds of material available to him or her. The problem, insofar as we have a problem, lies not with the Bible over against other allegedly more objective, more trustworthy, more factual witnesses to the past. The problem lies rather with the histo-

---

school of thought regarding Hebrew Bible and history such as I described in "Ideologies" and yet accepts the adjective "neo-Albrightean" for the group of scholars to whom he belongs and describes the methodology of this group in terms similar to my own description of it (note especially the emphasis on the verification of sources on pp. 694, para. 2, and 697, para. 1). He seems to imagine that this is not truly a particular school of thought both because scholars in the group do not agree with each other on individual aspects of Israel's history (pp. 693-695), and yet also because so many people in so many different countries now think in the same way about how to approach that history — there has been a "paradigm shift" in the field of history since the 1960's (696-697). It is for these reasons that my "conspiracy theory" cannot be right (p. 696). I never suggested, in fact, that there was any conspiracy. I suggested only that a broad prejudice currently seemed to exist with regard to the usefulness of large sections of the Hebrew Bible to the historian of Israel. It is an inadequate response to that critique to remind me of the diversity of scholarly views on individual matters (of which I am naturally aware; cf., e.g., "Ideologies," p. 589, opening sentence), and that the paradigm under discussion is widely adhered to (since a paradigm is only a paradigm, and not by virtue of that fact beyond criticism — although it is abundantly clear that it is regarded as such by many of those working within it). On the question of whether there has in reality been any recent paradigm *shift* see further below. The extent to which the paradigm is indeed widely adhered to among scholars is any case constantly and massively exaggerated by Thompson, who appears to believe that repeated assertion (combined with the repeated suggestion that those scholars who do differ are not truly scholars at all) will make it so; see now T. L. Thompson, "Historiography of ancient Palestine and early Jewish historiography: W. G. Dever and the not so new biblical archaeology," in V. Fritz and P. R. Davies (eds.), *The Origins of the Ancient Israelite States*, JSOTS 228 (Sheffield: Sheffield Academic Press, 1996), pp. 26-43, esp. pp. 33, 36 with n. 36, 37-38 and *passim*.

10. Grabbe, "Creatures," 29 n. 25.

rian, faced only and ever with witness to, and interpretation of, the past rather than with the past itself (which is gone, and never existed as a single story to be discovered in any case), but required by his profession nevertheless to weave a meaningful story about it out of the data available to him. The very business of writing history is problematic. It is this far more fundamental problem upon which, in my view, much scholarship on the history of Israel has failed to reflect in sufficient depth. It is aware of the problem of the Hebrew Bible and history. Of the problem of history more generally it is seemingly partially or wholly unaware. Only thus is it possible to explain why it is so often the case in recent discussion that it is the problem of the Hebrew Bible that has loomed so large, while the problems presented by other data are either ignored completely or minimalised. Indeed, the perception of just how problematic the Hebrew Bible is has in large measure arisen because scholars are so prone to compare it with other data that they are apt to regard as giving virtually unmediated or at least minimally mediated access to naked fact.[11] My impression is that many do this in all innocence, entirely unaware that they are thus making unargued assumptions which have already predetermined the results of their study of the texts. To that extent, I assert, much recent scholarship is indeed unaware of the epistemological problems involved in writing history, even where epistemology is otherwise mentioned or discussed.[12] It has a narrow idea of the nature of the problem we confront, and

11. For illustration of these points, see further the extended example discussed later in this essay.

12. *Contra* Grabbe, "Creatures," p. 29, n. 25. Grabbe himself provides a good example of how it is possible both to articulate some of the epistemological problems involved in writing history (as he does throughout his paper) and yet to make a fundamental error of the sort I describe when dealing with sources in respect of a particular era of *Israel's* history. Comparing the Hebrew Bible and other ancient Near Eastern texts in respect of their testimony concerning the later monarchy (pp. 24-26), he seems to assume that the latter, as "literature or inscriptions approximately contemporary with the events purported to be described," and notwithstanding the word "purported," simply describe for us the facts of the matter. Only thus can we understand how it is that the biblical text is thought to be "judged" by the extra-biblical information (p. 24), and how it is that Grabbe can go on to assert that "the text is reasonably accurate about the framework" but that the details are at times "demonstrably misleading or wholly inaccurate and perhaps even completely invented" (p. 26). It is entirely unclear, however, why one should embrace such a straightforward view of the Assyrian sources, nor grant them such epistemological primacy; cf., e.g., the brief summary discussion of the highly ideological nature of Assyrian scribal compositions in M. Z. Brettler, *The Creation of History in Ancient Israel* (London: Routledge, 1995), pp. 94-97, with extensive footnote references. Other scholars are in my view similarly muddled on epistemological questions, and I do not accept that in seeking to demonstrate this muddle I have misrepresented any of them, including Ahlström (*contra* Grabbe again,

indeed a narrow view of reality as it seeks to confront it.[13] To that extent — ironically in view of its frequent assaults on others for being insufficiently critical — it is itself somewhat naïve and uncritical, and indeed often involves itself in self-contradiction and incoherence. That is the thrust of my criticism of it in the *JBL* article.

Knowing about the Past

I hope that it is now clear what I have hitherto argued and why. In this paper I return to the argument and seek to develop it. I ask again: is the attitude of principled suspicion toward the Hebrew Bible with regard to history, which is now so commonly found in writing on the history of Israel, justified or indeed sensible? I begin by returning to that other, fundamental question mentioned a moment ago: how do we know what we claim to know about the reality of the past? I assert the following in response to this question: we know it, to the extent that we know it at all, primarily through the testimony of others about it. Testimony lies at the heart of our access to the past. There is the

---

p. 29, n. 25). *Of course* my quotation is "selective" (what else could it be?); I disagree, however, that my selection somehow distorts Ahlström's position. What Grabbe must demonstrate in order to substantiate his accusation of "misreading" (leaving aside the speculative and offensive "wilful") is that Ahlström (a) does not in fact believe that there is such as thing as "what history really looked like"; (b) does not regard the ideology and selectivity of the biblical texts as presenting a serious problem to the modern historian who wishes to reconstruct the past; and (c) does not believe (albeit with gross inconsistency in the argument) that archaeology grants us much more reliable access to the past than do the biblical texts. I do not believe that Grabbe can in fact demonstrate this. For comments on Ahlström's work which are somewhat consistent with my own, see H. M. Barstad, "History and the Hebrew Bible" in Grabbe (ed.), *History*, pp. 37-64, on pp. 47-48.

13. The fact of the matter appears to be that modern historians of Israel are on the whole remarkably not very well informed about the broader philosophical debates of the last several centuries about epistemology in general and historical knowledge in particular, and are thus seemingly unaware of just how far it is *not* self-evident that an historical method inherited from 19th century Germany is the only way (or indeed the best way, intellectually considered) in which to approach the past. Only thus is it possible to explain why this kind of "scientific" approach, founded as it is on a starkly developed but indefensible Cartesian dualism, can be advanced as the only properly critical approach to the history of Israel without the slightest hint that the position needs to be argued for rather than simply asserted (along with references to others who agree), and in studied ignorance of the devastating critiques of it in scholars like H.-G. Gadamer, *Truth and Method*, ET (London: Sheed and Ward, 1975) and W. Pannenberg, *Basic Questions in Theology*, ET, vol. 1 (London: SCM, 1970).

testimony of people(s) from the past about their own past, communicated in oral and written forms. There is the testimony of people(s) from the past about the past of other peoples, also communicated in oral and written forms. There is also the testimony of figures from the present about the past, whether the past of their own peoples or of others — figures like archaeologists, who make certain claims about what they have found and what it means in respect of what has happened previously. It is such testimony that gives us access to the past, to the extent that anything does. There is no way of doing any historiography which does not involve testimony. Even if I am the very person who digs up an artifact from the Palestinian soil, I am still entirely dependent upon the testimony of others who have gone before me in trying to make sense of its significance, in trying to decide how I shall add my testimony to theirs.[14] Testimony, story-telling if you like, is central to our quest to know the past; and therefore interpretation is unavoidable as well. All testimony about the past is also interpretation of the past. It has its ideology or theology; it has its presuppositions and its point of view; it has its narrative structure; and (if at all interesting to listen to or to read) it has its narrative art, its rhetoric.[15] We cannot avoid testimony, and we cannot avoid interpretation.[16] We also cannot avoid faith. I began this paragraph by using the language of knowledge: how do we know what we claim to know about the past? In truth, however, this is a concession to the view of what we are about as historians from which I wish to distance myself. What we call knowledge of the past is more accurately described as faith in the testimony, in the interpretations of the past offered by others. We consider the gathered testimonies at our disposal; we reflect on the various interpretations offered; and we decide in various ways and to various extents to invest faith in these, to make these

14. Cf. F. Brandfon, "The limits of evidence: Archaeology and objectivity," *Maarav* 4 (1987), pp. 5-43, the implications of which, not to mention the extensive bibliography touching on archaeology and theory, have seemingly (if recent discussion of the history of Israel is any measure) still to be digested by biblical scholars in general.

15. For an excellent theoretical discussion of history, ideology and literature which ranges much more broadly than Provan, "Ideologies," and provides voluminous bibliographical referencing, see Brettler, *Creation*, pp. 8-19.

16. This is again as true of the archaeologist as it is of anyone else. Cf. C. Schäfer-Lichtenberger, "Sociological and biblical views of the early state," in Fritz and Davies (eds.), *Origins*, pp. 78-105, on pp. 79-80: "Data derived from archaeological artifacts exist only in linguistic form. Being elements of a linguistic structure, however, they are subject to interpretation as well. The description of archaeological findings is already interpretation and it is subject, like any other literary form of expression, to the singular choice of the narrative procedure, to the concept of explanation, as well as to the value-orientation of the descriptive archaeologist."

testimonies and interpretations our own. If our faith is very strong, or we are simply not conscious of what we are in fact doing, then we tend to call our faith knowledge; but it is a dangerous term to use, since it too easily leads us into self-delusion, or deludes others who listen to us or read our books, as to the truth of the matter. It is this delusion, indeed, that seems to me to lie at the heart of the problem, so far as much of our recent (and not so recent) writing on the history of Israel is concerned. I shall return to consider it in due course.

We "know" what we claim to know about the past, then, by listening to testimony, to interpretation, and by making choices about whom to believe.[17] What sense does it make, then, in our pursuit of knowledge of the history of Israel, to adopt a principled distrust of major sections of, or even the totality of, the Hebrew Bible? In this literature we evidently have, among other sorts of texts, testimonies about (interpretations of) Israel's past in narrative form.[18] To tell us about this past is certainly not the only purpose of these narratives; it is arguably not even their main purpose. Yet so far as can be deduced from the texts themselves, it is clearly one of their purposes.[19] Whether

17. The constraints of space prevent a more detailed outworking of the epistemological stance outlined here, and this is in any case rendered unnecessary by C. A. J. Coady's excellent *Testimony: A Philosophical Study* (Oxford: Clarendon, 1992) as well as many of the other works mentioned in these footnotes which do not adopt a positivistic view of the historian's task.

18. I naturally accept (*contra* the impression given by Davies, "Method," p. 701) that not all stories are intended to refer to a real past, and that even stories which generally are so intended may for various reasons not do so in specific instances or for specific reasons. My observation in "Ideologies," nevertheless, was that biblical stories about the past have been *without good reason* increasingly marginalised in recent discussion on the history of Israel. Davies' comments here are, therefore, very much beside the point.

19. This is, on the basis of a reading of the content of most of the narrative texts, at least as clear as any other purpose that may be suggested by a reading of the same texts. I find no basis at all for Grabbe's assertion ("Creatures," pp. 32-33) that theological or religious intent is clearer than historical intent in the biblical text. In respect of his argument on these pages I grant that writers may in fact fall short of what they intend, or indeed that their communication may exceed their intention. Nevertheless, it is fundamental to the task of taking literature seriously that the reader try to form some judgment as to what the author is seeking to do; and it requires some narrowness of perception, in my view, to miss the obvious fact that biblical narrative overall is seeking to speak about Israel's past. The question as to whether every narrative seeks to do this in precisely the same way is a different question. I certainly see no reason to accept the (again unargued) assertion that "the biblical writer would have made no distinction between the account of creation in Genesis 1, the narrative of the exodus, or the story of Solomon's accession" (p. 32; cf. also Barstad, "History," p. 45, but contrast B. Halpern, *The First Historians: The Hebrew Bible and History* [San Francisco: Harper and Row, 1988], pp. 266-278). Whether it were true or not, of

it were one of their purposes or not, they might indeed still succeed in doing it.[20] How is it, then, that we have come to a place where a principled avoidance of the Hebrew Bible as a whole by historians of Israel can be advocated by some, and many more have come to regard entire sections of this Bible as being of little usefulness in getting at historical truth?

Verification or Falsification?

As we review the literature, it is evident that one of the reasons scholars have for their doubts is that it is difficult, if not impossible, to verify so much of biblical tradition; and without verification, it is asserted or implied, we cannot have great confidence in the material as source material for the doing of historiography. Thus Miller and Hayes, to take one example, are concerned about the general lack of what they call "non-biblical control evidence" throughout Genesis-Samuel and into 1 Kings. They do not think that one can presume the historical reliability of the Genesis-Joshua narrative in the absence of it; they are extremely hesitant about using the Samuel narrative in writing about Saul because of lack of external verification of the truth of the kernel of the stories there; and they would clearly prefer to have the same kind of verification in the case of David.[21] In the absence of such verification, which they regard as essential to the task of properly writing a critical historiography, they are to be found either not attempting to say anything (in the case of Genesis-Joshua) or virtually apologising for what they are indeed attempting to say.[22] Soggin, the author of the other watershed history of Israel dating from the 1980's, is just as unwilling in general to presume historical reference in biblical accounts without external verification.[23] Both histories

---

course, we should still have to make our own decisions (having sought to grasp the author's communicative intentions) as to how, precisely, to receive the testimony offered.

20. Barstad, "History," p. 62. I have struggled, but failed, to find an *argument* in Thompson, "Historiography," pp. 38-43, which might provide some basis for his rather different view of the biblical texts, discovering instead only assertion. We are apparently to believe simply that the character of the texts as theologically shaped narratives precludes any intention on the part of their authors to refer to a real past and any access for us via the texts to such a past.

21. J. M. Miller and J. Hayes, *A History of Ancient Israel and Judah* (London: SCM, 1986), pp. 74, 129, 159.

22. For the crucial nature of verification, cf. Miller and Hayes, *History,* p. 78. For examples of virtual apology, cf., e.g., pp. 129, 159-160.

23. J. A. Soggin, *A History of Israel: From the Beginnings to the Bar Kochba Revolt,* AD 135 (London: SCM, 1984), e.g., p. 98 on the patriarchal narratives; p. 110 on the Exodus.

are indeed regarded as *watershed* histories in part precisely because they apply the verification principle to the extent that they do. If some more recent scholarship has found them deficient, it is not because they are thought to have gone too far in this direction, but because they are considered not to have gone far enough. External verification for the Davidic and Solomonic periods, it is claimed, is just as absent as for the earlier periods, and indeed is also far more sparse than hitherto suspected for the period of the later monarchy. Since it is well known that we are struggling somewhat for verification in the post-exilic period as well, it is unsurprising that a number of scholars are calling for what they see as simple consistency in the approach adopted to the Hebrew Bible and history. If Genesis through to sections of 1 Samuel is not to be considered primary source material at least partly for the reason that verification is not available, why treat any differently the remainder of 1 Samuel through to 2 Kings and into Ezra-Nehemiah? Thus it is made to seem inevitable that any truly critical scholar will adopt a principled suspicion of the whole Hebrew Bible in respect of historical work; and, conversely, that those who partially or generally adopt the biblical story-line in writing their histories of Israel are, to the extent that they do this, religiously motivated obscurantists rather than critical scholars.

It is my view, on the other hand, that this headlong rush to scepticism is a result, not of being more purely critical, but rather of being insufficiently critical. Criticism is indeed widely employed; but it is not employed in respect of the sacred cow at the heart of the matter — the verification principle itself. Why should verification be a prerequisite for our acceptance of a tradition as valuable in respect of historical reality? Why should not ancient historical texts rather be given the benefit of the doubt in regard to their statements about the past unless there are compelling reasons to consider them unreliable in these statements and with due regard (of course) to their literary and ideological features? In short, why should we adopt a verification rather than a falsification principle — why should the onus be on the texts to "prove" themselves valuable in respect of history, rather than on those who question their value to "prove" them false? I have raised these questions before. I have still not received, in my view, an adequate answer to them. It cannot be, as many seem to assume, that verification is necessary because of the merely general *possibility* that any given biblical text is not in fact reliable as historiography.[24] I grant the possibility in

---

24. E.g., P. R. Davies, "Whose history? Whose Israel? Whose Bible? Biblical histories, ancient and modern," in Grabbe (ed.), *History*, pp. 104-122, on pp. 104-105, asserts that "the use of biblical historiographical narrative for critical reconstruction of periods that it describes (rather than periods in which it was written) is precarious and only possible where

any given case; but the individual case still must be examined in order to come to an individual decision about it. I do not therefore see how the general possibility leads on logically to the methodological stance just described.[25]

I use the inverted commas around "prove" in any case advisedly, for it is not at all clear whether the notion of verification or "proof" under consideration

---

there is *(sic)* adequate independent data." I can see nothing in his preceding discussion, however, that justifies this conclusion, and, indeed, I find his earlier assertion that "the historical testimony of any work will be relevant in the first instance to the time in which it was written" itself ungrounded and out of step with both logic and experience. *Why* should we believe (if not simply for the reason that Wellhausen asserted it; cf. for a discussion Halpern, *First Historians*, pp. 26-29) that the historical testimony of texts is relevant in the first instance to their own times, and can only be used in a secondary respect "to build a picture of the periods *which they claim to be describing*"? It is from this (itself precarious) starting point in assertion that Davies once more moves on to criticise those who in constructing a history of Israel synthesise biblical texts and extra-biblical data. He truly has no adequate *grounds* for such criticism, however. For ungrounded assertion of the same kind, in defence of the same view of texts, cf. T. L. Thompson, "Defining history," pp. 166-187, on p. 180: "We all know that the real world which such so-called [ancient] 'historiographies' reflect is that of their author; and they are never any better than that."

25. The general possibility, e.g., that the biblical authors *may* have been rather like James Macpherson, who is alleged to have invented the Celtic poet Ossian (Carroll, "Madonna," pp. 86-88), or Shakespeare, who recontextualised historical figures in fictional works (p. 91), does not demand that we take a general stance against presumption in favour of reading the Bible as historical (cf. p. 87 and the remainder of the article). Examples like these merely help us to form some idea of the range of possibilities that might exist in respect of any individual text (whether biblical or non-biblical) that "looks" historical in some way. A particularly intriguing aspect of much of this kind of citation of possible analogues to stories in the Hebrew Bible with a view to demonstrating its problematic nature is the way in which it is so readily forgotten that the "knowledge" we possess about the analogues has itself often been accumulated by scholars who operate with precisely that "scientific method" whose viability is here in question. It is thus naturally the case that the "evidence" brought to bear on the discussion of the history of Israel should favour biblical scholars committed to this same method. Whether that "method" gives us any more reliable access to historical reality when applied to non-biblical rather than biblical texts is, however, entirely open to question. The non-existence of Ossian, e.g., is by no means universally accepted among Scottish historians. More to the point, Grabbe, "Creatures," pp. 31-32, thinks that Herodotus showed "wonderful critical acumen" in questioning (on the basis of an Egyptian tradition) the "quasi-canonical" Homeric version of the story of Helen of Troy, and indeed that Herodotus placed the burden of proof on those who wished to continue to accept it at face value. I, on the other hand, can find no reason to think that one version of the story is more or less likely to be true than the other, and would indeed be interested in exploring further the relationship between Herodotus' "critical acumen" and his attitude to women ("... no nation would allow itself to be besieged for ten years for the sake of a mere woman ...," p. 32). The burden of proof has not, in fact, been moved one inch in any direction whatsoever by Herodotus' expression of his opinion.

here is at all coherent. How exactly is verification thought to be possible? Suppose that we have an archaeological datum which is consistent with the claims of a biblical text about the past. Does this "verify" that the text is historically accurate? This is certainly the kind of thing that has often been argued or assumed. Yet that piece of data, even if a written text, is still itself only another testimony to the past; it does not "prove" that the event to which the text refers happened. Non-written data are even less precise and more ambiguous.[26] How many testimonies are needed, then, before verification happens? And for whom does it happen — for everyone, or only for some? Recent discussion on the history of Israel has clearly suggested that the answer is indeed "only for some." One person's sufficiency of data is another's insufficiency, or even another's forgery.[27] This raises the interesting question as to how far verification lies in the eye of the beholder, and whether it is not one's primary attitude to the texts in the first instance that is far more decisive in terms of one's approach to the history of Israel than the discovery of this or that piece of external data.[28] This very question then thrusts us back to our opening questions on the point of method, and indeed sharpens them. Why, exactly, is verification commonly regarded as so central to the historiographical task, especially when it is so unclear in what it consists? To this question we may add another, which sharpens the point still further. How much history, ancient or otherwise, would we know about, if the verification

26. Cf., again, Brandfon, "Limits."

27. This is most clearly illustrated by the recent discussion of the Tel Dan inscription. For a convenient summary, cf. F. C. Cryer, "Of epistemology, northwest-Semitic epigraphy and irony: The 'bytdwd'/house of David inscription revisited," *JSOT* 69 (1996), pp. 3-17; and for an even more recent reassessment, K. A. Kitchen, "A Possible Mention of David in the Late Tenth Century B.C.E. and Deity *Dod as Dead as the Dodo," *JSOT* 76 (1997), pp. 29-44; A. Lemaire, "The Tel Dan as a Piece of Royal Historiography," *JSOT* 81 (1998), pp. 3-18.

28. This is to my mind well illustrated in the debate between W. G. Dever, "The identity of early Israel: A rejoinder to Keith W. Whitelam," *JSOT* 72 (1996), pp. 3-24, and K. W. Whitelam, "Prophetic conflict in Israelite history: Taking sides with William G. Dever," *JSOT* 72 (1996), pp. 25-44, concerning material culture and ethnicity. The debate is ostensibly about what it is that the archaeological data reveal to be true about the inhabitants of the central highlands of Palestine during the late 13th and early 12th centuries B.C. Decisive for the positions ultimately adopted in each case, however, is the attitude of each scholar to the biblical traditions, in terms of their usefulness to the historian as interpretative keys for the archaeological data. Cf. further Thompson, "Defining history," pp. 167-176, with whose comments on the difficulty of deducing ethnicity from material remains I tend to agree; and more generally, Brandfon, "Limits." It would greatly help scholarly discussion about what it is that *particular* archaeological data "suggest" or "prove" if scholars were able to articulate more clearly their views on what it is that such data are *generally* able to "suggest" or "prove," and on what part their own interpretative theory plays in producing "suggestion" or "proof."

principle were consistently applied to all testimony about it? The answer is clearly "very little" — which is precisely why those who employ the principle, whether historians in general or of Israel in particular, only do so selectively, choosing their targets for rigorous scepticism most carefully.[29] The delusion that I mentioned earlier — the delusion that we possess knowledge unmediated by faith — is indeed only possible if scepticism is directed at certain testimonies about, and interpretations of, the past, and not at others.[30] Method that holds verification to be centrally important can only ever be method that is partially (in every sense) followed through. The more consistently the method is applied, the more it collapses in upon itself, until the point is reached where it is realised that nothing can truly be known at all. It is one of the remarkable (if also tragicomic) aspects of recent writing on the history of Israel that a number of its practitioners seem to imagine that it is an advance in knowledge as a result of empirical research that has led to the end of "ancient Israel," when in fact it is only an advance in ignorance as a result of the quasi-consistent application of the verification principle.[31]

29. Knowing any history aside from the history in which we are personally involved in fact requires trust in unverified testimony. Selectivity in application of the verification principle is thus an essential prerequisite for writing about the past; and so every historian of Israel is to be found selectively applying it. The testimony of archaeologists, above all, has been privileged by a lack of suspicion until fairly recently, although there are signs that this is at least partially changing (cf. K. W. Whitelam, *The Invention of Ancient Israel: The Silencing of Palestinian History* [Routledge: London, 1996]; and my review article on this book, I. W. Provan, "The End of (Israel's) History? A Review Article on K. W. Whitelam's *The Invention of Ancient Israel*," *JSS* 42 [1997], pp. 283-300). The testimony of extra-biblical texts has also been privileged in many quarters and continues to be so (cf. n. 12 above on Grabbe and the Assyrian texts). It is naturally essential that some sources of information should be exempted in this way from any rigorous demand for verification, since nothing remains otherwise to be appealed to in respect of verification of the data being "tested."

30. I do not myself believe that an historian should always feel honoured when called a "sceptic" (Davies, "Whose history?" p. 109); cf. further below. If scepticism is indeed to be the denoting feature of the historian, however, (s)he should at least attempt to be consistent about it.

31. Cf., e.g., N. P. Lemche, "Clio is also among the Muses! Keith W. Whitelam and the history of Palestine: A review and a commentary," in Grabbe (ed.), *History*, pp. 123-155, on pp. 147-148, who paints a portrait of scholars "forced" successively to lower the time of composition of the biblical narrative; of scholars innocently engaged in "looking for traces" of early Israel, but compelled by lack of evidence to abandon use of the biblical narrative for historical purposes. I have no reason to think that Lemche does not sincerely believe this story, but it is, I believe, a fiction. It is the method itself that has determined the outcome of the enquiry, not such empirical evidence as has been gathered along the way. The fuller narration in N. P. Lemche, "Early Israel revisited," *CR:BS* 4 (1996), pp. 9-34 (in which Lemche himself figures particularly prominently among the heroes of the story),

I continue to reserve further comments on the delusion to which I refer, however, for a moment. In summary of this section of my argument, I simply affirm that I can see no reason why any text offering testimony about the past, including the Hebrew Bible, should be bracketed out of our historical discussions until it has passed some obscure "verification test."[32]

---

makes this especially clear. It is above all a decisive "shift of emphasis" (p. 17) in recent years, rather than any decisive shift in the evidence, that has led to the current state of the debate about the history of Israel; and it is a shift of emphasis in relation to historical method that was already committed in large measure to the verification principle, particularly in respect of archaeological investigation. The precise character of the "shift" in respect of the Old Testament traditions is transparently clear in the closing pages of Lemche's essay (pp. 25-28), marked as they are throughout by the presence of ungrounded assertion and the absence of convincing argument. The last (if not entirely comprehensible) word here, however, must go to T. L. Thompson, "Historiography of ancient Palestine and early Jewish historiography: W. G. Dever and the not so new biblical archaeology," in Fritz and Davies (eds.), *Origins*, pp. 26-43, on p. 32: "It may well be ironic that it is this recognition of our ignorance of this period's history — indeed that the recognition of such ignorance is the hallmark of our field's cutting edge — that marks the most conclusive results of this generation's historical research!" That ignorance would be the inevitable endpoint if the method employed could have been safely predicted some time ago.

32. It is characteristic of Thompson's response to my *JBL* article that he fails to address the substantive issue here and contents himself simply with assertions about the centrality of verification to historical method ("School," pp. 694, para. 2; 697, para. 1). Acceptance of the verification principle is indeed apparently one of the tests of orthodoxy in respect of critical scholarship, to express doubt about it is to be a dreaded "fundamentalist" (p. 694). Naked assertion aside, a central feature of his strategy in attempting to avoid having to address the main thrust of my argument is to suggest that I have engaged in deliberate and widespread distortion of his and others' views. I entirely reject this accusation. There is, for example, no case in which I have attributed a quotation to Thompson that belongs to an author he is citing or discussing (*contra* "School," pp. 683-684), and he never demonstrates that I have. Nor is he very accurate even in describing that which I have indeed placed in quotation marks (cf. his p. 685, line 17, with "Ideologies," p. 586, line 12; and especially his p. 685, n. 5 with "Ideologies," p. 586, lines 6-7, where the phrases in question are neither placed by me in quotation marks nor attributed to anyone). My use of what he calls "dots" in abbreviated quotations, moreover, in no case leads to misrepresentation of what he or anyone else has written (*contra* "School," pp. 687, lines 28-33; 688, lines 24-32; 689, lines 18-33; 690, lines 7-11; 693, lines 23-27). Apparently uneasy about resting his entire case against me on allegations of misreading his *Early History*, he characterises those sections of the book from which I quote as "rhetorical . . . often originally designed as much to provoke as to enlighten," and blames me for not reading some other writings of his instead (p. 684). It is true, of course, that I do expect scholars writing serious books to say what they mean. This appears to me to be a reasonable expectation. As to Thompson's other writings, there is in fact nothing to be found in them which suggests that my sketch portrait of his approach to the history of Israel is in the least degree unfair.

Specific "Rules" of Evidence

There is a second, connected reason, however, why scholars have increasingly expressed doubts about whole sections of the biblical tradition. It is not just that the Bible has "failed" in its own terms to verify itself. It is also because so much of the biblical literature is now widely considered intrinsically deficient in its very ability to testify about the past that it claims to reflect. Here we have to do with an accumulated inheritance of rules about which kinds of testimony really count, so far as the historian is concerned, and which kinds of testimony do not count as much or at all. These rules have apparently been designed, like the rules of textual criticism (for example), to make life easier for the historian, on the one hand, by absolving him from thought in specific instances; and, on the other hand, to reduce the subjectivity otherwise inevitably involved in deciding between witnesses to the past. We may list the most influential of these rules, as appropriated, comprehended and used by historians of Israel in particular, as follows. First, eye-witness or otherwise contemporaneous accounts are to be preferred on principle to later accounts.[33] Secondly, accounts which are not so ideological, or not ideological at all, in nature are to be preferred to accounts which are ideological in nature.[34] Thirdly and finally, accounts which fit our preconceptions about what is normal, possible, and so on, are to be preferred to accounts which do not fit such preconceptions.[35] These rules have, of course, been in operation for some time, and as such have been applied for some time to smaller or greater sections of biblical tradition. What has changed in recent times is not the rules, but the extent to which the biblical text is seen as unsatisfactory in respect of them. Scholars have found in the Bible fewer of the kinds of traditions that score highly in respect of their granting of direct access to the past (e.g., eye-witness or early sources), and more and more of the kinds that do not score highly. Thus once again there has seemed a certain inevitability about the marginalisation of the Bible by historians, as the places where "history" might

---

33. Thus, e.g., E. A. Knauf, "From history to interpretation," in D. V. Edelman (ed.), *The Fabric of History: Text, Artifact and Israel's Past*, JSOTS 127 (Sheffield: JSOT, 1991), pp. 26-64, on pp. 45-47, accepts that the historian should be first and foremost concerned with primary sources, produced in the course of the events as they were happening, rather than with sources produced after the events, which he (tendentiously) describes as designed "to clarify for future generations how things were *thought* [my emphasis] to have happened" (p. 46).

34. Thus, e.g., G. W. Ahlström, "The role of archaeological and literary remains in reconstructing Israel's history," in Edelman (ed.), *The Fabric of History*, pp. 116-141.

35. Thus, e.g., P. R. Davies, *In Search of "Ancient Israel,"* JSOTS 148 (Sheffield, 1992), pp. 32-36: cf. further the discussion of these pages below.

be found therein have been by degrees eliminated. And again, this perceived inevitability has led also to the perception that those who insist on finding history, say, in the books of Samuel are simply committed to being conservative and are not properly critical scholars.

Once again, however, the interesting question is: who is it that is really being critical? For the rules I have just enunciated are by no means self-evidently "true." The claims that are made about them (taken together and labelled as rules of "scientific method") in terms of their capacity to lead us into all truth, or at least to enable us to pronounce upon the probability that something did or did not happen in the past, are inflated. I leave aside for the purposes of the present discussion the question of whether scholars are in fact correct to see the Bible as more problematic than before in respect of the rules. There is certainly an interesting question here, for those who believe in verification, as to the status of many of the scholarly hypotheses about the dating of biblical texts in particular, and as to the defensibility of any rejection of the Bible as testimony to Israel's past on the basis of these unverified hypotheses. I leave this question aside, however,[36] and press the more radical question about the rules themselves, which I consider highly problematic. There is no good reason at all to believe that eye-witnesses are, any less than later reporters of events, interpreters of those events, nor any reason to assume on principle that their testimony is going to be more or less trustworthy.[37] There is, indeed, no reason to believe that earlier accounts are generally more reliable than later accounts,[38] even *if* the literary coherence of the latter

36. My view on dating and its implications is in summary as follows. I do not believe that those who have plausibly argued for the ongoing shaping of, e.g., Genesis-Kings in the post-exilic period have thereby demonstrated that Genesis-Kings is essentially and substantially itself late, and there are on the contrary many good reasons for thinking that it is not. There is in any case no good reason to think that the late date of a composition (if it were established) would inevitably imply that the composition would be less helpful than other sources of information to the modern historian interested in Israel's past. No implication follows from dating in itself.

37. B. Becking, "Inscribed seals as evidence for biblical Israel? Jeremiah 40.7–41.15 *par exemple*," in Grabbe (ed.), *History*, pp. 65-83, on p. 68, asserts that a detective pursuing a murder inquiry is better off than an historian, since the former is in a position to check eye-witness reports. I cannot see, however, how mere access to eye-witness reports places one person in a better or worse position in respect to the other. There is no necessary correlation between the sort of interaction that "witnesses" have with events and the quality of access to events provided to others through it.

38. H. Niehr, "Some aspects of working with the textual sources," in Grabbe (ed.), *History*, pp. 156-65, on p. 157, insists that a clear distinction between primary and secondary sources must be upheld, on the ground that the primary sources "did not undergo the censorship exercised by, for example, the Deuteronomistic theologians nor were they submit-

can plausibly be argued to be a late feature in their development.[39] Certainly most modern historians do not believe this, or they would not write their own books on history.[40] Nor is there reason to believe that there is any account of the past anywhere (including the archaeologist's account)[41] that is not ideological in nature, and thus in principle to be trusted more than oth-

---

ted to the process of canonization." This is to assume, of course, rather than to reason. It is to assume that we already know that the Hebrew Bible is problematic in respect of the way in which it mediates the past (because of "censorship" and "canonization") and that other sources of information are not. Niehr believes, in fact, that the historical reliability of the Assyrian sources has recently been "shown" to be very high (p. 158). The delusion of knowledge thus returns to wreak its havoc on rational argument. In relation to which "facts" do we "know" that Deuteronomistic redaction and canonical process have distorted the past in passing it on, and that Assyrian sources have not? What real basis is there for a distinction between these two kinds of data?

39. Thompson's view, e.g., is that an "understanding of the coherence of the biblical tradition, as arising out [sic] first within intellectual milieu [sic] of the Persian period, causes great difficulty in affirming the historicity of the Israel of tradition at all" (T. L. Thompson, *Early History of the Israelite People from the Written and Archaeological Sources*, Studies in the History of the Ancient Near East 4 [Leiden: Brill, 1992], pp. 353-354; cf. my "Ideologies," p. 597, for reference to other comments along the same lines). I do not myself believe that he has demonstrated (or can demonstrate) that the coherence of the biblical tradition overall indeed arises only at such a late date. Even if he is correct, however, there is simply no reason to assume that a particular rendering of earlier tradition at a later date cannot also be a truthful rendering, any more than there is reason to assume that an early rendering cannot be false. Certainly modern historians have typically wished to argue that *their* very late renderings of earlier tradition are truthful — and, indeed, more truthful than earlier attempts — even though (and precisely because) they supply fresh coherence in articulating the tradition.

40. Davies, "Method," p. 703, para. 4, objects to this same point in "Ideologies," defending the reliability of (demonstrably late) modern historians over against (allegedly late) biblical writers by referring to both archaeological excavation reports and comparative ancient Near Eastern materials in terms of their capacity to provide the "possibility of confirmation." The fallacy of verification thus rears its head once more (as it does throughout his response; e.g., p. 701, last three lines; p. 702, lines 4-6, 19-20, 34-36). It is not (as Davies suggests) that I "dislike" the possibility of confirmation at all. It is, rather, that I consider the whole notion of "confirmation" problematic.

41. The idea that archaeologists' "texts" are no more "objective" than others in respect of the past is slowly imposing itself on biblical studies (cf., e.g., Carroll, "Madonna," *passim*), albeit that there is little consistency in the way that scholars are handling the idea. It is mainly appealed to when scholars wish to question possible correspondence, rather than possible conflict, between archaeology and the Bible (cf. esp. my comments on Whitelam in "End," pp. 289-292). That Syro-Palestinian archaeologists themselves should generally have failed hitherto to see the need for epistemological reflection on their own discipline is nothing short of astonishing (cf. Brandfon, "Limits," p. 37; Dever, "Identity," p. 9, n. 8). For an excellent brief discussion in this area, see Schäfer-Lichtenberger, "Sociological and bib-

ers;[42] nor indeed to believe in any case that an ideological account cannot also be an historically accurate account.[43] There is no good reason to believe that just because a testimony does not violate our sense of what is normal and possible, it is more likely to be true than one which does, nor that an account which describes the unique or unusual is for that reason to be suspected of unreliability.[44]

---

lical views," pp. 79-82, whose closing words on the limited usefulness of archaeology to the historian of Israel in respect of the 10th c. stand in stark contrast to many of the statements from those of a more positivistic orientation: ". . . it is not up to archaeology to decide an essentially theoretic debate, whose course until now has demonstrated only that the so-called hard facts are determined by the discussants' perspectives" (p. 82).

42. There has been a general tendency among historians both recent and not so recent, and whether focusing on biblical or extra-biblical material, to view material which "looks" less ideological (e.g., annalistic material) than other material (e.g., narrative material) as if it really were so in reality. The assumption is a curious one, as Barstad ("History," pp. 45-46, n. 25) points out.

43. There is no reason to think (e.g.), just because the narrative of David's rise to power is pro-Davidic, seeking to acquit David of guilt, and follows a literary pattern found elsewhere in the ancient Near East, that "the traditional materials about David cannot be regarded as an attempt to write *history* as such" and do not grant us access to the real past (N. P. Lemche, *Ancient Israel: A New History of Israelite Society,* The Biblical Seminar 5 [Sheffield: JSOT, 1988], pp. 52-54). This is a straightforward *non sequitur* (of the kind also found, e.g., in Carroll's puzzling discussion of Omri, "Madonna," pp. 95-96). The fact that we are dealing with apologetic material here, with what Lemche calls "an ideological pro-grammatic composition," does not of itself demonstrate that what the text claims is untrue (e.g., and centrally, that David was indeed innocent); cf. the balanced comments of Brettler, *Creation,* p. 143. Thompson ("School," p. 686) seeks to redeem Lemche from the *non sequitur* by having him say (which he does not) that the stories, being ideological, can-not be *assumed* to be historiographical, suggesting that in "Ideologies" I misrepresent Lemche by lifting a quotation out of context. I assuredly do not; cf. further now Lemche, "Clio," p. 140, n. 25, where Lemche himself makes clear, in addressing the same point in my article and in spite of his objection to it, that he does not allow for the possibility that ideo-logical literature can truly represent the past. He allows only the possibility that historical information is *concealed* (my emphasis) in OT historical narrative (cf. also the text with which his n. 25 is associated: the fact that the history of Israel in the OT is a religious story "ensures that simple-minded paraphrases of it will, from a historian's point of view, never lead to anything but a false understanding of ancient Palestinian society, including also the two historical states of Israel and Judah").

44. Cf. my comments on analogy in "Ideologies," p. 601, n. 71. It is worth underlining here the intellectual incoherence of that modern approach to the past, reaching back at least as far as Hume, which claims to eschew dependence upon testimony, yet moves on to ground its beliefs about the past in "common human experience." This latter can itself only ever (at best) be a construct dependent upon testimony (that which some others whom we happen to believe have claimed to be their experience), and appeal to it often seems in fact to represent nothing other than a smokescreen in which it is hoped that the

In sum, there is no way that "rules" of evidence can prejudge whether particular testimonies are in fact worthy of faith or not. It is an illusion to think that they can. There is no intellectually defensible way of avoiding, in the particular case, the inevitable consideration of all testimonies together, weighing them up on their own terms and in comparison with each other and asking how far they are each likely (or not) to be in relationship to the events to which they refer. In that respect historical criticism is indeed directly analogous to textual criticism, but not in the way that was once supposed. There is no way, in either case, in which the application of a general set of "rules" to any particular case settles anything of itself. All that the so-called "rules" do is to provide a helpful background in terms of generalities, an accumulated wisdom which may or may not help in the resolution of any particular case. In the final analysis there is no substitute for the judgment of the individual reader of the testimonies in coming to some resolution in each particular case. In the final analysis there is no substitute for the judgment of the individual reader of the testimonies in coming to some resolution in some particular case — in deciding in which testimonies to invest faith (as to "better" text or historical event), in deciding which reading makes better "sense." All this being the case, there is once again no good reason to marginalise the testimony of the Hebrew Bible in our pursuit of the history of Israel.[45] There is every reason, in fact, to place its testimony at the heart of our deliberations.

---

very limited nature of the writer's individual experience might be lost sight of. Real human experience (as opposed to the construct "common human experience") is vast, differentiated and complex.

45. One occasionally comes across the assertion in current debate on our topic that, even if some of our biblical authors are indeed properly called historians, the fact that they are not *critical* historians (like some of the Greeks) makes access to the past for us through their texts problematic. This is a proverbial red herring. It is questionable enough to "deduce" from the *claims* of certain ancient Greeks about their critical intentions and the *absence of such claims* in ancient Hebrew texts (as in other ancient Near Eastern literary traditions) that there is inevitably a substantive difference in reality between (some) Greeks and (all) Hebrews. What is entirely curious, however, is the assumption that there is any necessary correlation between the *stated intentions* of an historian and the usefulness of his account of the past to *us*. One can as well imagine an author whose intentions to be critical caused him to fail to pass on important testimony about the real past, as one can imagine an author who uncritically passed such testimony on. Perhaps the imagination of some modern contributors to the debate on the history of Israel is limited at this point, however, as a result of an incapacity to believe that any gulf is possible between *their* intention to be critical, on the one hand, and their grasping of and transmission of historical truth, on the other.

Faith and Knowledge

We "know" what we claim to know about the past, I have suggested, by listening to testimony, to interpretation, and by exercising faith. There is no good reason, I have further argued, to think that any testimony and interpretation should be required to "verify" itself in some way before being listened to. Nor is there any good reason to think that any testimony and interpretation can be prejudged either positively or negatively by "method" rather than being listened to on its own terms. The only rational course of action for the person interested in the reality of history is, in fact, to consider all the testimony and interpretation available to him or her and to make his/her best judgments on a case-by-case basis about whether and how far it is to be believed.[46]

I would characterise this as a position of epistemological openness to past reality. It is the position that I adopt in respect of reality in general, and which would be widely recognised, I trust, as rational in that regard.[47] To illustrate this point, let me return briefly to verification and rules of evidence. I asked earlier how much knowledge we would have of past reality if the verification principle were consistently applied to testimony about it. The answer

46. I thus stand much closer to the position adopted by, e.g., Brettler, *Creation*, pp. 142-144, than to that adopted by, e.g., Thompson: note in particular the former's n. 53, which itself helpfully distinguishes the two positions. Cf. also Halpern, *First Historians*, p. 28: ". . . history cannot base itself on predictability. . . . Lacking universal axioms and theorems, it can be based on testimony only"; and, anticipating my next paragraph, "Our understanding of human history resembles our knowledge of the contemporary world."

47. It is naturally the case that our approach to the past will be very much tied up with our approach to and experience of the present (cf. D. V. Edelman, "Doing history in biblical studies," in Edelman [ed.], *Fabric*, pp. 13-25, on pp. 15, 19; J. M. Miller, "Is it possible to write a history of Israel without relying on the Hebrew Bible?" in Edelman [ed.], *Fabric*, pp. 93-102, on p. 100). In this sense we always tell our own story in the course of attempting to tell others' stories. It is in fact a good test of the worth of any "method" adopted in respect of external reality, whether past or present, to consider whether we are in fact able to (and do) live with it consistently. The running of such a test in relation to everyday life, I submit, would have saved more than one historian of Israel (and indeed more than one literary critic) from adopting implausible positions on a whole range of matters. Sufficient *contemplation* of everyday life in all its complexity, indeed, would have increased the capacity for imagination in historiographical work far beyond that which is often apparent. Narrowness of vision in the present can only ever produce narrowness of vision in respect of the past. Cf. further D. Edelman, "Saul ben Kish in history and tradition," in Fritz and Davies (eds.), *Origins*, pp. 142-159, on p. 143: "Most histories are created by linking together individual data into chains of cause and effect based on logical processing; real life does not necessarily operate by the same neat, rational principles. What is plausible, then, is not necessarily what actually happened." The whole discussion of method on pp. 142-148 is most perceptive and illuminating, underlining the complexity of the historian's task.

was "very little." Now I ask: how much knowledge of reality in general would we possess if we truly and consistently functioned in this suspicious manner, demanding of all and sundry that they validate their testimony to us before we accepted its veracity? Again, the answer is "very little." We generally regard it, indeed, as a sign of emotional or mental imbalance if people ordinarily inhabit a culture of distrust in testimony at the level of principle, and most of us outside mental institutions do not in fact inhabit such a universe. It is true, of course, as the old joke goes, that just because we are paranoid, this does not mean that someone is not out to get us. Suspicion may sometimes, or often, be justified. Yet we recognise that healthy people generally place trust in the testimony of others, reserving suspicion for those who have given grounds for it. The adoption of a thoroughgoing hermeneutic of suspicion is not considered sensible in terms of our apprehension of general reality. Nor is the adoption of a "method" in respect of testimony about present reality considered sensible either. We do not always, if we are intelligent, critical people, invest faith in eye-witnesses as opposed to those people who testify to us secondarily, nor vice versa. Indeed, if we characteristically believe one sort of person rather than another (e.g., consistently accepting "insider" accounts of reality over against "outsider" accounts), then we are considered, not intelligent, but prejudiced. Reality is more complex than is allowed for by method. We do not, therefore, if we are intelligent, critical people, allow method overly to influence us in seeking to apprehend it.

Whether it is historical reality, then, or present reality, or indeed textual reality,[48] epistemological openness (I assert) is the only rational stance in respect of the reality that is beyond us. With regard to the history of Israel in particular, it is thus in my view the most rational thing in the world to approach the Hebrew Bible with an *openness* of mind in respect of the major testimony it bears to Israel's past, acknowledging that we have to *bear* in mind the other important reasons for which these texts have been handed down in the form they have been handed down. It is in my view an historiographical virtue, not a vice, having identified what that testimony is, to employ it fundamentally in any modern re-telling of the history of Israel, whether or not other testimonies are available to us to consider alongside it (although certainly *along with* such other testimonies as *are* available to us), looking for coherence and incoherence among the testimonies and making our assessment

---

48. It is just as possible to lose confidence in external textual reality as it is in any other sort of reality, if we press our doubts in respect of it further than is sensible and are not epistemologically open to the text as "other." The recent history of literary criticism more than adequately illustrates this point.

of how far each reflects reality. It is to my mind absurd to adopt any other approach.[49]

Any other approach, in fact, is not truly epistemologically open. It is, rather, an approach that is only selectively open. It is to that extent an irrational approach.[50] This is indeed how I would characterise the approach adopted in some of the recent scholarship on the history of Israel of which I am critical. It is open to receive testimony about Israel's past predominantly or entirely from non-biblical sources, and generally exercises a high level of trust in these sources. It is predominantly or entirely closed to testimony from the Bible itself, generally exercising a high level of distrust in these sources. The main reason for this selectivity, so far as I can determine it, is precisely that delusion about knowledge that I mentioned earlier.[51] In spite of all their

49. Thus, to answer Thompson's question in "School," p. 687, I certainly have no objection in principle to returning to what he calls "Nothian paraphrases," or the "uncritical harmonizations" linked to the old Albright school, if what he means is a careful synthesis of biblical and non-biblical data to produce a composite portrait of the past which takes the biblical testimony about that past with great seriousness. I do not think that Noth, e.g., was always right; but he had a far more sensible approach than Thompson to the relationship between biblical and extra-biblical evidence (cf., e.g., M. Noth, *History of Israel*, ET, 2nd ed. [New York: Harper and Row, 1960], pp. 42-49).

50. As the remainder of this essay itself should make clear, I am not here suggesting a distinction between those who approach reality with sets of general beliefs already in place about it, and those who do not. No-one is "epistemologically open" in the sense that they possess no such beliefs. A rational person will, nevertheless, recognise the provisional nature of all beliefs, and will wish to be sufficiently open to the entire realm of reality external to him/her that false belief stands some chance of being discovered.

51. An associated reason has to do, I believe, with the particular socio-historical location of the historians. It is clear enough, as Barstad argues ("History," pp. 50-51, 63), that there has not in fact been any "paradigm shift" among historians since the 1960's of the kind claimed by Thompson and Lemche. What there has clearly been, however, is an increase in scepticism with regard to the Bible as an historical source. In reflecting upon the reasons for this, I find Thompson's comments ("School," pp. 694-695, n. 32) quite fascinating, inasmuch as they reveal how far a romantic attachment to "1968" shapes his approach to reality. It is not surprising, in the light of these comments, that biblical tradition, as well as scholarship pre-dating the 1960s that depended so much upon it in formulating its ideas about Israel's history, should attract such emotionally charged scepticism from him. Nor is it surprising, indeed, that an academic culture shaped directly or indirectly by the *Zeitgeist* of the 1960s should have been in general so devoted to "freedom" and so antagonistic to "tradition." Many of us younger scholars, on the other hand, find ourselves wondering whether this anti-conservative, anti-traditional passion aids clarity of thought any more than the anti-liberal, anti-critical thought that it opposes, and asking whether it is has noticeably improved the world. "1968" is long ago now, and those of us who did not experience it as adults find it difficult to see any reason why it should be taken as a (the?) defining moment in history.

claims to the contrary, and indeed all their claims about others misrepresenting their views, significant numbers of historians of Israel seem to believe deep in their souls that the attainment of historical knowledge, beyond testimony and interpretation and without faith, is possible. At least, they appear to believe that some types of testimony and interpretation communicate knowledge more directly, and with less investment of faith, than others.[52] Not only is attainment of such knowledge thought possible, it is commonly regarded as having been achieved. Sometimes statements to this effect are explicit. Towards the end of his response to my 1995 *JBL* article, in which he claims that I thoroughly misrepresent him, Thomas Thompson re-asserts precisely the kind of position for which I criticise him in the article, when he says: "There is no more 'ancient Israel.' History no longer has room for it. This we do know. And now, as one of the first conclusions of this new knowledge, 'biblical Israel' was in its origin a Jewish concept."[53] "Knowledge" of the past is obtained somehow, and held over against the construct "ancient Israel," which previous scholars have created in considerable dependence on the Hebrew Bible, and over against the Hebrew Bible itself, which is evidently thought of as providing us with something other than knowledge of this past.[54] The explicit statement of this kind of position is not so common, how-

52. There is a particular prejudice against *religiously motivated* testimony (cf., e.g., the two quotes from Ahlström cited in "Ideologies," p. 600, n. 70, to which may be added Becking, "Seals," p. 70: "In view of the religious character of the composition, DtrH cannot be viewed as a primary historical source" [cf. also p. 71 on Jeremiah]). I am not unaware that this prejudice is of long standing (Grabbe, "Creatures," p. 21, n. 6). I am only surprised that the length of time it has survived is thought to be sufficient justification of it, doubting as I do that scholars would allow the defence of any other prejudice on similar grounds. Are there any good *reasons* why this tradition of reading should be maintained? The prejudice in question is, in my view, not unrelated to the commonly found prejudice against religiously inclined *scholars* (magnificently expressed in Carroll, "Madonna," pp. 85-86).

53. Thompson, "School," p. 697, following Davies, *Search*, while ignoring my criticism of Davies' argument ("Ideologies," pp. 599-600). Becking, "Seals," p. 68, rightly notes (consistent with my own criticism of Davies) that: "He, correctly, sees 'ancient Israel' as a product of the mind of biblical scholars. He fails to see, however, that what he calls 'historical Israel' is a product of the mind too."

54. Thompson is right to say ("School," p. 690, lines 17-18) that he himself never explicitly stated that "events . . . may be directly observed," and it was careless of me to word my criticism of his position on "knowledge" in the way I did, not least because it has given him the opportunity to distract attention from its weaknesses. What he explicitly said (Thompson, *Early History*, p. 61) was that the heart of historical science is ". . . the specific and unique *observation* [my emphasis] of what is known," distinguishing this from processes involving probability and analogy. He appears to repeat the distinction a few lines further on in his response to me ("School," p. 690), when he differentiates between knowl-

ever, as the implicit adoption of it. Knowledge is simply assumed to have been accumulated in various ways. This knowledge can then be used as a yardstick against which to measure biblical testimony and come to some judgment upon it, or indeed as a basis upon which to build a "scientific" history in complete independence of it.[55]

Yet whence, exactly, did the knowledge under consideration spring, in the light of which the Bible's testimony is now to be assessed? Here, as when watching the accomplished magician, it is important to watch carefully for the sleight of hand. For the reality is that this so-called knowledge is really faith in disguise. When Thompson says, "There is no more 'ancient Israel'. . . . This we do know," *he* actually knows nothing of the kind, and "we" certainly do not. *He* simply believes it strongly, and "we" are drawn into the faith statement to offer some community support for the faith expressed. What he "knows," he "knows" because he has decided to invest faith in certain testimonies about the past rather than others, the most notable of the "others" being the testimony of the Hebrew Bible. The grounds upon which this epistemological privileging of non-biblical testimony can be defended are, however, entirely unclear. The wisdom of it is equally unclear. For the delusion that one possesses knowledge when one is only exercising faith is ever prone to lead on to a refusal to exercise faith when there are good grounds for doing so. We

---

edge (connected with texts and potsherds) and speculation (moving beyond these and beginning to guess), as if the process of "observing" were a straightforward one. Events, he claims, ". . . can be *directly described* [my emphasis] on the basis of evidence." It is precisely this sharp contrast between hypothesis, on the one hand, and direct access to events, on the other hand — between guesswork and knowledge — that I was questioning at this point in my paper. One does not have to read far into Thompson's writings to discover that the distinction, however questionable, is fundamental to his thinking (cf., e.g., "Defining history," p. 182, where "independent historical knowledge" will one day supposedly enable us to make judgments about the biblical tradition; or T. L. Thompson, "The intellectual matrix of early biblical narrative: Inclusive monotheism in Persian Period Palestine," in D. V. Edelman (ed.), *The Triumph of Elohim: From Yahwisms to Judaisms* [Kampen: Kos Pharos, 1995], pp. 107-124, on p. 108). As Barstad ("History," pp. 50-51) rightly points out: "Lemche and Thompson, apparently unaware of the fact that what we may call a conventional concept of history today is *highly* problematic, still work within the parameters of historical critical research, assuming that history is a science and that one must work with 'hard' facts."

55. Thus, e.g., Grabbe, "Creatures," pp. 24-26, and implicitly in his closing comments on p. 29, n. 25. In respect of his challenge to me here to deal with Joshua 1-15, I respond thus (in the context of this section of my current paper): I will accept his challenge to measure the distance between story and history if he will first of all tell me where the history is, outside the story, in respect of which I am to measure this distance. Presumably he is referring here to testimony embodied in non-biblical sources.

claim that we already know, and on that basis we close ourselves off from testimony that challenges our already preconceived knowledge.[56] "Knowledge"
becomes the wall that we build around ourselves to protect ourselves from reality, whether individually or as a group. It becomes the excuse for narrowness of vision and intolerance of other points of view. It is, when manifest in
this way, an obstacle rather than a means to the apprehension of reality. We
may hold the opinion that we are enlightened; but in truth we inhabit
epistemological darkness. It is one of the ultimate ironies, indeed, that when
Enlightenment scholarship gets to this point, it is essentially no different
from the fundamentalist religion that it so profoundly despises.[57] It is closed
in on itself, unable and unwilling to hear voices from the outside. It is an irrational approach to reality indeed.

I conclude this section of the paper with some further comments on toler-
ance and intolerance. I have sometimes been challenged when in dialogue
about matters historical to say whether, on my view of the way in which history should be approached, there is any way of saying that one history of Israel
is better than another. Is it not the case, on my view, that any story about the
past is as good as any other? I am glad to be able to clarify here that I certainly
do not believe that any story about the past is as good as any other, any more
than I believe that any reading of a text is as good as any other. There are histories that in my view do a good job of weaving testimonies about the past together to make a coherent story, and histories that do not. There are histories
that in my view do better justice than others to the various testimonies and interpretations upon which we depend for access to the past. There are histories,
indeed, that in my view falsify the past in all sorts of ways (i.e., do not deal convincingly or at all with the evidence as I see it). I do not believe, in other words,
that the past is simply an indeterminate mess out of which one can make any-

---

56. Cf. Davies, "Whose history?" p. 105: "If we have no positive grounds for thinking
that a biblical account is historically useful, we cannot really adopt it as history. True, the
result will be that we have less history than we might. But what little we have we can at least
claim to know (in whatever sense we 'know' the distant past); this, in my opinion, is better
than having more history than we might, much of which we do not know at all, since it
consists merely of unverifiable stories." The fact of the matter, however, is that history *is*
the telling and retelling of unverifiable stories (Collingwood's "re-enactment" of the past),
and that the kind of historical knowledge beyond tradition and testimony that Davies
seeks is a mirage. We should certainly expect the story now told to have internal coherence
and comprehensiveness in terms of the "evidence" that is drawn into it; but that is all that
we can sensibly ask. To press the point in respect of Davies himself: is the story that he tells
of the Assyrian invasion of Judah (see further below) itself truly a *verifiable* story?

57. Cf. Halpern, *First Historians*, pp. 3-29, who characterises scholarship in this mode as
"negative fundamentalist."

thing one wishes. We are constrained by testimony and interpretation in our reading of it, if we are as attentive as we should be to that testimony and interpretation. However, I also do not believe, on the other hand, that history is one objectively observable story which has one empirically verifiable "correct" interpretation. It is not simply that we have such a relatively small amount of data to go on in respect of the ancient past, and therefore must fill in thousands of gaps in the narrative of the past according to our own view of the world's story. That in itself, it is true, would lead us to different renderings of the story, each of which might be argued to be consonant with the "facts." More seriously, however, even if in some inconceivable world we had access to all the millions and millions of "facts" of history — every conversation, every action by every person, every "event" — we would still be found rendering the story in different ways, selecting and shaping the "past" in respect of the themes that we wished to develop. It is not lack of data that is our problem. Greater amounts of data would not improve matters. There is an inevitably subjective aspect to all our story-telling about the past, connected with the reality of our own contingency as mortal beings, which means that our stories will always be different from each other even if we all accept as a fundamental principle that we should be epistemologically open to testimony and interpretation, accountable to "the facts." It is thus a logical (and I would say moral) consequence of epistemological openness to the reality of the past that we should also be maximally tolerant of each other as we each render the past, listening with respect to each other's stories as we attempt to tell our own. In short, intellectual humility and charity, informed by a pluralist perspective, comprise the entailment of epistemological openness. This is not because any rendering of the past is as good as any other. It is because we recognise that what we call "good" has a considerable amount to do with judgments about matters other than what constitutes the "data" to be accommodated, and that those judgments are themselves a matter of debate and indeed choice.[58]

---

58. It is encouraging, in the aftermath of "Method," to find now such a healthy emphasis on pluralism in historiography in Davies, "Whose history?" pp. 117-120. The essay itself, one must say, still leaves the impression that the generosity implied by this section of it is not to be extended to those who think it acceptable, for good reasons, to use the Hebrew Bible as their major source in composing their historiography. The theoretical pluralism stands in some tension with the total argument. I am happy to accept the author's verbal assurance to me, however, that broad pluralism is indeed what he now advocates.

An Example: Davies and Provan on
Sennacherib's Invasion of Judah

I am moving in due course to my conclusion. It will be helpful, however, to illustrate with an example what I take to be the difference in approach to the matter of the Hebrew Bible and history between myself and those who hold the more sceptical view of the biblical texts with which I have been engaging above. My chosen example is the invasion of Judah by the Assyrian king Sennacherib around the year 701 B.C. Accounts of this invasion of Judah are found in 2 Kings 18:13–19:37; 2 Chronicles 32:1-23; Isaiah 36–37 and in an account repeated almost verbatim in all the later descriptions of Sennacherib's reign, including the Taylor and Oriental Institute Prisms[59] — the Rassam Prism Inscription of the Assyrian king (700 B.C.). There is some archaeological evidence that seems to touch on the details of the events described by these texts, but it is not directly relevant to our present inquiry.[60] The Kings account opens with a passage not found in the other biblical passages (2 Kgs. 18:13-16), which tells us of Hezekiah's initial unsuccessful attempt, after Sennacherib had taken "all the fortified cities of Judah," to buy off the Assyrian king. Thereafter the Kings and Isaiah accounts proceed in tandem, telling of Hezekiah's refusal to surrender Jerusalem to the besieging Assyrians; his consultation with the prophet Isaiah and Isaiah's promise of deliverance for the city; his later prayer and Isaiah's response to that prayer; the eventual miraculous deliverance of Jerusalem through an angel, and Sennacherib's death. Chronicles provides us with a much shorter account, not only omitting any reference to the attempted payment, but also abbreviating the account in other ways (particularly by omitting Isaiah's prophecies). Some details are nevertheless added (e.g., the building works of 32:3-5 and the speech of 32:7-8). The Assyrian account, in those places where it concerns Judah in particu-

---

59. For a clear and helpful summary of the number and character of the Assyrian data relating to Sennacherib's third campaign, see A. R. Millard, "Sennacherib's attack on Hezekiah," *TynB* 36 (1985), pp. 61-77.

60. Cf. O. Borowski, "Hezekiah's reforms and the revolt against Assyria," *BA* 58 (1995): pp. 148-155, for a convenient summary. With regard to "Hezekiah's tunnel," J. Rogerson and P. R. Davies ("Was the Siloam tunnel built by Hezekiah?" *BA* 59 [1996], pp. 138-149) allow only that Warren's Shaft may be Hezekian, arguing that the tunnel is Hasmonean, although I find convincing the rejoinders on the basis of the palaeography of the Siloam inscription by R. S. Hendel ("The date of the Siloam inscription: A rejoinder to Rogerson and Davies," *BA* 59 [1996], pp. 233-237) and on the basis of the archaeology and history by J. M. Cahill ("A rejoinder to 'Was the Siloam tunnel built by Hezekiah," *BA* 60 [1997], pp. 184-185). For discussion of the economic context of Hezekiah's revolt, cf. D. Hopkins, "Bare bones: Putting flesh on the economics of ancient Israel," in Fritz and Davies (eds.), *Origins*, pp. 121-139.

lar rather than Palestine in general, also does not mention any initial payment by Hezekiah after the fall of his cities. It moves straight from description of their fall to description of the siege of Jerusalem. It does not explicitly tell us the circumstances in which the siege ended, although it implies that Hezekiah at this point did agree to pay tribute, which he is then described as sending to Assyria after Sennacherib had departed from Judah.

Epistemological openness leads me in the first instance to read all these accounts with great seriousness as apparently offering testimony to the past, and further consideration does not lead me to the conclusion that I should revise my opinion. I recognise, of course, that each of the accounts is an ideological account of the past — it could not be otherwise. I shall not rehearse the ideologies of the three biblical accounts as they become apparent to us through consideration of the individual passages and their wider literary contexts. It is unlikely that any reader of this paper requires such a rehearsal.[61] For reasons that will become clear in a moment, however, I do wish to comment briefly on the ideology of the Assyrian text as it, too, is evidenced in the text itself and on the basis of broader considerations. As Younger has underlined,[62] all Assyrian royal inscriptions cater to preconceived ideological requirements in the way that they are structured. Their stereotypical nature instils in the readers a sense of anticipation of the obvious outcome of the campaign described, and hence of the relentless efficacy of the Assyrian king's actions as he seeks to reinstate (what is from the Assyrian point of view) order, righteousness, and life. They are concerned to exalt the reputation of the king concerned; to glorify the gods of Assyria, especially Ashur; and to encourage loyalty and submission among his subjects. This is presumably why such inscriptions are not noted for any frank admission of failure, even where the readers of other, non-Assyrian texts might reasonably deduce that failure has occurred. Any reader of this particular Sennacherib text who is interested in

---

61. Those who do require it can consult, for a brief account of the Kings and Isaiah passages, I. W. Provan, *1-2 Kings*, OTG (Sheffield: Sheffield Academic Press, 1997), pp. 57-60. The Chronicler, in pursuit of a vision of Davidic kingship relating to the future messiah, tends to avoid mentioning the failures of Judean kings. This perhaps explains the omission of the attempted Hezekian compromise. Aside from that, however, his message is much the same as that of Kings. Faithfulness to the living God and his laws makes a difference to Israel's historical experience; Israel knows blessing in obedience, even in the face of overwhelming odds (the addition of 32:7-8 makes this explicit). For a fuller discussion of the ideology of Chronicles, see H. G. M. Williamson, *1 and 2 Chronicles*, NCB (London: Marshall, Morgan and Scott, 1982), pp. 24-33; S. Japhet, *The Ideology of the Book of Chronicles and Its Place in Biblical Thought*, BzEATAJ 9 (Frankfurt: Peter Lang, 1989).

62. K. L. Younger, Jr., *Ancient Conquest Accounts: A Study in Ancient Near Eastern and Biblical History Writing*, JSOTS 98 (Sheffield, 1990), pp. 61-124.

history will have to take these broader realities into account, in just the same way that the ideologies of the biblical texts require to be taken into account.

I repeat, nevertheless, that further consideration of our four texts, helping me as it does to understand them as ideological texts, does not lead me to the conclusion that I should generally revise my opinion of them as testimonies to the past. It reminds me that each is indeed a *story* about the past, and that I must be alert for features of each which perhaps have more to do with the particular requirements of the story than with anything else. It does not compel me to any generalised attitude of suspicion or distrust, however. It compels me only to caution on a case-by-case basis. We move, then, to the detail. What kind of story do our four ancient stories allow us to construct about Sennacherib's invasion of Palestine?

Let me suggest the following outline reading. Hezekiah had prepared himself well for the expected invasion, not least in making a pre-emptive strike against Philistine territory associated with Gaza, whose king Sillibel (we deduce from Sennacherib's own account of the campaign) remained loyal to Assyria throughout the revolt, and in imprisoning the similarly loyal king Padi of Ekron.[63] All this may imply that Hezekiah was one of the moving forces of the revolt. This may in turn help to explain the opening of the Kings account (2 Kgs. 18:13-16). Hezekiah offered renewed tribute, the text claims, if the Assyrian king would withdraw.[64] Sennacherib, however, chose, while Jerusalem's gates remained closed to him, to continue to regard Hezekiah as a rebel. An army was thus sent from Lachish to Jerusalem, in order to persuade Hezekiah fully to surrender (2 Kgs. 18:17ff.).[65] We might plausibly suggest that

---

63. 2 Chronicles provides further information on these preparations (32:3-5), and there is no good reason to doubt its account.

64. This is unsurprising when it is realised that according to Sennacherib's own account the coalition had already early in the campaign collapsed. Luli king of Sidon had fled, and his cities had been brought to submission; others had also submitted, or, in the case of Sidqia of Ashkelon, had been deported to Assyria.

65. This move is not unparalleled. The practice of besieging a major city while continuing operations elsewhere in the surrounding region is known also from Tiglath-pileser's campaigns in Syria in 743-740 B.C. Lachish was itself soon overwhelmed by Sennacherib, as implied by 2 Kings 19:8; claimed also by the Assyrian reliefs and associated text which portray the siege and conquest of the city; and illustrated by the discoveries of archaeologists: cf. W. Dever, "Archaeology, material culture and the early monarchical period in Israel," in Edelman (ed.), *Fabric*, pp. 103-115, on pp. 106-108. I am puzzled by Dever's assertion, however, that we cannot "sidestep" the challenge of archaeology to biblical historiography here "by insisting that we simply have two differing but complementary versions of what really took place." I see nothing in the data that he describes that leads me to think it *is* "sidestepping" anything to suggest such a reading of our sources.

it was because of Hezekiah's prominence as an instigator of the revolt that Sennacherib was so insistent. All the biblical accounts and Sennacherib's own account agree, in any case, that Jerusalem ended up being besieged by an Assyrian army because Hezekiah was perceived as not submitting to Assyrian overlordship. At some point during the campaign, Kings, Isaiah and the Assyrian records also agree, an Egyptian army appeared on the scene. The Assyrian text describes its appearance, and the ensuing battle, before it describes the siege of Jerusalem. It does not clearly intend in so doing to be strictly chronological, however (the arrangement of the text may be according to topic), whereas Kings and Isaiah do clearly imply that the Egyptian advance occurred after the siege had begun, and this perspective is thus the one that I weave into my account. Sennacherib claims to have defeated this Egyptian force at Eltekeh, and we have no reason to disbelieve him. It may be that it was after this Assyrian victory that Hezekiah, in an attempt to buy more time, released Padi of Ekron, whom Sennacherib claims to have "made" come from Jerusalem and to have re-established on his throne. Whether this is the case or not, Sennacherib does not claim to have taken Jerusalem at any point, nor even to have received tribute from Hezekiah in the immediate aftermath of the siege. He tells us only that after his return to Nineveh, whose occasion he does not describe, Hezekiah sent tribute. The silence on this matter of the conclusion of Sennacherib's assault on Hezekiah, when compared to what Sennacherib says in his inscription about other kings in the region, begs some explanation, and our biblical sources give us some hints in the direction of such, when they tell us of a mysterious reversal suffered by the Assyrians while Jerusalem lay at their mercy.[66] It is entirely plausible that Hezekiah sub-

---

66. I take the opportunity here to correct a misunderstanding in Carroll, "Madonna," p. 90, n. 19. I have never argued that any narrative event is "historical rather than legendary because the 'miraculous' must be factored into any competent historical reading of the Bible by historians today." One cannot (should not) short-circuit the genre issue, nor indeed any other issue, by the appeal to miracle, and one certainly cannot ignore, even in a case where one is convinced that the text overall means to refer to past reality, the question of how far narrative art and theology are playing their part in shaping the text. There is no reason to think, on the other hand, that past reality will always conform to the expectations we may have of it, and that unusual or unique (and even unexplainable) events cannot occur. Everyday reality, I suggest, is likewise a mixture of the "normal" and the surprising. I do not press the word "miracle" in the context of a general discussion with others whom I know do not share my religious world-view, any more than I press, in the particular case under discussion here, the interpretative "the angel of Yahweh . . . struck down." I certainly assert, however, that anyone seriously interested in the past rather than only in their own ideology should be as open to the possibility of "highly unusual events" in the past they are sensitive to issues of literary genre, and should not foreclose consideration of

sequently decided to reaffirm his vassalship to Assyria by sending tribute on to Nineveh, as Sennacherib claims.[67] 2 Kings 18:13-16 suggests that he had wished to settle things in this manner in the first place; and in the aftermath of Sennacherib's campaign Hezekiah was evidently very isolated, with much of his territory annexed by Ashdod, Ekron and Gaza, and significant portions of his army having deserted him.

This is, of course, only an outline reading. Much more could be said in explication of it. The main point to be made about it in this context, however, is that it is a particular sort of reading. It takes the biblical and other data equally seriously as testimony, while recognising the perspectival nature, rhetorical features, and ideology of each testimony and seeking to take intelligent account of these. It recognises the possibility that any testimony may mislead; yet it takes a positive attitude to testimony, open to the possibility that the reading which is based upon it may be falsified, but resistant to any foolish demand that it should be verified.

With this reading I now wish to contrast another: the reading of Philip Davies, in his book *In Search of Ancient Israel*,[68] to which I have previously referred in my *JBL* article and elsewhere.[69] Davies takes the Assyrian invasion as a particular example in the course of his argument about the folly of looking for any "ancient Israel." He is prepared to allow that *behind* our extant ac-

---

individual cases as a result of a method which in practice (if not always in theory) equates improbability with impossibility. On the importance (and rationality) of openness to the "incredible report," cf. further Coady, *Testimony*, pp. 179-198.

67. The Kings account differs from the Assyrian account in what it has to say about the timing and content of the tribute paid by Hezekiah to Sennacherib; and it may well be the case that here we must make a decision about how far what one or both accounts has to say on this point has more to do with the overall purposes of the texts than with the past which they describe (see, e.g., Younger, *Conquest Accounts*, pp. 122-124, for some interesting comments on the significance of material goods in the Assyrian texts). There is no reason to think, however, that Hezekiah did not indeed both attempt to buy Sennacherib off before the siege and provide future security for himself after it was over. In this case our texts are simply selecting differing aspects of the events for their narratives.

68. Davies, *Search*, pp. 32-36.

69. Provan, *Kings*, pp. 57-64. I choose this example again because it is an especially good one, and not because I have any particular reason to concentrate on Davies' unique contributions to recent debate on the history of Israel. I take the opportunity to comment, however, on his response to my *JBL* article, in which he at one point joins Thompson in his accusations of distortion, and with just as little justification (Davies, "Method," p. 704). His claim that I have engaged in "outright falsification" of his argument is, in fact, nonsense. I myself refer to one of the passages Davies cites on p. 704 precisely to show that, while he *claims* to have given reasons for his distinction between earlier biblical texts and Ezra-Nehemiah, these reasons are not convincing ("Ideologies," p. 604, n. 80).

counts there does lie an historical reality. A vassal king of Judah rebelled against the king of Assyria, and the Assyrians in response devastated Judah, depriving Hezekiah of virtually all his kingdom except Jerusalem. Jerusalem was not captured, but Hezekiah paid a large tribute, and afterwards remained a vassal of Assyria without the power of rebellion. This is "what happened" in the history of Palestine. The biblical story, on the other hand, tells us of a victory by the God of Israel over the Assyrian king which left Judah ever after free of Assyrian control — for such control is never referred to again. Why this story is as it is can in the last analysis be explained only if we recognise that it is not simply giving us a different version of an historical event, but is rather telling us a story of something that is not historical. The analogy which Davies offers is that of Shakespeare's *Julius Caesar,* where things happen because of the play's own dramatic logic. Whatever any historical Brutus may or may not have done does not either explain the actions of Shakespeare's character of that name nor make this character into an historical figure.

Davies thus provides an excellent example of precisely the kind of approach to the matter of history that I have already criticised. As he comes to consider the biblical text, he already knows "what really happened" in that part of the history of Palestine which concerns the Assyrian invasion of Judah; and this is then contrasted in particular with what the biblical story has to tell us (although also to some extent with the Assyrian story as well). Where does this knowledge of "what happened" come from? Closer attention to the argument reveals that it originates in what is described as a "reasonable guess."[70] How we get in the course of a few lines from this "reasonable guess" to the kind of solid "what really happened" which may be contrasted with what the ancient texts say is unclear. It is particularly unclear because the description of "what happened" is itself partly based upon these same ancient (biblical and Assyrian) texts. It is, in fact, a new story derived from the ancient stories, which takes on a mysterious solidity which they apparently lack for reasons which are not fully spelled out. At least part of the solution to the mystery, however, lies in this statement:

> The events are described as they are because Israel is involved. And to this Israel happen things that as an historian I do not accept happen in history here or anywhere else.[71]

The reference is clearly to the idea of supernatural deliverance through "the angel." Davies, "as an historian," does not accept that such things happen

70. Davies, *Search*, p. 34 (top).
71. Davies, *Search*, p. 35.

in history. How he knows this "as an historian" is, however, something of a mystery. He may well choose, as Davies the non-theist, to differ with the theological interpretation of the biblical writers with respect to the events they are describing. What is it, however, that drives him as Davies the historian to think that the Assyrians could not have suffered an unexpected reversal which caused their withdrawal from Palestine? Even as an historian deeply committed to the rules of historical method he would only be permitted to consider such an eventuality, by analogy, improbable. If that were what he were arguing, then I would press him further to explain why I should believe that it did not happen in this specific case, improbable or not. In fact, however, there is no argument here at all — only a statement of belief accompanied by the customary appeal to community support for the faith expressed ("as an historian"). We are left to decide why we should accept Davies' assertion as to what cannot happen over against the testimony of the texts as to what did happen.

Reasonable guesses and general prejudices aside, whence otherwise does Davies derive his "knowledge" of the past against which the biblical text can be measured? The answer appears to be: from the Assyrian account of the invasion and its aftermath. Only thus is it possible to understand his assertion that the biblical story tells us that Judah was ever afterwards free of Assyrian control, whereas the "facts" were otherwise. Here we find that classical combination of maximal suspicion of the biblical text and maximal naiveté with regard to other sources of information about which I was so critical earlier — a naiveté most puzzling in view of Davies' own general awareness of the ideological nature of the Assyrian texts.[72] It is in truth by no means clear why, if the biblical text were indeed in conflict with the Assyrian text with regard to its testimony, we should think that the latter provides us with access to the facts and the former only to the minds of the biblical authors. In fact, however, the assertion that the texts are in conflict is in any case mistaken. Davies himself allows that the biblical text does not actually say that Judah was ever after the Sennacherib invasion free of Assyrian control; and non-reference to the Assyrians cannot of itself be taken to indicate that this is what is implied, in a text which is selective in the first place (especially regarding Assyria) about what it records. The conflict is imagined. Even if it existed, however, we should at least require an *argument* as to why we should favour one account

---

72. Davies, *Search*, p. 34: ". . . Sennacherib's account belongs with a number of other similar texts which serve the vanity of the Assyrian monarchs, sustain the loyalty and cohesion of the Assyrian nation, and probably intend to cow would-be rebels into renouncing thoughts of rebellion."

over the other. An assertion would not — should not — be considered sufficient.

The difference between the two approaches should now be clear. I am inclined in the first instance to listen to the varied testimony that we possess about the Assyrian invasion of Judah and to try to form a broad judgment about the course of events that might lie behind the testimony. I am much more inclined to form these judgments in the first instance on the basis of ancient claims about the past than on the basis of modern "reasonable guesses" about it. I am indeed much more interested in listening to claims about what did happen than in listening to guesses about what must have happened, for the simple reason that I am vastly more interested in finding out about the past than about the present. I am not unaware of the inevitably ideological nature of all the ancient testimony to which I am listening. Each of the four texts that testify do so within their larger literary and sociological contexts, and with some intention to persuade and to influence. It is precisely because I am aware of this, however, that I do not succumb to the temptation to think of one or other of my accounts as providing me with more or less unmediated "knowledge" of the past in contrast to the others. Davies certainly seems to imagine that the Assyrian text grants him some degree of knowledge of this kind — as if it were not really an ideological text at all in the same sense that our biblical texts are. I find no reason to see any distinction of this kind. I grant, then, that all four texts are ideological. I do not, however, adopt a fundamentally suspicious attitude in respect of any of them, but rather an open attitude. It may be that I shall find specific reasons to think that one or other of them is unreliable or deficient in their testifying; but I await specific reasons, and do not fall back on general prejudice. It is indeed prejudice, and not reason, that I see as lying at the heart of the alternative approach — a lack of openness to data which precludes the acquisition of knowledge that is not already known. Thus it is that the pursuit of "how it really was" results, as it so often has in the past, only in the projection of a narrow present view of reality onto the past — "how we truly expected it to be."[73] It is not the first time in the history of Israel that this has happened. That history demonstrates more than adequately the general truth, in fact, that we either respect and appropriate the testimony of the past, recognising the forms in which it is cast and allowing it to challenge us even while we engage in critical thinking about it, or

---

73. It is worth recalling in this context that Leopold von Ranke (1795-1886), to whom scholars often refer when they articulate the ideal of seeking *wie es eigentlich gewesen ist,* was himself "the foremost myth-maker of the Bismarckian National State" (A. Richardson, *History Sacred and Profane* [London: SCM, 1964], p. 175).

we are doomed, while believing that we alone possess objectivity regarding the past and can start afresh in accurately describing it, to create highly individualistic experience and imagination and to have them masquerade as representations of the world outside our minds.

A final quotation from Davies, in a different publication, enables me to bring this section of my paper to a close:

> It is only in religious language that to believe is good and to doubt bad; for a historian, to doubt is good and to believe is bad![74]

I think, on the other hand, that whether practising religion or historiography, or indeed simply living life, it is necessary and good both to believe and to doubt as it seems sensible and appropriate so to do.[75] I find Paul Ricoeur's approach to hermeneutics, in fact, much more persuasive than Davies' apparent approach, in that the former (unlike some of those biblical scholars indebted to him) incorporates a hermeneutic of suspicion without allowing suspicion to dominate, and indeed balances it with a hermeneutic of belief: "Hermeneutics seems to me to be animated by this double motivation: willingness to suspect, willingness to listen; vow of rigor, vow of obedience."[76]

Conclusion

I began this paper with the picture of the dwarves in the stable. They were happy to be without humbug; determined not to be taken in. They considered themselves enlightened. The reality was that their enlightenment was darkness, and that, through misplaced commitment, they had put themselves beyond ever discovering that this was so. As the lion Aslan himself put it, in reality they were inhabiting the prison of their own minds, ". . . so afraid of being taken in that they cannot be taken out."[77] This is the fate, it seems, of all who are so convinced that they possess knowledge that they are unprepared any longer to hear testimony and interpretation; unwilling any longer to exercise faith; committed ideologically, if inconsistently, to doubt. It is certainly possible, taking such a stance, to construct very plausible and comforting ac-

---

74. Davies, "Whose history?" p. 109.

75. Davies himself elsewhere appears to accept the wisdom of this approach to life, if not to history: P. R. Davies, "Introduction," in Fritz and Davies (eds.), *Origins*, pp. 11-21, on p. 13.

76. P. Ricoeur, *Freud and Philosophy: An Essay on Interpretation*, ET (New Haven: Yale University Press, 1970), p. 15.

77. Lewis, *The Last Battle*, p. 135.

counts of reality, historical and otherwise. It is certainly possible that these accounts will find group affirmation. Whether they actually correspond to reality outside one's own head, or outside one's group, is another matter. Without an openness to complex reality itself, there is no possibility of ever finding out. Without such openness, indeed, all that one is ever going to discover is "facts" that confirm one's own first-articulated world-view. It is an unhappy position in which to find oneself, if one has any aspirations after truth. By all means, therefore, let us embrace criticism, and let us use it to deconstruct idolatry and dogmatism. But let us ensure in embDracing it that we do not fall into the trap of being so obsessed with criticism of the Bible that we fail to be sufficiently critical of everything else, including our own prejudices and presuppositions, and thus end up simply with new idolatries and dogmatisms to replace the old. I doubt whether the dwarves required great faith in Aslan in order to hear his voice. They only needed, in the first instance, to match their scepticism respecting him with due scepticism regarding their own beliefs.

Editors and Contributors

David W. Baker is Professor of Old Testament and Semitic Languages at Ashland Theological Seminary.

Richard S. Hess is Professor of Old Testament at Denver Seminary.

Brian E. Kelly is Chaplain at Canterbury Christ Church University College.

Kenneth A. Kitchen is Brunner Professor of Egyptology (Emeritus) at the University of Liverpool.

Jens Bruun Kofoed is Lecturer in Old Testament Studies at Copenhagen Lutheran School of Theology.

V. Philips Long is Professor of Old Testament at Regent College, Vancouver, British Columbia.

Alan R. Millard is Rankin Professor of Hebrew and Ancient Semitic Languages at the University of Liverpool.

Iain W. Provan is Marshall Sheppard Professor of Biblical Studies (OT) at Regent College, Vancouver, British Columbia.

Gordon J. Wenham is Professor of Old Testament at the University of Gloucestershire.

Peter Williams is Lecturer in Hebrew and Aramaic at the University of Cambridge.

Nicolai Winther-Nielsen is Lecturer in Old Testament Studies at Lutheran School of Theology, University of Aarhus.

Index of Names

Index of Names

Rorty, R., 47n.3

Saebo, M., 7n.12
Sass, B., 88
Schäfer-Lichenberger, C., 178n.41
Schneider, T., 116n.9
Schniedewind, W., 144
Schorn, U., 152
Searle, J. R., 54, 61
Shakespeare, W., 172n.25
Shapin, S., 39
Soggin, J. A., 136, 170
Sternberg, M., 50-51, 77, 132-33n.3
Stone, L., 11-12, 63n.40
Strauss, D. F., 9

Tadmor, H., 139n.24
Thiselton, A. C., 13n.22
Thompson, T. L., 1n.1, 7, 10-11, 20, 23-41,
    90n.9, 164n.7, 9, 170n.20, 173n.28,
    174n.31, 175n.32, 178n.39, 179n.43,
    183nn.49, 51, 184nn.53, 55, 185, 192n.69
Tomlin, R. S., 69

Uglow, J., 73
Ussishkin, D., 88

van Keulen, P., 140-41
Vanhoozer, K. J., 52n.18, 57, 68n.49
von Ranke, L., 195n.73

Watson, F., 50n.10
Weeks, S., 129n.26
Wellhausen, J., 19, 134, 135, 136, 138,
    147-48, 172n.24
Welton, P., 136n.17, 137, 139n.26, 143-44
Whitelam, K., 173n.28, 178n.41
Widdowson, H. G., 65
Williams, P., 7, 19-20, 21
Winther-Nielsen, N., 7, 13-14, 21
Wittgenstein, L., 54

Young, I., 15, 82, 95n.62
Younger, K. L., Jr., 189n.62, 192n.67
Yule, G., 59

Zagorin, P., 8n.15

Index of Scripture References